the G___ __Nomad's

GUIDEBOOK

Cindy and Jeremy Gough

Right: A giant tingle tree near Walpole in southwest Western Australia.

Previous page: Bell Gorge is one of the many highlights of a trip along the Gibb River Road (J and C Gough)

Below: The magnificent wildflowers at Koolanooka Springs near Morawa in Western Australia have to be seen to be believed.

Above: The unmistakeable majesty of South Australia's Flinders Ranges.

Despite the growing number of grey nomads on the road, there's still solitude out there.

Above: Contos Beach near Margaret River in southwest Western Australia is impossibly beautiful.

Cooktown in Queensland's tropical north is a grey nomad mecca during the dry season.

An off-road van negotiates Cockatoo Creek on Cape York.

Jeremy and Cindy Gough spent two years travelling around Australia, visiting everywhere from the Kimberley to Cape York and from the Territory to Tasmania. Their extensive on-the-road experience, as well as numerous campfire conversations and caravan park meetings, has given them a unique insight into the grey nomad lifestyle. They have written many travel articles for newspapers and magazines and have also launched a website specifically for grey nomads: www.thegreynomads.com.au

the Grey Nomad's
GUIDEBOOK

CINDY AND JEREMY GOUGH

PAN
Pan Macmillan Australia

First published 2007 in Pan by Pan Macmillan Australia Pty Limited
This Pan edition published 2009 by Pan Macmillan Australia Pty Limited
1 Market Street, Sydney

National Library of Australia
Cataloguing-in-Publication data:

Gough, Jeremy.
The grey nomad's guidebook : everything you need to know about
hitting the open road / Jeremy and Cindy Gough.

9780330424929 (pbk.)

Automobile travel–Australia–Guidebooks.
Camping–Australia–Guidebooks.
Retirees–Australia.
Retirement–Australia–Planning.
Australia–Guidebooks.

Gough, Cindy.

919.40846

Typeset in 12/15 pt Adobe Garamond Pro by Post Pre-press Group
Printed in Australia by McPherson's Printing Group
Cartographic art by Laurie Whiddon, Map Illustrations
Text design by Bland Design

Acknowledgements

Thanking by name all of the people who have helped us gather information for this book would be a near-impossible task. We are nonetheless extremely grateful to the numerous national park rangers, recreational vehicle manufacturers and others who have so willingly shared their knowledge.

There are also a few people who have given so generously of their time that we feel we must single them out for special mention. So, in no particular order, we would like to express our gratitude to Steve Jones, Sarah Thomas, Ross Robinson and Lynne De Groot for their unfailing assistance and support. Last but not least, we would like to thank Oliver, Dominic and Madeleine for sharing the journey . . . and living the dream.

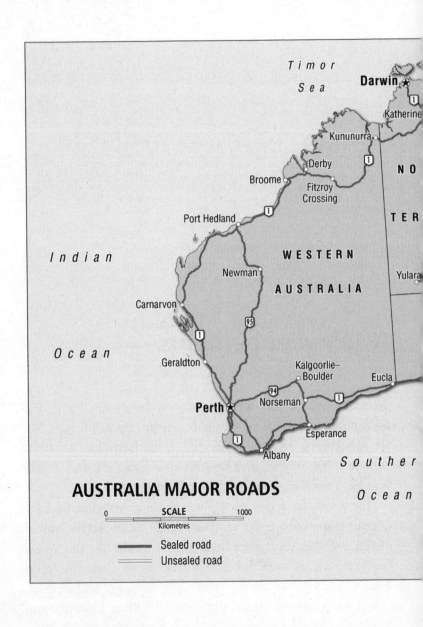

AUSTRALIA MAJOR ROADS

SCALE
0 ———————— 1000
Kilometres

——— Sealed road
········· Unsealed road

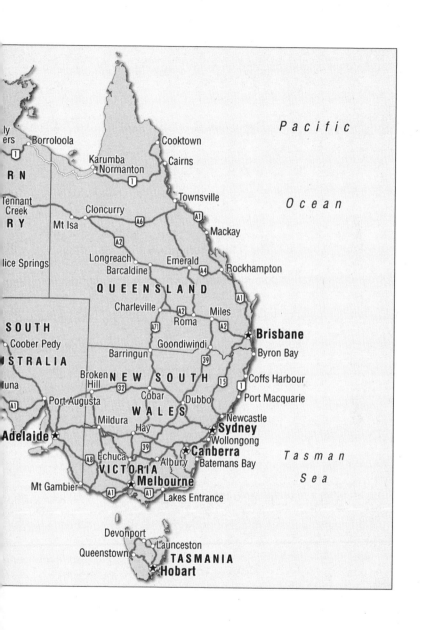

Table of contents

Vital documents: Power of attorney, Document storage, Vehicle registration, Driving licence renewals

Preface

The 'big lap' around the country has become something of a rite of passage for older Australians. Statistics tell us more grey nomads are out there than ever before, with some 60 per cent of new caravans being purchased by the over-55s. Researchers explain the trend by saying this generation of retirees is simply fitter, more financially secure, and more adventurous than their predecessors.

But that doesn't begin to tell the whole story. The grey nomad revolution is really about an army of individuals. People who have worked long and hard – and who are now ready to live the dream.

If you are a mature person planning an extended road trip,

this book is for you. It is intended to help you make the most of your wonderful new lifestyle. It offers you a comprehensive guide to financing and planning a long-term trip, as well as advice on how to manage your affairs while you are away, and how to keep things fresh and exciting even after years on the road. From the cities and the caravan parks to the bush camps and the campfires, this guide will prove an invaluable companion.

We look at everything from western wildflowers and remote-area health care to communications and stargazing; everything from fossicking for sapphires and happy-hour socialising, to buying the right rig and vehicle maintenance.

While many grey nomads travel indefinitely, others choose to test the waters with shorter trips. Whether you are travelling for three weeks, three months, or three years, you are all but guaranteed an incredible adventure, and we hope this book will help enrich the experience.

It does not pretend to be a comprehensive 'where to' guidebook. There are plenty of excellent publications that list the top tourist spots for every Australian region. Although we look at the attractions of the various states, discuss the best times to visit, as well as looking at some excellent budget campsites, this book is about a lot more than showing people how to get from A to B.

This revised edition of *The Grey Nomad's Guidebook* has been comprehensively updated to include the latest news on superannuation rules, mobile communications, wireless internet connections, global positioning systems, caravan park prices and electoral registration. All phone numbers and websites have, of course, also been updated. We are also pleased to have added a brand new chapter. In Chapter 10, Six of the best, we speak to several grey nomads about their experiences on half a dozen of the most iconic Australian roads and tracks. Hopefully, their stories will bring back happy memories to those of you who have already been there, and perhaps inspire and excite those of you who are about to strike out on your own grand adventure.

This is a holistic guide to an amazing lifestyle being led by a growing number of very special people . . . people like you. The grey nomads.

For our part, we will never forget pulling out of our driveway, savouring that magical moment when our own big adventure officially began. We remember being excited but also being apprehensive. Leaving behind family, friends and the familiarity of your own neighbourhood to strike off into the great unknown is a massive step. What if we didn't like it? What if we found we couldn't support our new lifestyle? What if we were out there on our own?

We need not have worried. Out on the road, the hassles of our old existence seemed to instantly melt away and we were able just to concentrate on making the most of each and every day.

We fell immediately in love with our new life and the wonderful people we met. We were amazed not just by the number of grey nomads out there in the caravan parks and the camping areas, but also by the warmth, openness and friendliness of them all. In two years on the road, we can count on the fingers of one hand the number of fellow travellers who were anything other than incredibly helpful, sociable and relaxed. If you ask any long-term nomad what the best thing about travelling around Australia is, they will almost always say 'the people'.

Running a close second, of course, would be the places you see. We had travelled a bit before the 'big one', but we had always been on a schedule. Suddenly, instead of rushing from Tourist Destination A to Tourist Destination B, we had the chance to linger, to venture down the smaller roads, to check out that camping wonder spot we'd been told about the previous evening. We quickly realised that no amount of time would ever be enough to see properly what there is to see, to soak up the essence of this amazing country.

Everything and everywhere was simply magnificent. From the vivid greens and amazing contrasts of Tasmania to the dusty outback towns and surf beaches of South Australia, from the magnificent national parks and stunning coastal drives of Victoria to the crocodile-infested waterways of the Northern Territory, it was all so much better than we had dared dream.

We decided to stay a fair while in Western Australia as it was so far from our home and we thought we might never get back out there again. Wrong. Even though we spent nine months in Western Australia we will *definitely* go back again. We loved the rugged gorges of the Kimberley, the white sandy beaches of the southwest and the uncrowded, unhurried atmosphere in the remote regions. Similarly, the vast open spaces of Queensland and the magic of the Great Barrier Reef will live with us forever, as will the amazing beachside camps and fossicking areas of New South Wales.

In nomad hotspots such as Broome, Darwin and Port Douglas, we cheerfully joined the dry-season throng for happy-hour drinks and made friends for life as we did so.

Although we tried to spend most nights in free and budget campsites enjoying the campfires and the night sky, we also looked forward greatly to the time we spent in caravan parks. The anticipation we felt driving into a well-appointed park after a spell in the bush was simply delicious. We'll certainly never take the pleasures of hot showers and flushing toilets for granted again!

That said, we're back in a house for a while now and we're finding it something of a challenge to re-adjust to 'normal' life. But we know there's still so much to do and so much to see that it won't be long until we're pulling out of our driveway once more, revelling in the magical moment when another grand adventure gets under way. Perhaps life on the road *is* 'normal' life, after all.

1

Financing the trip

The prospect of endless days of carefree camping with new friends, surrounded by spectacular scenery, is enough to persuade thousands of older Australians to hit the open road each year. Beyond doubt, a wonderful lifestyle awaits most of those adventurous enough to join the swelling ranks of the grey nomads.

However, not every story from the highways and byways of this great southern land has a happy ending. For the most part, it is those travellers who don't properly plan their trip and who don't make a realistic assessment of how they expect to live who end up disappointed.

Finances, inevitably, have a huge role to play here. It is true that life on the road can be incredibly cheap but camping in the bush and basic living is not for everyone. Sorting out your financial affairs before you leave and making a sensible on-road budget that will suit the lifestyle you want is essential.

And then, of course, there are the getting-ready-to-go costs. Taking an extended trip, whether it is for three months or three decades, is not simply a matter of locking up the house and hitting the highway. A lot of thought – and, importantly, money – has to be invested in getting the right rig and set-up for the trip you want. In Chapter Two we look in detail at the sort of rigs that are available but, for now, it is important to bear in mind that you can spend anywhere up to $500,000 getting ready to go. It is obviously not necessary to splash out anything like that amount but, if you are planning to travel tens of thousands of kilometres in often-remote country, you will need a rig that is both reliable and comfortable. When it comes to setting yourself up, trying to save money can be a costly exercise!

But, however you choose to travel, the essential rules remain the same. Do your sums and have a good time.

Estimating costs

ONGOING EXPENSES
While your on-road budget will be dominated by necessary evils such as fuel, food and camping fees, it is important not to forget about ongoing costs, some of which will be throwbacks to your old life as a 'house dweller'.

House expenses
The majority of grey nomads choose to keep the family home by either renting it out or allowing friends or family to look

after it. Inevitably this choice entails a host of continuing expenses:

- *Mortgage* – those still paying off a mortgage will, of course, have to continue to make their payments and will need to be aware of the possibility of interest rate rises.

- *Rates* – domestic rates in most places in Australia have risen sharply in the past year or two, so possible increases need to be taken into account. Most councils allow you to pay your rates in advance for the year, or you can arrange a quarterly direct debit.

- *Utilities* – unless your house is rented and the tenants have agreed to pay them, water bills and other utilities will need to be taken care of in your absence. Arranging direct debits to cover these kinds of bills is an effective way to ensure you don't miss any due dates.

- *Insurance* – although you may no longer be residing at your house, it is vital that you maintain your home insurance. Most insurance companies offer customers a choice of paying their annual premiums in advance or by monthly instalments. Make sure you keep the payments up to date so your policy doesn't lapse. If you are leaving your house vacant and are relying on friends or relatives to collect the post and mow the grass, check with your insurance company about its rules and limits for leaving the house vacant. The policy and/or the premium may have to be adjusted. For those renting out their homes, acquiring specialist land-lord insurance usually incurs a higher premium.

For more information, see 'What to do with your property' later in this chapter.

- *General maintenance* – while you may have left your home in perfect condition, maintenance issues ranging from a leaking tap to a leaking roof can still deliver an unwelcome blow to your budget. You must allow for this possibility. A handyman's bill of a few hundred dollars can have a massive impact.

While none of these extra expenses would be overly significant on their own, you need to be aware that they could come up and you must plan for them.

Car insurance

Comprehensive car insurance is a must-have for long-term travellers. It is designed to cover your vehicle and contents for eventualities including accidents, theft, vandalism and even storm damage. Some policies provide accommodation costs and car rental while your vehicle is being repaired. The cost of the policy is calculated on the year, make, model and condition of the car, where the vehicle is garaged, and the age and driving record of the drivers.

There are two main types of comprehensive car insurance: agreed value policy and market value policy. An agreed value policy is when the person buying insurance and the insurer agree on a sum that the car is worth and the premiums are based on that value. Market value policies are usually cheaper but, if the car is a write-off, the insurer determines its value – and this may be less than the car is worth to you.

Many insurance companies offer discounts to over-55s and to those who take out more than one policy with the company. Some firms even offer discounts to people who buy their policy online. As a general example, an agreed value comprehensive policy for a nomad with a good driving record and a 4WD wagon worth about $33,000 will cost in the region of $700 per annum. Shop around and check policy features so you know how your claim would be handled if something does happen.

Caravan/motorhome insurance

As well as your ongoing vehicle insurance costs, you may well now have caravan, motorhome or camper trailer insurance to worry about. Depending on the level of cover you choose, which state you reside in, and the insurance company you go with, insuring, for example, a $50,000 caravan will cost you around $600 a year. A policy for a $200,000 motorhome can set you back around $1300 per annum. It's certainly not an expense you want to forget about if you are living on a tight budget.

Your rig becomes your home on the road so it's crucial to protect it with a high-quality insurance policy in case of accident, theft, storm damage or sudden illness. A comprehensive policy will also provide you with alternative accommodation if your van/motorhome is being repaired. In addition, it will ensure your vehicle is returned to your address if, for any reason, you are unable to bring it back yourself. Most caravan/ motorhome policies also provide coverage for contents so you can insure everything from your laptop and camera to your bicycle, fishing gear and jewellery.

As with car insurance, some policies provide market value coverage while others offer agreed value coverage. Also, if you've carried out any improvements to your van, such as installing a new air-conditioning unit or re-upholstering the seats, be sure to tell the insurance company so a realistic valuation can be made.

Although the whole point of a caravan or motorhome is to travel in it, most insurance companies calculate your premium based, in part, on where your rig will be garaged. If you plan to keep your house on and eventually return there, the address you provide to the insurance company will be your home address. If you plan to sell your house and travel indefinitely, you may have difficulties securing coverage from some insurers. Ask if this is a problem or if it will be sufficient to supply contact details, including some sort of 'care of' postal address.

Although every rig and situation is different, some useful caravan/motorhome insurance features you may wish to look for in a policy are:

- Cover for returning your caravan to your home if you are no longer fit to drive.

- Cover for returning your caravan to your home if your towing vehicle is no longer in a fit state to be driven.

- Cover for travelling on gravel roads and/or 4WD tracks if you think you might take them.

- Cover for accidental damage, theft and attempted theft.

- Cover for storm, hail and flood damage.

- Cover for legal liability claims.

- Cover to pay for alternative accommodation if your van is uninhabitable following an accident.

- Contents cover.

- Cover for emergency repairs if your caravan cannot be towed after an accident.

- Cover for delivery of your motorhome back to you after it has been repaired.

Remember to obtain a few quotes from different sources and compare levels of coverage and premiums. As already mentioned, insurance companies often offer discounts to customers who take out other policies, such as motor insurance and home insurance, with them.

Vehicle registration

When you're on the road it's easy to lose track of time but you can rest assured that your vehicle registration and associated expenses are coming around quicker than you would like. The charges are slightly different in each state. At the time of writing, in New South Wales, for example, you will spend more than $380 renewing registration for a heavy vehicle like a 4WD. There is also the small matter of the compulsory insurance certificate which, again in New South Wales, will cost you around $250 if you are over 55 with a good driving record and you also have comprehensive insurance.

A small caravan with a tare weight of between 1155 kilograms and 1504 kilograms will cost around $270 to register in New South Wales, while the bigger vans cost around $380.

In some states you also have the cost of an inspection to think about, depending on the age of your vehicle and caravan. All in all, this is one annual obligation not to look forward to.

Family commitments

While grey nomads are frequently famed for their ability to travel and live on a shoestring, that miserliness sometimes doesn't extend to dealing with other family members. Older Australians often playfully refer to themselves as being part of the SKI (Spending the Kids' Inheritance) generation, but that tag doesn't always sit comfortably with the truth.

Many younger nomads have children going through tertiary education or in the early stages of getting themselves established in the workforce. In this day and age, particularly with real estate prices as high as they are, there is an expectation among many youngsters that parents will always be there to offer financial support. That can be an expensive proposition for poor old Mum and Dad. It is important for you to discuss with the family just how your decision to travel long-term could impact on your ability to provide a financial safety net.

Each family is different and you may well be happy – and able – to keep helping out with your kids' accommodation costs or study expenses, or your grandchildren's school fees or field trip expenses. That is up to you, but the extent to which you expect to be helping others out is something that needs to be taken into account when you draw up the financial blueprint for your trip.

DAY-TO-DAY EXPENSES

A realistic on-road budget is vital to a relaxing trip. You can't properly enjoy a happy-hour beer or glass of wine with the couple who've just pulled up in their Coromal caravan if you're preoccupied with money worries. Remember, though, even the most carefully thought-out budget can be destroyed by unforeseen circumstances such as a surge in fuel prices, an interest rate hike, an illness or accident, or a family emergency. Whether you're travelling in a 30-year-old Millard or a $400,000 Winnebago you'll need to make a budget, stick to it – and then keep your fingers crossed!

Camping costs

When budgeting your trip, three costs will dominate the expenditure column – food, fuel and camping fees.

While you can make some minor adjustments to your food and fuel outgoings, they are still relatively fixed expenses. In contrast, the amount spent on camping can vary wildly, and personal preferences come into play here. Caravan park-loving travellers can easily spend $200 a week to park the van, while their bush-dwelling counterparts can stay in paradise for nix. If you visit virtually any established free camping spot in the country during the right season, you will nearly always find a cluster of nomads settling in for the night. They have all they need for a pleasant stay and figure they may as well save some money on accommodation expenses.

For most nomads, the answer to a relaxed and enjoyable trip lies in finding a happy medium. They spend some time in free or inexpensive camping spots, as well as occasionally enjoying the comforts of caravan park facilities.

Below is a rough indication of the fees attached to the camping options available to you. You will find a detailed analysis of the pros and cons of each of them in Chapter Six under the heading 'Which sort of camp?'.

Caravan parks

A stay in a caravan park will typically cost in the region of $25 to $30 for two people per night, although this figure can rise depending on the level of services provided, the time of year you stay, and the location of the park. If you are not planning to use the facilities offered at resort-like parks, such as kids' clubs and tennis courts, then you should think long and hard about paying for them. You will also tend to pay more in or near big towns, or if you are right on the beach, although it is a sad fact that many spectacular beachfront caravan parks are now being sold to developers.

Remember also that school holidays are an expensive time

to stay in caravan parks. Prices shoot up and yet there is still no shortage of people willing to book in. If you are watching your bank balance, try to find a nice, quiet, secure free camp or national park camp before the holidays start and stay there until they are over. Everything will return to normal once the 9–5ers are back at work and their kids are back at school. Oh, and you won't have to queue to use the shower, the toilet or the pay phone either!

If you intend to use caravan parks regularly, you may find it will pay to join one of the caravan park membership schemes available. BIG4 Holiday Parks, Top Tourist Parks and Family Parks of Australia are three of the biggest caravan park groups offering membership schemes. In general, the schemes provide members with a discount for stays in affiliate parks, while the member parks must meet certain requirements in terms of facilities and cleanliness.

For example, BIG4 Holiday Parks offer a ten per cent discount to members on accommodation fees – although the discount is limited to $30 per stay. At the time of writing, new members must pay $40 for a two-year membership, which entitles them to the accommodation discount, a directory mapping out all the BIG4 parks in Australia and other special offers. Assuming you save around $2 per night, you can quickly make up the cost of membership. Top Tourist Parks and Family Parks of Australia offer similar schemes, although their membership fees are about half that of BIG4. All three chains boast more than 160 parks nationwide.

OzParks is another caravan park group established in 2005 to cater to people who want clean amenities and competitive rates. OzParks has approximately 45 parks nationwide, charges $16.50 for two years' membership and provides a ten per cent discount on accommodation for members.

If you are thinking of joining one, it may be worth staying at a couple of parks in each one of these groups to determine which suits you best. Bear in mind, however, that parks which are part of these schemes aren't always the cheapest in town.

Contact information

BIG4 Holiday Parks
Website: www.big4.com.au
Tel: 1800 632 444

Family Parks of Australia
Website: www.familyparks.com.au
Tel: 1300 855 707

OzParks
Website: www.ozparks.com.au
Tel: (03) 5983 0251

Top Tourist Parks
Website: www.toptouristparks.com.au
Tel: (08) 8363 1901

National parks

The cost of staying in national parks varies from state to state and sometimes from camping area to camping area. Indeed, in many of Tasmania's national park camping areas there is no charge at all. As a general rule, you can expect to pay around $10 to $20 for two people per night, with a drop toilet and not much else in the way of facilities. However, times are changing and at Ormiston Gorge in the Northern Territory, for instance, you will find solar-heated showers and running water. In some regions, notably in the Northern Territory and Western Australia, you may also find free gas barbecues. This is perhaps the precursor to the demise of the great Aussie tradition of campfires in national parks, which is slowly being eroded due to concerns about bushfires and potential damage to the environment caused by cavalier firewood gatherers. There is also a charge for entry to national parks in some states, although you would have to pay this whether you were camping or not.

See Chapter Six for details of national park entry charges and the availability of discount annual passes.

State forests, bush camping and rest areas

Why pay for camping every night when you have everything you need in your rig? A lot of the best camping spots are out in the wilds somewhere. You will need to have a degree of self-sufficiency to maximise the use of these camps. Camping in state forests is often free or there may be an honesty box on display with a nominal charge requested. There are also a number of publications available that give you the run-down on where to find some other terrific free camping spots. Many of the established camps provide drop toilets and some even have water. Rest areas on the sides of highways and roads offer decent facilities for travellers and some are well set up for overnighters.

See Chapter Six for more about bush camping, free camps and roadside stops.

Fuel

The ever-changing price of fuel plays havoc with the task of budgeting for a big trip. This is normally the biggest on-the-road expense and yet is certainly the most difficult to estimate.

It's not so long ago that $1.50 a litre was considered a

psychological barrier that fuel prices might never exceed. Now all bets are off, and how high prices could go over the next few years is anybody's guess.

While it's bad enough that the political volatility of the oil-producing countries of the Middle East makes fuel prices go up and down (usually up) on a daily basis, city-based nomads have to be ready for a further shock when they get out into regional Australia. Prices at the bowser can be higher – much higher. At certain places on the Nullarbor Plain, or the Kimberley, or the Northern Territory, you may pay up to 50 per cent more than you have become used to. Nomads must do their homework and be prepared to pay for the privilege of passing through some wonderful country.

It is easy to get indignant about exorbitant fuel costs but, before you start shouting 'profiteering' from the rooftops, bear in mind that freight costs – as well as the costs of luring staff to often lonely and unattractive roadhouses – can be considerable. Besides transport costs and the level of competition, prices may also vary across the country due to the different fuel subsidies in each state. Nonetheless, it's hard to explain away a 20 or 30 cent per litre price difference between fuel at equally lonely Nullarbor roadhouses.

Be warned, though. Urban myths abound about travellers who have dared to complain about the price of fuel in these places. The stories go that they then find themselves stranded as an ornery roadhouse manager refuses to fill their tank. It's hard to know whether the stories are true or not, but are you game enough to put it to the test?

How far will you travel?

One of the most accurate methods of assessing how many kilometres you will travel on a big trip is to overestimate the distance wildly, then double that estimate, and hope you are getting close. It's a big and interesting country.

From a day-to-day expense point of view, it is not the overall distance you will travel that matters, it is the speed at which you do it. A number of excellent websites and maps can help you plan your trip. See the Maps section in Chapter Three for details.

How much fuel per kilometre

Slower travel is cheaper travel and the grey nomad who isn't in a rush will find he or she has more to spend on the good things in life – like a meal out or a zebra rock necklace! A large diesel 4WD towing a caravan will use around 15–20 litres per 100 kilometres. A similar-sized petrol 4WD will use around 20–25 litres per 100 kilometres. It is a sobering statistic when you bear in mind that prices could be around the $2 mark in some parts of Australia.

Putting that into more concrete terms, the RACQ estimates that a diesel 4WD towing a caravan would consume 685 litres of fuel on a trip from Brisbane to Cairns and back, at an average 17 litres/100km. If diesel were $1.50 per litre, the trip would cost $1027.50; if it were $2 per litre, the cost would rise to $1370.

How to improve fuel efficiency

There are a number of commonsense ways that nomads can improve their fuel efficiency whatever rig they are travelling in. WWF-Australia has produced these simple, fuel-efficiency driving tips to save money on fuel and reduce the greenhouse gas emissions produced by your car.

1. Drive in high gear

Your car engine runs most efficiently in high gear (around 1500 to 2500rpm, lower in diesel-run cars), so change up through the gears as soon as you can. Automatic cars shift up gears more quickly if you ease back on the accelerator once the car gathers momentum.

2. Drive smoothly

Braking and accelerating back up to full speed uses more fuel than driving at a consistent speed. Avoid unnecessary acceleration and braking by driving at a good distance from the car in front, so you can anticipate and travel with the flow of traffic.

3. Turn your engine off instead of idling

Minimise fuel wasted on idling by turning off the engine whenever your car is stopped or held up for an extended period of time (even as little as 30 seconds). Having the engine switched off even for a short period will save more fuel than is lost from the burst of fuel involved in restarting the engine.

4. Reduce your speed

Slow down! At 110 km/h your car uses up to 25 per cent more fuel than it would cruising at 90 km/h.

5. Reduce your drag

Additional parts on the exterior of your car – such as roof racks (and the things you put on them), and having the window open – can increase 'drag' and how much fuel you use by more than 20 per cent.

6. Look after your tyres

Inflate your car tyres to the highest pressure recommended by the manufacturer (including your spare) and ensure your wheels are properly aligned. Looking after your tyres will not only reduce your fuel consumption, it will also extend tyre life and improve handling.

7. Use the air-conditioning sparingly
Car air-conditioning uses around ten per cent extra fuel. But at speeds of more than 80 km/h, air-con use is better for fuel economy than an open window. Make sure that your air-conditioning is properly serviced to prevent the leaking of CFCs from the seals.

8. Travel light
The more a vehicle carries, the more fuel it uses, so don't carry more cargo than you need to and clear out your boot. An extra 50 kilograms of weight can increase your fuel bill by around two per cent.

9. Service your vehicle regularly
Keeping your vehicle well tuned will mean it is operating at its most efficient, which means it will use less fuel.

Where to find the cheapest fuel
One of the most powerful attractions of the grey nomad life-style is the camaraderie and companionship it offers. Wherever you pull up, there's a fair chance that a like-minded traveller will soon be parking close by and, sooner or later, the conversation will wend its way to a subject close to both of your hearts – fuel prices. There's no better way to find out where to get the best deal than to talk to someone who has just been where you are going. Fuel prices vary widely, even in smaller towns, so don't always rush to the first place you see.

Of course, another way to keep costs down is to use the discount fuel vouchers given out by the major supermarkets. Similarly, wherever possible, it is plain commonsense to fill up in the bigger towns or cities, where competition generally ensures prices are kept lower.

Many grey nomads also like to fill up jerry cans when they do have access to cheaper fuel, and this can save significant dollars when travelling in remote areas. On the other hand, it is a waste of money to lug an extra 40 litres of fuel around if it is never going to be used. Some people find it reassuring always to have extra fuel with them as an emergency stock but, if you plan your trip properly, it's unnecessary to carry it all of the time.

A number of websites, such as www.motormouth.com.au, are dedicated to helping travellers find the cheapest fuel. These can be useful, although they are not always practical to access for the on-the-move nomad. They also tend to have a city-centric focus and may do more to keep you informed about what you would be paying if you'd stayed at home rather than helping you find the cheapest prices where you are.

While there are a number of valid ways to help reduce your fuel bills, it's impossible to drive around Australia without pumping thousands of dollars worth of fuel into your tank. Do what you can to keep costs down but don't become obsessive. Many grey nomads are travelling on a tight budget but all are on the road because they want to see the country. The cost of missing out on a once-in-a-lifetime opportunity to see a magnificent gorge or spectacular waterfall normally outweighs the cost of 20 litres of fuel. See what you came to see and enjoy it.

Vehicle maintenance

The cost of keeping a rig on the road depends on many factors. As a general rule, the newer the vehicle, the lower the ongoing maintenance costs. Similarly, grey nomads who stick to the bitumen rather than venturing onto the rough stuff will tend to save dollars on mechanics' bills. Each car and journey is different but your rig is now your home and, as such, it needs looking after properly. Prevention is better than cure and a thorough service in a major city is considerably cheaper than a long tow from the middle of nowhere. While it is possible to save cash by carrying out basic vehicle maintenance tasks yourself, for most people a regular professional service is a necessary and sensible precaution.

Manufacturers generally recommend a major service every 20,000 kilometres and a minor service every 10,000 kilometres. A minor service – where things like fan belts are checked, grease points greased, and oil and filters changed – will cost you between $150 and $300. It can be a heavy hit to the budget but it's probably money well spent. The cost of a major service will depend, to a large extent, on what work your vehicle requires.

While regular servicing and maintenance checks may minimise the risks, a budget-busting breakdown could still be just over the next hill. Hope for the best and budget for the worst.

Another ongoing fact of life will be wear and tear on your tyres. While there are stories of people going all the way around the country without getting a flat, they are few and far between. As previously stated, having regular wheel rotations, balancing and alignments will all help to prolong the life of your tyres, as will keeping them inflated to the recommended pressure. If you are planning to get off the blacktop and onto some dirt tracks you can expect your tyre maintenance bills to rise sharply. A straightforward puncture in a tubeless tyre can normally be repaired relatively cheaply, for maybe $25 or so depending on where you are. You can also buy puncture repair kits for tubeless tyres, which is a surprisingly uncomplicated job as long as you use your commonsense and follow the instructions properly. You will, however, need to bring your own compressor.

When only a new tyre will do, expect to pay anywhere from $150 to $300 or so for a 4WD tyre. Obviously, a second-hand tyre is a cheaper alternative but extreme caution is required when going down that route. It is never worth compromising your safety to save $100.

See Chapter Nine for a full guide to vehicle maintenance.

Food

Food budgets are subject to the tastes and dietary requirements of individual travellers. Nevertheless, many couples find aiming to spend $100 to $150 a week purely on food items is a realistic target. If you are travelling in a comfortable rig with good cooking and refrigerating facilities, it's possible to eat as well as you do at home and spend only slightly more doing it.

Commonsense rules apply when it comes to keeping food bills low. Remember to shop up in the big towns or cities and make full use of your freezer and fridge. The more remote you go, the higher the food prices get, and it can be quite painful to part with $6 for a loaf of frozen bread. Some nomads, however, are happy to pay a little more to help support rural communities.

Depending on the area you are in and the season, you can pick up some super-cheap fruit and vegies from roadside stalls and markets.

For those who are really counting the cents, cooking over the campfire is a fantastic way to make your gas cylinders last longer and to make you the envy of the camping area. Delicious smells wafting from a simmering camp oven are guaranteed to draw people over for a chat, too.

Similarly, making use of the myriad free gas and electric barbecues available in many reserves and national parks can also help to keep cooking costs down.

Travelling around Australia should never be an endurance test, however, and many long-termers find it nice to break the cooking routine occasionally with a cheap and hassle-free meal at an RSL club or somewhere similar. These nights out can be a real morale booster and may be just as cheap as cooking at your camp.

Finally, of course, you've always got the trusty fishing rod option. Who needs a supermarket when there's a seemingly endless supply of barramundi, Australian salmon, bream and flathead waiting to be landed? Good luck . . . and don't forget to take your crab trap as well.

Entertainment

The best things in life are free. It won't cost you anything to visit Australia's endless unspoilt beaches; nearly all of the magnificent gorges and waterfalls can be enjoyed for nothing; and there is no price tag attached to the craggy mountains and the mighty rivers.

However, as the popularity of every area grows, so too does the number of tourist operators eager to offer you new ways to spend your money. It's worth deciding in advance what your policy is in regard to tourist attractions. If you spend $10 for a guided tour of every cave you come across on your trip, you'll probably end up having to live in one! Depending on your budget, think through what you are prepared to spend entertainment dollars on and what you're not. A gold coin donation to visit some of the excellent small museums may seem reasonable; a once-in-a-lifetime trip out to the Great Barrier Reef may seem essential, so too the Yellow Waters cruise in Kakadu National Park. And then there's the fee charged by the traditional owners to visit Standley Chasm in the Northern Territory's Macdonnell Ranges, plus the spectacular helicopter flight over Mitchell Falls in Western Australia. The list goes on.

Work out what you want to see and what you can afford to see and, while you will always need to be flexible, try to stick to your plan.

Remember, too, that many caravan parks, particularly those in outback areas, offer free entertainment such as bush poets or country singers. Take advantage.

When you are in a town, read the local paper and inquire at the visitor information centre to find out what cheap and free attractions are in the area and when local markets are held. Many regions hold produce and craft markets; both provide opportunities to take in the atmosphere, meet people and pick up a couple of bargains.

On the road, often the best entertainment is the company of others, and the grey nomad tradition of a happy-hour drink with new friends offers rich rewards. Just remember, as you enjoy your favourite tipple in paradise, that the cost of alcohol goes up steeply as you head further out of the major population centres. Cheers.

Seniors Card discounts

Every state and territory government around Australia issues the Seniors Card to Australians over the age of 60. The card is issued in recognition of the contribution that seniors have made, and continue to make, to the Australian community.

The range of government benefits attached to the card is determined by each state or territory and may include discounts on transport, motor vehicle registration, entry to tourist attractions and national parks, fees for educational courses and many other items.

Numerous private businesses also offer Seniors Card holders discounts on their goods and services. A statewide directory of participating businesses and the discounts they offer is usually provided to Seniors Card recipients. Most discounts are also offered to interstate card holders – so it is always worth asking for the discount.

The Seniors Card websites listed below contain lots of useful information for older Australians and – in addition to the list of government and private benefits attached to the card – there are special offers for travel, accommodation, events and courses. Each state and territory has slightly different requirements to qualify for the card in terms of employment and residency. Check with the authority in your state or territory to find out whether you are eligible for the card and associated benefits.

Contact information
General
Website: www.seniorscard.com.au

Australian Capital Territory
Website: www.seniorscard.act.gov.au
Tel: (02) 6282 3777

New South Wales
Website: www.seniorscard.nsw.gov.au
Tel: 1300 364 758

Northern Territory
Website: www.seniorscard.nt.gov.au
Tel: 1800 777 704 or (08) 8922 7354

Queensland
Website: www.communities.qld.gov.au/seniorscard
Tel: 1800 175 500

South Australia
Website: www.familiesandcommunities.sa.gov.au
Tel: 1800 819 961

Tasmania
Website: www.dpac.tas.gov.au/divisions/cdd/seniors_card
Tel: 1300 135 513

Victoria
Website: www.seniorscard.vic.gov.au
Tel: 1300 797 210

Western Australia
Website: www.seniorscard.wa.gov.au
Tel: (08) 6217 8855 for metro areas;
1800 671 233 for country areas

What to do with your property

Working out what to do with the house is a massive challenge
for soon-to-be grey nomads. While to a large extent this decision will depend on individual circumstances, careful thought
is always required.

A large number of wannabe nomads, however, consider
the choice to be a simple one. They have hundreds of thousands of dollars of equity locked up in their home and they
want to use it to finance their dream trip. It's that simple. This

temptation is strongest when the plan is to travel for many years. While selling may well be the only realistic option for some, all the implications need to be properly analysed and all other options thoroughly explored. It's a big step and you don't want to get it wrong.

SELLING UP

The vast majority of grey nomads will probably have paid off their mortgage and seen the value of their home shoot up in recent years. For some, it is this surging equity that will have given them the impetus to take to life on the road in the first place.

While the sudden arrival of hundreds of thousands of dollars in your bank account can make you feel extremely wealthy, stop before you invest in a luxury motorhome instead of a camper trailer. Have you considered all the consequences of cashing in on the family home?

- *Centrelink implications*: The family home is considered an exempt asset by Centrelink, even if it is worth more than $1 million. Bear in mind that it is only considered an exempt asset for the first year that you are away. Once the family home is sold, the proceeds of the sale will be taken into account and may easily result in the loss of a pension and associated fringe benefits. For example, a couple which sells its home for $500,000 and spends $150,000 getting its rig organised will suddenly have an extra $350,000 that Centrelink will want to know all about. As a consequence, the couple may miss out on some pension payments. Living on the road can be very cheap, so weigh up which is more important to you – the cash in the bank or the pension payments.

- *Emotional impact*: Selling a home is not an easy thing to do, particularly if you are not about to buy a new house or build a new home. Your neighbours will never be your neighbours again; the living room where your grandchild took his or her first steps will soon be a room collecting someone else's memories. Living in a van or a motorhome is exciting and it's different but how will you feel about not having a place to go 'home' to at the end of your journey? On the other hand, some people feel a sense of freedom and relief at the prospect of not having a property to tie them down or to worry about.

- *What next?* Even the longest journey must come to an end. Despite the fact you may be selling up in order to travel for the next decade or two, there will come a time when you are no longer financially or physically able to keep going. What will you do then? It is important to have a plan in place as even living permanently in a caravan park is not always all that cheap. Some grey nomads travel around Australia keeping half an eye out for a desirable – and sometimes cheaper – place to buy property and to live at some time in the future. This can work out well. However, if you don't find that dream spot, you must realise it may no longer be possible to return to your old stomping ground. Depending on where your old home was and how the real estate market performs there, you may well find yourself priced out of the market. Another option favoured by many is to move in with family members when it is all over. Depending on family dynamics, this can work out fine but it's probably wise to let your kids know what you've got in mind first!

REVERSE MORTGAGE

The reverse mortgage concept has received plenty of publicity in recent years and not all of it positive. It remains, nonetheless, a realistic way to finance an extended trip that might otherwise be unachievable. It also allows grey nomads to return to their own home after an extended tour.

Basically, reverse mortgages enable homeowners to convert some of the equity in their property into a lump sum or an income stream in the form of a loan. Interest, fees and charges accrue until the loan is finally paid off with the sale of the house or from the borrower's estate. In effect, the longer you have the loan, the more the debt will grow.

A number of financial institutions, including the Commonwealth Bank and the St George Bank, offer reverse mortgage products. While this may appear to be a perfect solution, the reality is that you will pay compound interest on the loan, so you can end up with a big debt. For example, a loan at seven per cent compound interest will just about double in ten years, so if you borrowed about $40,000, you will owe about $80,000. When considering any reverse mortgage, you should be clear who is liable for this possible loss.

This also means that you will not be able to pass on the family home to children or grandchildren when you die. It's an issue you may wish to discuss with your family.

Be aware also that if you live with a partner or spouse but the house is only in one name, the loan will have to be repaid when the partner who owns the house dies.

If you are contemplating taking the reverse mortgage route with a lump sum payout, remember that any spare money you don't spend on your rig or other items is counted as an asset by Centrelink and may impact on your pension entitlements.

The case study below, provided by the Australian Securities

and Investments Commission (ASIC), should help you to get a better understanding of how reverse mortgages work. It shows how your loan could double in less than ten years, just through the force of compound interest. If interest rates increase (with a variable rate loan) you could end up owing even more.

CASE STUDY

Kim is 70 years old and decides to borrow a lump sum of $100,000 at an interest rate of 8.32 per cent per year. Kim's home is worth $400,000. Here's what Kim could owe at the end of various periods.

Number of years since Kim took out the loan	What Kim's home may be worth if housing values increase 3.5 per cent every year	What Kim or Kim's estate could owe if the interest rate is 8.32 per cent*	What Kim could owe if the interest rate increases to 11 per cent** after the first two years
5 years	$475,000	$154,000	$167,000
10 years	$564,000	$234,000	$290,000
15 years	$670,000	$356,000	$502,000
20 years	$796,000	$540,000	$869,000 Exceeds value of home, 'negative equity'

All figures rounded to nearest $1000

*assumes 8.32 per cent interest applies throughout

**assumes 11 per cent interest starts after two years and then applies throughout

Get advice

As always, it is simply commonsense to obtain sound advice before making a big financial decision such as selling your home or taking out a reverse mortgage. At the very least, it is worth talking to Centrelink to find out how your pension entitlement may be affected.

See page 45 for contact information.

RENTING OUT

The major advantage of renting out your house is that you have somewhere to come 'home' to when your travelling is over. It removes the feeling that you have gone out on a limb and are somehow risking everything to make the trip happen. Some of those who sell up to go on the road report feeling increased pressure to keep travelling and to 'enjoy' it. Long-term travelling is not for everybody and, if you rent out your own home, you can always go back to your old life and chalk your brief adventure up to experience.

Just like selling your home, renting it out has implications for your Centrelink entitlements. The changed circumstances that rental income brings about can lead to Centrelink reducing or even axing your age pension payments. Everyone's circumstances are different, so take good advice before proceeding.

Any rental income will have to be declared in your tax return but insurance, rates, and maintenance can then be claimed as tax deductions to offset the income. Importantly, you are allowed to rent out your home for up to six years without losing the capital gains tax exemption on your family home. However, you must not claim another property as your principal place of residence during this time.

Property management

If you are able to rent your property out to someone you know and trust, there shouldn't be too many dramas with property maintenance and respect issues. Your trusted tenants can contact you if there are problems and you can advise them how to proceed.

However, the situation changes dramatically when there are strangers in your house. Unfortunately, renting out a property is not always as simple as collecting the cash every week and you will need to appoint someone to keep an eye on things in your absence. Think it over carefully before asking a family member or friend to take on this role for you, as it can be quite a stressful and time-consuming task if there are 'problems'.

For this reason, many grey nomads seeking to rent their house out engage a property manager. They are normally professionals who work within a specialised division in a real estate agency.

Their main roles are to market the property, select tenants, collect rent, arrange repairs and represent the property owner at tribunal hearings if there is a problem with the tenant. Typically these property managers charge between seven per cent and nine per cent of the weekly rent for this service, as well as extra for finding a new tenant and for inspections. This fee is probably worth it for the peace of mind it gives you. Your family home is still your family home and you want to make sure it is properly looked after.

What to look for in a property manager:

- A track record of successful property management. Do they have letters of recommendation from previous customers?

- A commitment to communicate regularly with you, particularly if there are maintenance issues.

- A clear understanding that this is your home and you expect it to be looked after as such.

- A transparent accounting and payment structure that will deliver you regular and reliable payments. It is worth requesting that a direct debit arrangement be written into any tenant's lease so that you know exactly when rent money will be paid.

- A willingness to employ the handymen and tradespeople you recommend in the event of maintenance work being required.

Landlord insurance

This is a sensible safeguard against all manner of events that are not necessarily accounted for by your typical home insurance policy. Nevertheless, not all landlord insurance policies are the same and you should ensure that the one you choose covers things such as:

- Malicious damage by a tenant, including arson.

- Accidental damage.

- Loss of rental income due either to necessary repairs, tenants absconding, or payment default.

- Legal liability, which can protect you if a tenant sues you for an injury suffered in your house.

Assuming all of these items are included, compare the extent of the coverage and the excess required by the various policies very carefully.

Exploring Australia is a pursuit that should be carried out in a relaxed frame of mind. Put all of the necessary safeguards in place to protect your home and then look forwards, not backwards.

Contact information for renting out your home

The Department of Fair Trading offers fact sheets, brochures and guidelines for tenants and landlords.

Australian Capital Territory
Department of Fair Trading
Website: www.fairtrading.act.gov.au
Tel: (02) 6207 0400

New South Wales
Department of Fair Trading
Website: www.fairtrading.nsw.gov.au
Tel: 13 32 20

Northern Territory
Consumer and Business Affairs (division of Department of Justice)
Website: www.nt.gov.au/justice/consaffairs
Tel: (08) 8999 1999 or 1800 019 319

Queensland
Department of Fair Trading
Website: www.fairtrading.qld.gov.au
Tel: 13 13 04

South Australia
Office of Consumer and Business Affairs
Website: www.ocba.sa.gov.au
Tel: (08) 8204 9544

Tasmania
Department of Fair Trading
Website: www.consumer.tas.gov.au
Tel: 1300 654 499

Victoria
Department of Fair Trading
Website: www.consumer.vic.gov.au
Tel: 1300 558 181

Western Australia
Department of Consumer and Employment Protection
Website: www.docep.wa.gov.au
Tel: 1300 304 054

HOUSESITTERS

For people travelling for a comparatively short time or for those not comfortable with the concept of renting out their home, getting a housesitter is a viable alternative. There are a number of agencies in operation that thoroughly vet potential housesitters, giving you peace of mind when you are away on the other side of the country. Reassuringly, it seems that many of the people seeking to act as housesitters are grey nomads themselves, looking for a place to park the van for a while and enjoy some creature comforts before continuing their travels.

Housesitters will typically be required to provide professional, personal and business references and allow background checks to be made. Once a housesitter has been selected, agreement will be reached about the details of the arrangement. Normally, the housesitter will pay for things such as electricity and other utilities, while the owner may pay for things such as repairs and maintenance. Each arrangement can be tailored specifically to meet your needs.

Benefits

- No rent changes hands, so there are no tax or pension implications.

- You can rest assured that your house, its contents and its garden are being looked after.

- You are leaving your house occupied and therefore less susceptible to break-ins.

- There is no need to put your furniture and personal belongings in storage.

- The traditional grey nomad pet dilemma is resolved – have them looked after in the comfort of their own home.

- You have someone 'in situ' who can forward your mail to whichever post office you want and who can take phone and e-mail messages.

- You don't have to burden often-busy family members with 'keeping an eye' on your place.

Websites
www.aussiehousesitters.com.au
www.happyhousesitters.com.au
www.houseminders.com.au
www.housesittingservices.com.au
www.thegreynomads.com.au/featurespages/adverhousesit.html

STORING YOUR BELONGINGS

For those who choose to rent their house out while they are away or sell up completely, the next issue is what to do with all of their belongings. This is not always as simple – or as cheap – as you might think. Some of the possibilities are:

Family or friends

Depending on how many belongings you have, storing things with family and friends may not be a bad option. If you've sold your house and pretty much everything in it to become a permanent nomad, you should find someone happy to look after your old photos, a couple of boxes of your favourite books and that treasured golf trophy. However, few people are ruthless enough to shed themselves of their worldly goods and shackles to such an extent that their belongings will fit into the back of a station wagon. It's amazing how possessions stack up so, unless you have friends or family with loads of spare space in a garage or something similar, think carefully before imposing yourself on them.

Some people are comfortable storing their belongings in their own garage and then locking it up and making it clear to new tenants that the garage is off limits. This is more practical when the garage is a stand-alone structure.

However, if you are renting out your house and are hanging onto your TV, your lounge suite, your bed, your dining table and your fridge, you may want to consider some other options.

Professional storage

Self-storage is one of the fastest-growing industries in Australia, with more than 20 per cent growth in the past three years. Self-storage compounds basically allow you to keep your belongings in storage units – commonly sheds – for long periods of time. The area will generally be security patrolled and measures will be taken to counter the risk of rodents, insects or moisture damaging your property. The bad news is that the contents of an average three-bedroom home will just about fit into a 6-metre by 3-metre storage shed and this can cost from $2500 to $4000 a year. Extra costs can include removalists, insurance (although this may be included in your house and contents insurance – please check with your insurer) and your own padlock. There's no need to commit to a fixed-term lease so you can store your goods for as long as you like. You will, however, need to pay your fees in advance, generally a month, and you may also be required to provide a refundable deposit.

Contact information
Self-Storage Association of Australasia
This provides a list of members in your area.
Website: www.selfstorage.com.au
Tel: 1800 067 313

Building your own shed
Rather than spend a small fortune having your possessions stored in professional self-storage units, you may prefer to spend your hard-earned cash building your own shed. This can work well if you have a big yard and can put a shed somewhere out of the way, where it won't affect possible tenants. Alternatively, you might come to some arrangement to build a shed in the yard of a friend or family member. This will allow someone you trust to keep a close eye on your shed and to check on its contents occasionally.

A 6-metre by 3-metre zinc shed kit can be purchased from

hardware shops or from specialist shed and garage suppliers for around $1600. You must also factor in the cost of a concrete slab.

If you are handy or have some friends who are, building a shed of this size is certainly possible, although it is a task not to be taken lightly. Similarly, doing the formwork for a slab yourself and arranging for a concrete mixer to deliver the concrete can keep the slab price down to a few hundred dollars. Or you may choose the easy way. It will probably cost about $1000 to get a pro to put the shed together and slightly more to organise the slab. Also bear in mind that you will require council approval for a shed of this size and generally this will cost a few hundred dollars.

A big plus about the build-your-own-shed option is obviously that, at the end of your trip when you remove your belongings, someone will have a nice new shed to keep their lawnmower in. Another positive is that you won't have to consider the storage costs if you want to extend your trip. However, some caution is required.

- Check with your insurer that belongings stored in a garden shed will be covered by your existing policy.

- Don't build your shed where there is any chance of water flooding in. Build on high ground and make some drainage arrangements. It's one thing getting your garden fork wet, it's quite another giving your $5000 lounge suite and nearly-as-expensive sound system a bath.

- Build it properly and check for gaps. A fully grown rat can get through a hole the size of a 20 cent coin and can have a lot of babies while you're travelling. Put down some rat poison, just to be on the safe side.

- Ants can also be a menace. Put some poison down for them also.

- Don't build near trees that may fall or shed limbs during high winds.

- Moisture in the air is a fact of life but make sure your shed has good ventilation. Consider installing insulation to guard against condensation forming and dripping.

- Stack your goods carefully, keeping them off the ground.

Finances

SUPERANNUATION

Superannuation is a highly complicated area and professional advice should always be sought when considering your superannuation options.

While the prospect of laying your hands on hundreds of thousands of dollars, buying yourself that dreamed-of deluxe rig and living the life of Riley on the road may be tempting, taking a superannuation lump sum payout is not always the most financially sensible, or enjoyable, course of action.

Deciding whether to keep your money invested in super or to cash it in will depend on your overall financial circumstances, as well as how – and how long – you plan to travel. While there are strict guidelines governing how and when super funds can be accessed, it may be possible to take the entire amount as a lump sum. Check first, however, to find out if this has a significant tax implication or affects your age pension entitlements. Seek appropriate advice when deciding whether this is the right move for you.

Soon-to-be-retirees received a significant boost on 1 July 2007 when the tax on superannuation payouts for people over the age of 60 was abolished. Those over-60s who are already retired and are receiving a superannuation pension from a funded superannuation scheme now also pay no tax on their pension income.

While some pretty complicated rules and regulations have recently been clarified and simplified to some extent, superannuation is still not an issue that you want to try to get to grips with if you're suffering from a headache.

Understanding your superannuation statement

Superannuation amounts are divided into three categories that should be clearly marked on your superannuation statement.

- *Unrestricted non-preserved funds* can be accessed at any time, subject to the payment of the applicable tax.

- *Restricted non-preserved funds* can be accessed at any time once you have stopped working permanently for an employer who has contributed to the regulated superannuation fund.

- *Preserved benefits* include employer contributions, member contributions and investment earnings. Under most circumstances, the earliest you can access your preserved superannuation savings is once you reach your preservation age and have satisfied a condition of release.

Different types of superannuation

A few years ago, the Federal Government introduced rules to give you more options in making the transition from work to retirement. If you have reached your preservation age (55 if you were born before 1 July 1960) you will be able to draw on your super, if your fund allows, without having to retire permanently from the workforce. This may be particularly useful if you are planning to pick up some part-time work as you travel.

Under these rules, if you're still working, you will have to receive your super as a non-commutable income stream product, which means you won't be able to stop the pension and cash it in as a lump sum at that time. The transition to retirement allocated pensions will allow you to take a lump sum either when you retire or reach the age of 65. You can return it to the accumulation phase of superannuation at any time if you want to.

Income stream options and taxation

The main option available to people who do not want to continue working but want to keep an income stream through their retirement years rather than take a lump sum is to set up or purchase an Account Based Income Stream (ABIS). ABISs are very similar to allocated pensions. The main difference is that you only have to take a minimum percentage of the balance of your account and the maximum is the full balance of the account. For those over the age of 60 there is no tax liability, while for those between the ages of 55 and 60 years there is a tax offset (rebate) of 15 per cent and, depending on the make-up of your superannuation, there may be a deductible (tax-free) amount.

You can use immediate annuities provided they meet the minimum payment standards for superannuation pensions. They are becoming rare and ABISs are the preferred form of income stream.

ABISs also receive concessional treatment under the income test, which can be advantageous for some people.

Term-allocated pensions set up or purchased prior to 20 September 2007 are regular income streams you receive from your super savings over a fixed term. These products are no longer available, but those who already have them continue not to have all of their pension counted as income for Centrelink purposes and this could be beneficial to you.

Through a term-allocated pension you would have chosen how long your pension lasts within a given range (based on life expectancy) and your income is a set amount which is determined annually based on your account balance and the remaining term of your pension. You continue to receive income payments until the end of your chosen pension term. Term-allocated pensions are also treated concessionally under the asset test – 50 per cent of their value is exempt.

All new income streams are now fully asset tested. Existing complying pensions purchased prior to 20 September 2007 continue to have their 50 per cent asset test exemption, and those purchased prior to 20 September 2004 continue to have 100 per cent exemption.

From 1 July 2007 the asset test for receiving the pension has also been relaxed, effectively increasing the income that retirees can receive from savings before they lose the pension. Retirees now lose $1.50 of age pension a fortnight for every $1000 of assets above the asset test mark.

It's worth repeating that tax and pension implications of the various superannuation options available to you are both extremely complicated and extremely serious. Think long and hard and obtain up-to-date, independent advice from a qualified source. It is not only the success and enjoyment of your trip that depends on you making the right decision. It is also the rest of your life.

LIVING OFF INVESTMENTS

Many older Australians taking extended trips have more disposable cash at their fingertips than they have ever had in their lives. As previously discussed, this may be due to the sale of the family home or a large superannuation payout. This raises another possibility – investing. Some will have already accumulated considerable investment expertise; others may be playing catch-up as they try to make their new investments work for them. If you are new to the world of investments – or even if you are experienced – there are plenty of potential traps.

The Australian Securities and Investment Commission has the following tips for new investors.

- Work out your financial objectives and what sort of risks you are willing to take.

- Understand your financial situation and work out how much you can invest and where you can find the money.

- Develop your own financial strategy.

- Develop your own ground rules for investing so you can stay in control.

- Consider tax and social security issues.

Among the possible investment opportunities are cash and fixed-interest investments, managed funds, topping up superannuation and investing in real estate.

Shares

Many retirees choose one of the above options, particularly real estate investment, but large numbers turn to the stock market, often for the first time in their lives.

It's not an uncommon sight at caravan parks to see grey nomads lounging in their campchairs scanning their laptops for the latest market news. It can be a new, engrossing and sometimes profitable hobby for the novice but, when the numbers get big, it's time to talk to the experts.

Stockbrokers

The rise and rise of the internet has made share trading much more accessible and affordable for everyone.

For the occasional investor who is able to source information and trade online, the costs can be surprisingly reasonable. For example, at the time of writing, CommSec advertises charges of $29.95 for each trade up to $10,000 transaction value, and .31 per cent of the transaction value for trades above $10,000.

Although a wealth of useful information and statistics to help you trade successfully are available online, the internet cannot give you personal advice. This is the domain of professional stockbrokers, who charge depending on the level of their services. The cost of advice varies significantly between brokers and is also very much dependent on the frequency and value of your trades.

For investors seeking some share guidance without wishing to incur the often considerable expense of entering into a full-service arrangement, many stockbrokers offer a more affordable alternative. Goldman Sachs JBWere, for example, charges a minimum $99 fee for giving general share recommendations on the phone. Trades less than $20,000 cost 1.25% of transaction value and trades in excess of $20,000 cost .85% of transaction value.

It must be remembered that every stockbrokerage company is different and will structure its fees around the sort of customer it wants to attract. Shop around carefully to ensure you are getting the right service for what you want at the right price.

Benefits

Over the long term, history suggests that shares outperform other types of investment, including property. Nonetheless, values go down as well as up and so you need to be prepared to hang on in there when things aren't looking so rosy.

To many, the appeal of the share market is that it offers the opportunity to spread the investment risk across many different sectors, whether it be media, resources or financial. Unlike property, shares can be bought and sold quickly, and many find this liquidity appealing. Indeed, the accessibility to your investments contributes to the feeling of many that shares give you real control over your financial future. You are in charge of your own destiny.

Share investing tips

The Australian Stock Exchange provides the following general guidelines:

- Remember, shares are not short-term investments. Usually, the best returns will be gained over the medium or longer term.

- Past performance is not a reliable guide to future performance.

- As with any investment that offers capital growth, wide fluctuations in value can occur.

- Spread your shareholdings to include different companies across different market sectors, such as industry, mining or finance. This helps reduce your risk.

- Ask your stockbroker for information about the company's profile, performance, history and economic forecasts before buying or selling any shares. Much of this information is also now available online. Websites containing valuable research data include those of the Australian Stock Exchange and CommSec. See the end of this section for details.

- Balance the proportion of shares in your overall investment portfolio with the level of risk you are prepared to take. If a company goes into liquidation, shareholders are the last to be paid.

- Remember that even the most thoroughly researched information and advice, given with the best intentions, may still result in a loss.

Interest rates

The best-laid financial plans can come unstuck as a result of an unexpected change in interest rates. Many grey nomads remember all too well the anguish of paying off a property purchase when interest rates were running at 17 per cent. Similarly, self-funded retirees have recently been struggling due to historically low rates. No matter what the government or the banks tell you, no one can predict with any degree of certainty what interest rates will be in the medium to long term. There are simply too many variables to take into account. Just remember to do your investment sums based on what interest rates might be, rather than purely on what they are at the moment.

Contact information

The National Information Centre on Retirement Investments Inc. (NICRI) is an independent, confidential service funded by the Federal Government. As well as producing a number of brochures and leaflets explaining the various superannuation choices, it offers free information or guidance for people seeking help with financial matters.

Website: www.nicri.org.au

Tel: 1800 020 110

The Australian Taxation Office Superannuation Information Line

Website: www.ato.gov.au

Tel: 13 10 20

Centrelink

Centrelink's Financial Information Service can help you maximise your overall retirement income. It produces a range of relevant brochures and offers a number of free financial seminars, including one relating specifically to superannuation and one about understanding retirement income streams. To find out more about seminars, call Centrelink on 13 63 57.

To make an appointment with a Centrelink Financial Information Service Officer or to request booklets, leaflets and fact sheets about investment products, call Centrelink on 13 23 00. Financial Information Service Officers have no authority to make decisions about your pension or calculate the rate at which you can be paid but they may be able to work out approximately what your payments will be.

Centrelink's website: www.centrelink.gov.au

Australian Stock Exchange

This site contains comprehensive information about different kinds of investment, choosing brokers, trading shares, researching investment possibilities and many other tips and facts.

Website: www.asx.com.au

Tel: 13 12 79

CommSec

CommSec started in 1995 with the aim of making investing easy, accessible and affordable for all Australians. As well as enabling you to trade shares online, it offers access to free research, including detailed company profiles. You can also follow your favourite stocks with watchlists, share alerts and charting tools. Membership is free.

Website: www.commsec.com.au

Tel: 13 15 19

Australian Securities and Investments Commission

ASIC is the consumer protection regulator for financial services. Both websites listed below contain helpful information on a wide range of topics regarding financial matters.

Websites: www.asic.gov.au, www.fido.asic.gov.au

Tel: 1300 300 630

MAKING MONEY ON THE ROAD

Casual work

It is surprising how much casual work is available as you travel, particularly if you have a trade or are just plain 'handy'. General work is often available on cattle stations, at caravan parks, and in local businesses such as service stations. This is increasingly true the further away from the major cities you travel. Some of the smaller, more isolated towns struggle to enlist the sort of skilled and unskilled help they require. Furthermore, in the north especially, there is a seasonal aspect to the local job market. Places like Darwin change character in the dry season and the associated tourist influx means there are generally great opportunities to pick up work.

It is important that you have a clear idea of how much work you want before you begin your adventure, although circumstances can change. For many people, the chance to earn extra cash is vital to the trip but it does make it a very different experience. Think about:

- How long you are prepared to stay in one place because of work.

- Whether you want part-time or full-time work.

- How much your working will affect your partner's holiday.

- Whether working in one place for a significant period will mean you can't see all the parts of the country you want to.

- How working will affect your Centrelink payments.

- Whether you will enjoy working again and meeting new people through your job.

To get a better feel for casual employment opportunities, check the following:

Contact information
Department of Employment and Workplace Relations
Tel: 13 62 68

Websites
www.australia.gov.au/315
(This site provides a state-by-state link to job opportunities, work conditions, training and plenty of other interesting information.)

www.jobsearch.gov.au
(This site provides details of job opportunities throughout Australia, as well as lots of other useful information about employment.)

www.jobwise.gov.au
(This site is dedicated to providing help and advice to mature-age job seekers.)

www.thegreynomads.com.au/featurespages/adverthelp.html
(Cattle stations, caravan parks and farms all need extra help sometimes. See who wants what at this site.)

Private employment agencies
Private employment agencies may be found all over the country. Check the internet or Yellow Pages to contact them.

Fruit picking
If you think fruit picking is the sole domain of European backpackers working in slave-like conditions under the blazing Australian sun, then think again. Fruit picking has gone respectable and there is no shortage of grey nomads making a decent income from it.

Anecdotal evidence suggests that the September 11 terrorist attacks in the US had an unexpected knock-on effect in the fruit-picking world. As international tourist numbers plummeted, one of the traditional sources of seasonal workers for Australian farmers began to dry up and they had to fill the gap somehow. Older Australians travelling around in campervans and caravans were targeted, as they were perceived to have an established work ethic, their own ready-made accommodation, and a willingness to broaden their horizons.

At fruit farms these days you're equally likely to find a group of grey nomads playing cards outside their caravans in the evenings as you are to find backpackers partying the night away.

Right, so what about those slave-like conditions? Fruit picking is hard work. You will need to be fit and healthy and prepared to stay the distance. However, you do not need to be a triathlete. It is in no one's interest for you to keel over with heat exhaustion or dehydration, and working conditions are generally good. Normally you will start picking early in the morning and finish before the sun really begins to take its toll. Each fruit or vegetable is different and pickers soon work out what they do and don't like. Harvesting ground crops, such as strawberries, rockmelons, watermelons, cabbages and potatoes means you'll be bending down all day long and this can be a strain on your back. Tree fruits, such as avocados, oranges, apricots, macadamia nuts, apples, cherries and bananas, are more back-friendly as you stand and pick them from the branches of a tree or plant. Sometimes you'll need to climb ladders to reach the fruit.

Fruit pickers are either paid by the hour or by the bucket. The hourly wage is based on the Australian standard wage rate for casual farm workers. For experienced or enthusiastic pickers, the contract arrangement is generally more lucrative. You will be paid a set amount per bin and you are free to work as long and as hard as you like, although the farmer will obviously require a certain level of productivity.

Besides picking, there are plenty of other opportunities for seasonal farmwork, including pruning and weeding, grading and packing fruit that has already been harvested, and even driving tractors and heavy machinery if you have a licence.

Happily for hardworking nomads, Australia is a big country with a varied climate and therefore produces a wide range of fruits and vegetables at different times of the year, so you'll be able to keep yourself pretty busy. As a rule, the main picking season is in the summer months and your services will be in hot demand during that time.

The grey nomad fruit-picking trail has become a well-worn one and you'll see many of the same faces at different farms picking different fruits. Members of this growing community are eager to pass on their knowledge and relate their experiences, so it will quickly become known on the grapevine which farmers are difficult to work for and which farmers are not.

The following chart provides a general overview of when and where various fruits are harvested in each state (please note that this is not a comprehensive list).

New South Wales

Fruit and vegetable crops are harvested all over New South Wales. Among the towns to check out are Griffith, Bathurst, Forbes and Young for stone fruit; Tumut, Forbes and Orange for apples; the Hunter Valley, Mudgee and Griffith for grapes; Forbes, Orange and Young for cherries; and Bourke, Narromine and Leeton for citrus.

Month	Fruit
January	apples, cherries, citrus, grapes, melons, stone fruit
February	apples, cherries, citrus, grapes, melons, stone fruit
March	apples, cherries, citrus, grapes, melons, stone fruit
April	apples, cherries, citrus, grapes, melons, stone fruit

Month	Fruit
May	apples, citrus, grapes, melons, stone fruit
June	citrus, cherries, grapes, melons
July	citrus, prunes
August	citrus, melons, prunes
September	citrus, melons, prunes
October	blueberries, citrus, grapes, melons, stone fruit,
November	apples, blueberries, cherries, citrus, grapes, melons, stone fruit,
December	apples, blueberries, cherries, citrus, grapes, melons, stone fruit

Northern Territory

The tropical north of the Northern Territory boasts year-round harvesting of bananas, selected vegetables and cut flowers. Seasonally, both the Darwin and Katherine regions have melon and mango harvests.

Month	Fruit
January	citrus, tropical fruits
February	citrus, tropical fruits
March	citrus, tropical fruits
April	citrus, tropical fruits
May	tropical fruits, melons
June	melons, tropical fruits
July	melons
August	melons
September	citrus, melons
October	citrus, melons, mangoes
November	citrus, mangoes, melons
December	citrus, mangoes, tropical fruits

Queensland

Queensland offers fruit pickers a few year-round crops, such as bananas and sugar in Tully and citrus and tomatoes in other regions. Check out Emerald, Mundubbera and Gayndah for citrus; Atherton and Mareeka for avocados; and Bowen, Laidley and Ayr for tomatoes and other vegetables.

Month	Fruit
January	apples, peaches, plums, lychees, mangoes, melons
February	apples, avocados, lychees, mangoes, melons, pears
March	apples, avocados, lychees, melons, pears,
April	apples, avocados, melons
May	apples, avocados, melons
June	avocados, melons
July	avocados
August	avocados, melons
September	avocados, mangoes, melons
October	avocados, mangoes, melons, peaches
November	apples, avocados, lychees, mangoes, melons, peaches, plums
December	apples, lychees, mangoes, melons, peaches, plums

South Australia

South Australia has a range of crops, mainly in the state's more fertile south. Among the regions to check are the Adelaide Hills, the Barossa Valley, the Clare Valley and the Fleurieu Peninsula for apples, pears and grapes; Barmera, Berri, Cadell, Loxton, Paringa, Ramco and Waikerie for citrus; and Barmera, the Adelaide Hills, Berri and Renmark for cherries.

Month	Fruit
January	apples, cherries, citrus, grapes
February	apples, cherries, citrus, grapes, pears
March	apples, avocados, cherries, citrus, grapes, pears
April	apples, avocados, cherries, citrus, grapes
May	apples, avocados, citrus, grapes
June	avocados, cherries, citrus, grapes
July	avocados, citrus
August	avocados, citrus
September	avocados, citrus
October	avocados, citrus, grapes, peaches, plums
November	apples, avocados, cherries, citrus, grapes, peaches, plums
December	apples, cherries, citrus, grapes, peaches, plums

Tasmania

Thanks to Tasmania's great growing climate, there is a wide range of fruits and vegetables that require harvesting. Among the areas to check for picking opportunities are Devonport, Huonville, Richmond and the Tamar Valley for apples, cherries and grapes; and Ulverstone for tomatoes and other vegetables.

Month	Fruit
January	apples, berries, cherries, grapes, tomatoes
February	apples, berries, cherries, grapes, tomatoes
March	apples, berries, cherries, grapes, tomatoes
April	apples, berries, cherries, grapes, tomatoes
May	apples, berries, grapes, tomatoes
June	cherries, grapes, tomatoes
July	tomatoes

Month	Fruit
August	tomatoes
September	tomatoes
October	berries, grapes, tomatoes
November	apples, berries, cherries, grapes, tomatoes
December	apples, berries, cherries, grapes, tomatoes

Victoria

A large number of harvesting opportunities are available in Victoria. Look at Shepparton and Murchison for apples and cherries; Echuca, Shepparton and Werribee for tomatoes; and Mildura, Swan Hill, Wangaratta and the Yarra Valley for grapes.

Month	Fruit
January	apples, cherries, citrus, grapes, peaches, tomatoes
February	apples, cherries, citrus, grapes, peaches, pears, tomatoes
March	apples, cherries, citrus, grapes, peaches, pears, tomatoes
April	apples, cherries, citrus, grapes, peaches, tomatoes
May	apples, citrus, grapes, tomatoes
June	cherries, citrus, grapes, tomatoes
July	citrus, tomatoes
August	citrus, tomatoes
September	citrus, tomatoes
October	citrus, grapes, strawberries, tomatoes
November	apples, cherries, citrus, grapes, strawberries, tomatoes
December	apples, cherries, citrus, grapes, strawberries, tomatoes

Western Australia

Because Western Australia is so big, it can be divided into several distinct regions, each with its own weather pattern and season for fruit picking. Among the towns to look into are Kununurra for mangoes; Manjimup for apples and pears; Margaret River, Mt Barker and the Swan Valley for grapes; and Carnarvon and Kununurra for tomatoes and other vegetables.

Month	Fruit
January	apples, cherries, grapes, mangoes, tomatoes
February	apples, cherries, grapes, mangoes, pears, tomatoes
March	apples, cherries, grapes, pears, tomatoes
April	apples, cherries, grapes, tomatoes
May	apples, grapes, squash, tomatoes
June	cherries, grapes, tomatoes
July	tomatoes
August	tomatoes
September	mangoes, tomatoes
October	grapes, mangoes, tomatoes
November	apples, cherries, grapes, mangoes, tomatoes
December	apples, cherries, grapes, mangoes, tomatoes

Contact information

Jobsearch
Website: www.jobsearch.gov.au/harvesttrail
Tel: 13 62 68

National Harvest Labour Information Service
Tel: 1800 062 332

Fossicking

More than 100 years after gold prospectors turned remote regions of Australia into veritable beehives of activity, a new generation of 'old timers' is doing much the same thing.

From Harts Range in the Northern Territory to the gem-fields of inland Queensland, a small army of grey nomads is hard at work in the dust and the dirt.

Sapphires, zircon, rubies, agate, garnets, opals, topaz, thunder eggs and, of course, gold are all there for the taking – and as long as you stay in the designated fossicking areas, it's all legal and above board.

Digging, sieving, washing and sorting is a lot of hard work, doubly so when you don't find anything. But then, of course, there are the days that you do and it all seems worth the effort. Be warned that fossicking can be addictive and the permanent-looking camps of the dusty-looking veterans, back in the same spot for the eighth straight year, is proof enough of that. While cruel Mother Nature has worked it so that most of the gems are hidden in truly stark, dry and desolate parts of the country, the plus side is that only hardy, adventure-seeking treasure-hunters have made it out there. Okay, so you can't fossick on the beach under the shade of a gently swaying palm tree but you can enjoy the company of some marvellously warm characters by a crackling campfire.

There are different requirements for different sorts of gem hunting but generally speaking a pick, shovel, bucket, sieve, a good supply of water and a keen eye will get you started. The major exception is gold, which requires a specialised and often expensive metal detector.

Many fossicking areas allow free camping but quite a few don't. Check for your nearest and most suitable camping spot before striking out for your destination.

Probably the most famous fossicking area is Coober Pedy in South Australia, from where an incredible 70 per cent of the world's opals are mined. While significant amounts of opals continue to be pulled from the ground, fossickers – or 'noodlers', as they are called locally – are not permitted out to the privately owned mines, where giant machines blow out huge amounts of dust, and small opals, from underground.

It is important to find out as much as you can about fossicking before you go, but nothing beats hands-on experience. Normally, there'll be helpful veterans around who'll show you the ropes. Don't be too downhearted if they tell you they haven't been finding much – these gem hunters like to play their cards close to their chest.

In many areas there are also commercial operators who will hire out equipment and expertise as well as showing you the best place to dig. If you just want to give it a try for a couple of hours, this isn't a bad option.

If you are one of the lucky ones, be advised that you can keep as many gems as you like and Centrelink won't care. Once you start selling them, it becomes an income and, as such, should be declared. Don't start worrying about losing your pension yet, though. Go and find a football-sized sapphire first!

Where to fossick

Before you set off with your equipment, check whether a permit or licence is necessary. In some regions, you can purchase these at visitor information centres or online. Below is a chart detailing a small selection of the many fossicking areas state by state, as well as contact details to check the current licensing requirements.

NEW SOUTH WALES	
Location	Materials found
Inverell region Three free sapphire-fossicking areas and at least six other sites in the region for other gems	Sapphires, crystals, citrine, quartz, tourmaline, diamonds, topaz, garnets, gold
Lightning Ridge Region	Opals, topaz, agate, petrified wood
Ophir (near Bathurst)	Gold
Barraba (90km north of Tamworth) Woodsreef fossicking area	Gold, jasper, petrified wood, quartz

Licensing details
Currently no fossicking licence is required in New South Wales. Check with local tourist information centres for locations of fossicking areas.

NORTHERN TERRITORY	
Location	Materials found
Mud Tank Gemfields (90km northeast of Alice Springs)	Zircon, garnets, magnetite, microcline
Central Harts Range and Harts Range West	Zircon, garnets, quartz, muscovite, tourmaline
Wave Hill Extension (within Wave Hill Station). Closed 31 Aug–31 March due to station activities.	Prehnite, smoky quartz, agate, jasper, amethyst, calcite

Licensing details
A fossicking permit is required to fossick in the Northern Territory Department of Primary Industry, Fisheries and Mines – Minerals and Energy: (08) 8999 5322 Website: www.minerals.nt.gov.au

QUEENSLAND	
Location	**Materials found**
Anakie Gemfields (seven large designated fossicking areas centred around Anakie (45km west of Emerald))	Sapphires, zircon
Mount Hay (near Rockhampton)	Thunder eggs
Agate Creek (near Forsayth)	Agate, thunder eggs, chalcedony
O'Brien Creek (near Mt Surprise)	Aquamarine, topaz, quartz
Licensing details	
A fossicking licence is required to fossick in Queensland Department of Mines and Energy: 1800 657 567 Website: www.dme.qld.gov.au/mines/fossicking.cfm	

SOUTH AUSTRALIA	
Location	**Materials found**
Coober Pedy Noodle on site of old opal field in town	Opals
Mount Lofty Ranges Region Mt Crawford, Jupiter Creek Diggings, Chapel Hill Diggings	Gold, opals, garnets, beryl, tourmaline, diamonds, topaz
Andamooka Noodle in opal fields. Take advice from local tourist info	Opals
Licensing details	
Licensing rules are different for 'fossicking' and 'prospecting'. Check guidelines on the website under 'publications' and then 'information sheets' to find out more. Department of Primary Industry and Resources – Minerals: (08) 8463 3000 Website: www.minerals.pir.sa.gov.au	

TASMANIA	
Location	Materials found
Lune River Fossicking Area (100km south of Hobart)	Jasper, agate, petrified fern, petrified wood
Killiecrankie Bay Fossicking Area (on Flinders Island, 30km north of Whitemark)	Topaz crystals and pieces, smoky quartz, zircon and beryl
Weld River Fossicking Area (between Scottsdale and St Helens, off Tasman Hwy)	Sapphire, topaz, zircon

Licensing details
No licence is required for fossicking; however, a licence is required for 'prospecting'. Check website or phone DIER to determine whether you need a licence. Department of Infrastructure, Energy and Resources – Mineral Resources: (03) 6233 8377
Website: www.mrt.tas.gov.au

VICTORIA	
Location	Materials found
Victoria's Goldfields Region Large area in central Victoria including Inglewood, Bendigo, Heathcote, Ballarat and Maryborough, and many others	Gold
Beechworth Region	Alluvial gold, topaz, quartz, agate, amethyst, garnets, jasper, lydionite, sapphires, smoky quartz, tourmaline, zircon, tin crystal and citrine

Licensing details
A 'Miners' Right' is required to fossick in Victoria Department of Primary Industries – Minerals and Petroleum: 13 61 86 Website: www.dpi.vic.gov.au

WESTERN AUSTRALIA	
Location	Materials found
Pilbara Region (near Marble Bar)	Gold
Norseman	Gold, moss agate, gold lace agate, moss opalite
Licensing details	
A 'Miners' Right' is required to fossick for gold and most minerals in Western Australia. Department of Industry and Resources: (08) 9222 3333 Website: www.doir.wa.gov.au/1635.aspx	

Websites
www.aussiesapphire.com.au
www.gemfossicking.com
www.gold-net.com.au

Lapidary and Gem Clubs
Gemmological Association of Australia
Website: www.gem.org.au
Tel: State-by-state telephone numbers listed in the website

Australian Facetors Guild
Website: www.facetorsguild.org.au

Selling services
Driving around some of the bigger caravan parks, you might easily come across two or three 'hairdressing here' signs with a big arrow pointing to site 26 or site 51. Then there are the masseurs, the mobile welders and the mechanics, while professional gem cutters are normally found in force on the fossicking fields. Grey

nomads sometimes seem like a huge travelling army that, to a large extent, brings with it the skills and knowledge to keep itself on the move and to look after its own 'soldiers'. Those with the right skills have a wonderful chance to make some pocket money by providing services to their fellow travellers. There are few, if any, overheads in caravan park-based businesses so prices can be kept low and the customers are particularly happy because they don't have to leave the park to get what they want.

Unless you are at a camping area somewhere out in the bush, it always pays to check the caravan park is happy for you to put out your 'hairdressing here' sign. Some aren't keen but others are prepared to turn a blind eye as long as what you're doing doesn't become a serious, full-time business.

Given that you'll have to bring along with you the tools of the trade – and, depending on your business, that may or may not be a bulky load to lug around – think carefully before you set off about how much you are hoping to work and whether it is worth the effort and space.

Besides the extra cash it brings in, the other bonus about selling your service is that you get to know an awful lot of people. The friendly mobile hair snipper is normally about the most popular person in the park – as long as nobody loses an ear!

Arts and crafts

Whether you're into making dolls out of surplus shirt buttons, knitting woollen hats by the dozen or producing attractive sketches, the open road could well be paved with gold for you. More realistically, you might be able to make a few extra dollars peddling your wares every now and again. Selling to fellow travellers, however, is not the easiest thing in the world to do, as a lot of them will be travelling with the same budget and space restrictions that you are. Don't be shy.

Display your wares on a table outside your van one sunny afternoon. At the very least you'll meet a few nice people with similar interests.

The local market is usually another good place to sell your products. Cities like Darwin are awash with fascinating craft markets, so join the happy throng. Most towns will have similar markets on the weekends, particularly during the season. Call the local council to find out where the markets are held and how you get a pitch. At some established markets a small charge is made to set up, so you need to be reasonably confident that your product will sell before forging ahead.

Tax implications

Although any income you derive from a freelance venture must be reported to the tax office, many of your expenses for such things as tools, materials, uniforms, mileage and even accommodation in some cases, are tax deductible. Keep any relevant receipts as well as a vehicle logbook to present to the tax office with your tax return.

WORKING FOR FREE ACCOMMODATION

Camp hosting

The 'Camp Host Here' sign outside well-established caravans will become a familiar sight as you pull into camping areas throughout the country. So who are these relaxed characters hanging out in their campchairs waiting to greet you with a smile and a friendly piece of advice? And, more importantly, how do you get a piece of the action?

Camp hosting programs are on offer at national parks and other established camping areas in a number of states and are becoming increasingly popular among community-minded grey nomads. Under the arrangement, hosts enjoy free camping – at some truly magnificent locations – in return for keeping an eye on the campsite and liaising with national park rangers. Camp hosts are in particular demand during peak seasons. The period for which a camp host is required varies, but is normally for at least two weeks. On top of free camping, camp hosts also really get to know a park; they can relax in one beautiful spot for a while, meet loads of new people, and help out the national parks staff during a frantic time. Prospective hosts normally have to undergo some sort of training course and may be subject to police checks.

In most locations, camp hosts need to bring all their own food and camping equipment.

Specific camp host duties vary from site to site but may include:

- Providing information and advice to the camping public and other park visitors.

- Assisting in campsite allocation, check-in and check-out, and recording numbers.

- Giving directions and general information about the area and its attractions.

- Providing a contact point at campsites for both national park staff and the public. This may include regular radio or phone contact with ranger staff.

- Informing park staff of any problems and seeking ranger presence for any issues of compliance.

- Maintaining campgrounds, toilets and barbecues.

- Recording and posting bulletins.

Monitoring activities at camping sites, mostly remote ones, is not for everyone but many grey nomads find the experience addictive and hosting gigs can be in hot demand. Hosts are required at scores of places nationwide and these include such iconic destinations as: Cape Le Grand National Park, Karijini National Park, the Flinders Ranges National Park, Grampians National Park and Finke Gorge National Park. If you think camp hosting could be for you, the following are each state's contact details:

Camp host contact information
Northern Territory
The Parks and Wildlife Service runs a volunteer program for people who are keen to stay in selected parks and collect fees, perform light maintenance duties, etc.
Tel: (08) 8999 4555 (Darwin)
(08) 8973 8851 (Katherine)
(08) 8951 8250 (Alice Springs)

Queensland
Limited camp hosting opportunities are available at a number of national parks in specific regions of the state. The Environmental Protection Agency recommends that interested grey nomads make direct contact with rangers at individual parks to find out if camp hosting possibilities exist.

South Australia
Currently, the Department of Environment and Heritage offers roles for hosts in various national parks, conservation parks and reserves.
Website: www.environment.sa.gov.au/parks/involved/fpgroups.html
Tel: (08) 8124 4784 (volunteer coordinator)
Candidates will be asked to attend an interview.

Tasmania

The Parks and Wildlife Service in Tasmania uses campground hosts at several parks in the state and even more opportunities for hosting may arise in the future.

Website: www.parks.tas.gov.au

Tel: (03) 6264 8463 (regional volunteer facilitator)

Victoria

Parks Victoria utilises camp hosts at some of its popular parks during peak periods. Camp hosting candidates must consent to police checks, and a two-day training camp is provided for successful applicants.

Website: www.parkweb.vic.gov.au (follow the links to camp hosting)

Tel: 13 19 63

Western Australia

The Department of Environment and Conservation operates a campground hosting program at numerous sites throughout the state. Hosting candidates must provide a national police clearance and attend an interview to be accepted into the program.

Website: www.dec.wa.gov.au (follow the links from 'Community and Education' to 'volunteer programs')

Tel: (08) 9334 0251

New South Wales and Australian Capital Territory

Currently, no official, state-wide camp hosting programs are run in these places but they may be set up in the future.

Caretaking and housesitting

Just as many grey nomads leave their home in the care of housesitters while they are away, other grey nomads seek to do a little housesitting as they travel. Even though this is not generally a paid position, it does offer rent-free accommodation and a few of the often-missed comforts of home. For many long-term travellers, housesitting provides the perfect opportunity to catch their breath, take a break from the rigours of the road, and maybe to plan the next stage of the adventure. Housesitting opportunities range in length from a few weeks to many months. There are a number of established agencies that can help you to find a vacancy. Some of these charge a listing fee, carry out character checks and may require references. You will be going into somebody else's home, normally with all of their furniture and personal belongings still there, so they will want to be very comfortable with who you are.

Housesitters' duties normally include keeping the house and gardens neat and tidy, forwarding mail or phone messages, caring for any pets, and generally being a presence around the house to deter burglars.

Many wonderful friendships have been established this way and it's always interesting to get an insight into how people in a different part of the country live.

A list of housesitting websites can be found earlier in this chapter under the heading 'What to do with your property'.

Owners of small farms commonly seek reliable, experienced people to care for their property while they are away. These positions often include duties such as general maintenance and animal feeding – tasks that are heavier than typical housesitting – and for this reason may command a small wage. Enquire at local tourist information centres and check bulletin boards at shops, caravan parks and in the local paper.

CASE STUDIES

It's difficult to imagine how your finances are going to work out when you're travelling until you're actually out there doing it. Will you manage to stay out of caravan parks? Will you be able to live without champagne and caviar? Will the cost of fuel force you to take up fruit picking as a hobby? Below are four case studies that should give you a better idea of how much your budget can vary, and help you to identify areas where money can be saved.

Alan

Age: 68
Time on the road: three years
Rig: 60 Series LandCruiser towing 1975 caravan

Alan travels with his Jack Russell terrier, Smooch, after his wife of 45 years, Janice, died unexpectedly only weeks before he retired from his blue-collar job. During his working life, Alan went through several prolonged periods of unemployment and made some poor financial decisions. Nonetheless, after selling his home, he was able to put some money into an education fund for his two young granddaughters and to buy a second-hand 4WD vehicle and a second-hand caravan. He has also kept $10,000 in reserve as an emergency fund but lives off his age pension and occasional casual work. Alan loves his new lifestyle and now plans to travel indefinitely. Although he describes himself as a 'loner', Alan says he has made many good friends on his travels.

'I don't mind my own company and I have learned to appreciate so many things that I never really thought about before,' he says. 'Of course, I miss my two little granddaughters but I get back to my son's place every Christmas and I look forward to that.'

Alan is on a particularly tight budget and prefers to hunt out free camping spots wherever possible. He dislikes what he calls the crowded nature of caravan parks and prefers the bush.

'A lot of van parks don't like dogs and those that do seem to insist I keep Smooch tied up, which he doesn't like. I try to avoid them where I can, although I do need a good wash and scrub up now and again. Most places also charge me as if I am two people, which I don't think is fair.

'Of course, I have to watch how much I spend on diesel, but I am never in a hurry and if I find a nice spot I'll stay there a week or two . . . that helps to keeps things affordable. And when I'm picking fruit I might stay in the same place even longer than that.'

Alan has only recently started doing a bit of fruit picking work and plans to do more of this in the future.

'I've met up with a few other people who are in similar situations to me and we all get on pretty well,' he says. 'I hadn't realised there was quite such a well-established circuit so I might just see how I go. It's a great way of keeping fit and getting a few extra dollars, and I don't mind a bit of hard work.'

For Alan, travelling Australia was never about eating out in restaurants or paying to visit every tourist attraction along the way. He has learned to appreciate the simple pleasures in life, and sitting in the shade reading a book, taking a bushwalk with Smooch, or talking to fellow nomads are all well within his budget.

Rig setup costs

60 Series LandCruiser	$7000
1975 Millard Caravan	$3000

A week's costs

During this week, Alan stayed at Herron Point near Pinjarra in Western Australia for a couple of days, then moved to

Wellington Dam near Collie for a free camp and finally went to a caravan park in Bunbury on Saturday night.

	Sun	Mon	Tues	Wed	Thu	Fri	Sat	Totals
Accommodation ($)	5.50	5.50	5.50	free	free	free	22.00	38.50
Food ($)							80.00	80.00
Fuel ($)	65.00							65.00
Post ($)		1.10						1.10
Phone ($		5.00						5.00
Laundry ($)							4.00	4.00
Dog food ($)							8.50	8.50
Newspapers/mags ($)	2.00	2.00	2.00				2.00	8.00
Totals ($)	72.50	13.60	7.50	0	0	0	116.50	210.10

Steve and Margaret

Ages: 66 and 64

Time on the road: three weeks

Rig: Nissan Patrol towing genuine off-road caravan

Steve and Margaret are new to life on the road but plan to travel for somewhere between six months and one year. For their trip, they splashed out on a 'nearly new' off-road caravan, which is their pride and joy.

'We have spent most of the last five years dreaming about, and planning for, this adventure,' says Steve. 'I was keen to get out into some really adventurous country and Margaret was keen to have a decent level of comfort and so this was what we came up with . . . I guess it was our treat to ourselves. I have worked for many years in insurance and Margaret had a part-time clerical position at a school so we figured we'd earned it. We cashed in Margaret's super fund, which nearly paid for the rig, and we are able to live pretty well on my retirement income stream.'

Steve and Margaret own their home outright and plan to return there once the trip is over.

'Our daughter and her partner have moved into the place while we are away,' says Margaret. 'We thought about renting it out but we couldn't bear the thought of strangers in our home, plus we'd have had to pack up all of our belongings. This way, we left everything as it was and my daughter is storing her furniture in our garage. It really helps them out a bit as they have been spending a fortune on rent.'

The couple plans to spend a lot of time camping in national parks and out in the bush but so far have only spent one night out of a caravan park.

'I suppose I'm being a bit of a nervous Nelly,' says Margaret. 'But I'm not quite used to the idea of camping out there on our own yet. I don't mind if there are a few people around that we can be with but I suppose I'll slowly build up my confidence . . . everybody says there's nothing to worry about. Anyway, we've been having a great time in the parks and have met some lovely people.'

Steve and Margaret admit they are already spending more money than they had planned to, mainly because they hadn't budgeted for caravan park fees every night. They are also surprised by how much fuel they're getting through.

'Obviously, you have to spend what you have to spend to keep on trucking,' says Steve. 'But we seem to be doing an awful lot of extra kilometres just pottering around and exploring an area once we have set up camp. It's something we'll have to keep an eye on but, if the worst comes to the worst, I'll just have to catch a few extra fish to keep food on the table.'

Although Steve and Margaret are not what you would call wealthy, they are relatively comfortable financially and the fact they are only travelling for a limited time means it is not a total disaster if they break the budget a little bit. The most important thing to them is that they are both able to relax and enjoy what they see as their trip of a lifetime.

Rig setup costs

Nissan Patrol	$34,000
Off-road caravan	$75,000

A week's costs

During this week, Steve and Margaret took the ferry from Melbourne to Tasmania, where they plan to tour around for six weeks. They stayed in Devonport the first night and then headed to the east coast, where they stayed in a caravan park in St Helens and took day trips to explore Mount William National Park and the Bay of Fires.

	Sun	Mon	Tues	Wed	Thu	Fri	Sat	Totals
Accommodation ($)		24.00	22.00	22.00	22.00	22.00	22.00	134.00
Ferry ticket ($) (one way, shoulder season)	496.00							496.00
Groceries ($)		130.00					20.00	150.00
Fuel ($)						70.00		70.00
Post ($)			2.20					2.20
Mobile phone ($)						5.00**		5.00
Laundry ($)					6.00			6.00
Entertainment ($)		56.00*		5.00	10.00			71.00
Books/maps ($)		17.00						17.00
Newspapers/mags ($)			15.00	2.00	2.00	2.00	2.00	23.00
Dining out ($)	24.00					28.00		52.00
Totals ($)	520.00	227.00	39.20	29.00	40.00	127.00	44.00	1026.20

*National Parks pass

**Part of a $20-per-month plan

Peter and Gillian

Ages: 58 and 57
Time on the road: seven months
Rig: 7.3-metre motorhome towing small 4WD vehicle

Peter and Gillian are having the time of their lives travelling the country. They are in the fortunate position of being financially secure for life. Peter ran his own building business for many years and has acquired a significant property portfolio. He also likes to invest in the stockmarket and has been quite successful in doing so.

'The trip has been pretty interesting for me in as much as I've got out to a few mines and mining towns in the west,' he says. 'Over the years, I have done pretty well out of my resources shares so it was nice to actually see where the stuff is coming out of the ground.'

Peter has found the travelling lifestyle has not affected his ability to monitor his investments.

'I'm obviously not trading every day or even every week,' he says. 'I'm pretty happy with my portfolio as it is but I like to keep an eye on things and I'm able to do that with my laptop. I plug in at internet cafés when I can but otherwise I get my broker to e-mail me some relevant figures now and again. I can pick those up via my mobile phone, if necessary.'

While the motorhome is large and uses quite a bit of fuel, particularly as they're towing a 4WD, it's not something that Peter and Gillian worry about.

'We wanted this motorhome and it costs what it costs,' says Peter. 'There's nothing we can do about that. We've worked hard all of our lives and we've invested wisely, now we are just enjoying the fruits of our labour.

'We don't really have a budget as such. If we want to eat out, we eat out. If we want to stay in a caravan park, we stay a night in a caravan park. If Gillian wants to fly home for a week or so to visit the grandkids, then she flies home, that's all there is to it.'

Peter and Gillian no longer have a place to call home and plan to travel 'until we don't want to any more'. They say they are always keeping half an eye out for their dream house in their dream location as they travel but expect it will be a good few years until they are ready to park the motorhome.

Rig setup costs

Motorhome	$240,000
Small 4x4 car	$24,000

A week's costs

From Sunday to Thursday, Peter and Gillian stayed in a caravan park in the coastal Queensland town of Seventeen Seventy and they treated themselves to a day trip to Lady Musgrave Island on Tuesday. They set off for Yeppoon on Friday.

	Sun	Mon	Tues	Wed	Thu	Fri	Sat	Totals
Accommodation ($)	26.00	26.00	26.00	26.00	26.00	22.00	22.00	174.00
Groceries ($)		95.00				71.00		166.00
Fuel ($)						102.00		102.00
Post ($)		3.30						3.30
Phone ($)						10.00**		10.00
Laundry ($)	6.00				6.00		3.00	15.00
Entertainment ($)			320.00*					320.00
Books ($)				5.00				5.00
Newspapers/mags ($)	2.00	12.00	2.00	2.00	2.00	2.00	2.00	24.00
Dining out ($)	41.00			7.50				48.50
Totals ($)	75.00	136.30	348.00	40.50	34.00	207.00	27.00	867.80

* Lady Musgrave Island day trip
** Part of $40-per-month plan

Tom and Petra

Age: 77 and 74
Time on the road: Five months per year
Rig: Toyota LandCruiser towing pop-top caravan

Tom and Petra have been retired for many years and live on the age pension. They have spent every winter for the past seven years at a caravan park in Broome, Western Australia, and plan to keep going back.

'The weather's beautiful, the park is beautiful, the beach is beautiful and the people are beautiful,' says Petra. 'The same people tend to get the same sites each year and it's great to know everyone when you arrive . . . it feels more comfortable.'

Tom agrees. 'I can't see the point moving on every five minutes,' he says. 'I don't particularly like towing the van any more than I have to, and the fuel costs . . . I don't know how others can afford to keep moving. No, if you find paradise, why would you choose to leave it?'

Tom and Petra own their own home and their next-door neighbour keeps an eye on the place when they're away.

'We're lucky to have such good neighbours,' says Petra. 'They collect our mail and send it on to us, feed our birds, and generally check everything is okay. We do get a gardening man in to keep everything looking nice because we love our garden but, other than that, the place pretty much looks after itself. We've still got the usual utility bills, but we always say the money we save on heating costs when we are up north virtually pays for our caravan park costs . . . and anyway, you can't take it with you, can you?'

Rig setup costs

Toyota LandCruiser	$15,000
Pop-top caravan	$50,000

A week's costs

Tom and Petra stayed in their favourite caravan park in Broome. They treated themselves to a night out at a restaurant, bought a few treasures at the weekly markets and hosted a happy hour on Friday for two other couples.

	Sun	Mon	Tues	Wed	Thu	Fri	Sat	Totals
Accommodation ($)	31.00	31.00	31.00	31.00	31.00	31.00	31.00	217.00
Home expenses* ($)							85.00	85.00
Groceries ($)		86.00				42.00		128.00
Fuel ($)						48.00		48.00
Post ($)		2.20						2.20
Phone ($)						2.50**		2.50
Laundry ($)		6.00						6.00
Misc. souvenirs ($)	18.00							18.00
Entertainment ($)			5.00					5.00
Alcohol ($)						41.00		41.00
Newspapers/mags ($)	2.00	2.00	2.00	2.00	2.00	2.00	2.00	14.00
Dining out ($)	20.00			13.00				33.00
Totals ($)	71.00	127.20	38.00	46.00	33.00	166.50	118.00	599.70

* Includes electricity, landline phone, rates, lawn mowing, house insurance
** Part of $10-per-month plan

2

Rigs

Choosing your rig

WHAT TO CONSIDER

Choosing the right rig for your trip is perhaps the most important decision – other than the one to go in the first place – that you will have to make.

As the number of long-term travellers has increased, so, too, has the number of options. You'll probably be surprised by just how much relative luxury is now available. It's pretty standard for grey nomads to plan trips lasting several months or even several years, and manufacturers appreciate that certain levels of comfort are both expected and required. As they bend over backwards to attract grey nomads to their products, RV (Recreational Vehicle) manufacturers have tended to go down the US-inspired 'bigger is better' path. Indeed, it's fair to say that some Australian caravan parks have been struggling to keep up with the growing size of the RVs using their services. Many are simply unable to accommodate the larger rigs.

There are a number of angles you might want to approach your research from. Ask yourself the following questions:

What is my budget?

Work out in advance what you want to spend and try to be disciplined when you're out in the marketplace. Comfort is important but so is having enough money to put fuel in the tank and food on the table. Your lifestyle on the road is dependent on more than the vehicle you travel in. We are blessed in Australia with a magnificent climate and it's entirely possible to live most of your time outdoors. Naturally, there will be times when you would love to retire to your leather lounges to watch your satellite television with its state-of-the-art surround sound . . . but is it within your budget? If you have the money, then enjoy the pleasure that a luxury rig will bring, but don't overstretch yourself.

How long am I going for?

The longer you plan to travel, the more you'll probably be prepared to spend on your rig. Although you may be able to put up without a toilet and shower in your van for one week every January, you might not be quite so happy to do so for a six-month stint. The more weeks and months and years you're away, the more the little comforts of home will be appreciated and enjoyed. Also, the longer you travel, the more likely it is that your vehicle will require a little maintenance and the bills might start rolling in. Bearing all of this in mind, a newer or a higher-quality rig may be a worthwhile investment.

Where will I be staying?

If you're planning to spend 99 per cent of your time staying in van parks, then solar panels, generators and a massive water storage capacity are not really big buying points for you. Try not to spend cash on special features that you don't intend to use. However, if you're not an experienced traveller, don't back yourself in to a corner, either. You may find that, once you are on the road, you actually prefer camping in national parks to caravan parks. Many caravans now come with an auxiliary battery to accommodate lighting and perhaps a few other appliances if you're away from 240v power. Ask the dealer how the battery is charged up and what it can typically run and for how long without mains power.

For more information, see 'Rig power' later in this chapter.

Where will I be travelling?

If you envisage heading out into remote regions along rough roads, then you need to consider some sort of off-road setup that can cope with the rigours of corrugations and washouts. Some caravans are better equipped to handle extreme 4WD conditions than others – and they have hefty price tags to match.

Cheaper caravans that claim an off-road capability may not cope well with the most extreme tracks. However, they do offer the flexibility to enable you to take dirt roads into the national parks and to handle some of the less demanding 4WD routes, which may give you access to beautiful attractions or campsites.

Camper trailers are a popular budget off-road option and some nomads are even out there in converted 4WD trucks, similar to the ones used by outback tour companies.

What do I expect from the trip?

Talk to as many people who have travelled as you can, and try to imagine what it will be like when you are out there yourselves. What do you imagine yourself doing when the sun goes down? What do you imagine cooking? How much TV will you watch? Do you expect to have lots of people over to your van to play cards? Will you spend a lot of time sitting outside under your awning? Picture yourself on your trip and then, when you are looking around at various rigs, see if you can imagine yourself in that particular rig. Some rigs will feel like a fit and some simply won't – trust your instincts!

How will I feel driving it?

Unfortunately, the quality of Australia's roads is not rising as quickly as the number of vehicles using them. Driving for long periods is often a stressful experience, particularly when you are towing or driving a larger vehicle than you are used to.

Before you plunge into the market for a caravan or motorhome, make sure you've taken it out for a thorough test drive.

Towing a caravan or trailer reduces your vehicle's braking performance, its acceleration capability and your control and manoeuvrability. Driving a large motorhome or converted bus will place a different set of demands upon a driver. It's absolutely vital that you feel comfortable driving your new rig. You'll be spending a great deal of time at the wheel.

Do I want a second vehicle?

Caravans are pretty straightforward inventions. You tow them along until you reach a spot where you want to stay, you unhitch them and you can then explore the area to your heart's content in the towing vehicle. But times are changing and the caravan has competitors – campervans, motorhomes, fifth wheelers, and camper trailers. It's getting complicated.

With campervans and motorhomes, one of the biggest issues that people report is the lack of mobility once camp is set up. If you put up the awning, or simply leave the washing up on the draining board, you have to pack it all away before you can drive around the corner. Again, when you are in the throes of purchasing your rig, you must imagine how your trip is going to unfold and what your specific requirements are. Some people get around the problem by towing a small four-wheel-drive vehicle behind their motorhome. See the 'Motorhomes' section later in this chapter for more details.

SECOND-HAND OR NEW?

It's quite amazing how a second-hand caravan holds its value, particularly a well-made one. Surprisingly, some of the highly regarded off-road vans can cost as much second-hand as they do new. This is because there are so many orders in place for new vans that a buyer can wait many months to have his or her van built – and some customers aren't prepared to do so.

It's impossible to really know how far a caravan has travelled or how it has been treated other than by judging its condition. Plenty of dealers sell second-hand vans and motorhomes, and a few visits will give you an idea of how much you can save by going second-hand.

Buying from a private source is generally cheaper again and you can make your own assessment of the trustworthiness of the person you're buying from when they explain the vehicle's history. However, private sales do not include a warranty and by virtue of the fact that the van has been around the traps, there's a greater chance that it may develop a problem.

The good thing about buying a second-hand caravan or camper trailer is that there's no engine to worry about, so fewer things can go wrong. If you can see no rust and everything looks well maintained, then there's every chance that it will perform very well. Indeed, some people swear by older vans, claiming they're far better made than the average van of today. The number of 1970-something Millards still making their way up and down the nation's highways and byways suggests there may be something in the claim.

On the other side of the ledger, a new vehicle can be tailor-made to your exact specifications in terms of fittings, appliances and layout. New vans also come with a manufacturer's warranty.

Where to look for second-hand rigs

- Go to local caravan/motorhome dealers and look around the yard for second-hand models.

- Check newspaper classifieds (many local papers list their classified sections online as well as in the paper itself).

- Consider advertising in the 'wanted to buy' section of your local and regional classifieds.

- Check the *Trading Post* or equivalent in your area or online at: www.autotrader.com.au.

Where to look for new rigs

- Go to local caravan/motorhome dealers.

- Contact the manufacturer directly; some firms specialise in custom-made vehicles.

- Shop around at dealers and manufacturers initially and then attend a caravan/motorhome show to potentially pick up a bargain show model.

WHAT TO LOOK FOR

While choice of a rig is a personal matter, based on a series of subjective criteria, there are a number of specific issues to consider, such as the size of the fridge you want, whether to opt for single beds or a double bed and how much living space you need. Once you've had a look at a few rigs, it may be useful to compile a list of what you must have, what you want to have and what you can do without.

A few general points to consider are:

- When you are both inside, does it seem too crowded?

- Is the general layout logical and convenient?

- Do you want a toilet and shower?

- Is there enough headroom?

- Is there enough space for cooking and food preparation?

- Are the seats and beds big enough and comfortable enough?

- Are there enough windows and is there sufficient ventilation? To improve airflow, many nomads leave the heavy door of the van open at night, only locking the security screen door.

- Is air-conditioning an important inclusion?

- Is there enough storage space? Is there a facility for hanging clothes?

- Is a conventional oven important to you or can you cope with a microwave and perhaps a portable toaster oven?

Annexes, awnings and outdoor floor coverings

Annexes attach to the side of your caravan or motorhome, making a tent-like structure where you can set up your table, TV, and pot plants, if you wish. But they spark lively debates within the nomad community. For some, they are an effective way of more than doubling the living area while maintaining privacy. Their detractors say they are unnecessary and anti-social – after all, how much private space does one couple need? Although annexes are getting easier to set up, they are still time-consuming to erect and are really most suitable for long-term stays.

More popular with nomads are awnings, which slide out quite simply from the top of the van or motorhome, offering plenty of shaded area in which to set up a table and chairs, but no walls. While other campers may now be able to watch you reading and arguing about whose turn it is to put the billy on, they are also far more likely to stop for a chat and a joke.

> **Tip:** Carrying with you a cut-to-size section of shadecloth to put on the ground under your awning is an effective way of making the outside area seem more homely and comfortable. Similarly, a doormat outside the van helps to keep your interior clean, as well as adding a nice, welcoming touch.

Television

You'll probably be surprised at how frequently you can get decent television reception, as the number of transmitters has been increasing. Most new caravans and motorhomes have a TV antenna already included so all you have to do is plug in and view. If for any reason you don't have an antenna with your rig, the portable, foldaway types can be purchase for about $150. You can also buy signal amplifiers for little more cost. They will often improve the quality of reception in low-signal areas and can help to turn snowy pictures into clear ones. Some systems also boast remote control devices that can move and angle the antenna into the ideal spot to pick up the best reception.

Digital TV

The availability of digital TV has improved picture and sound quality for many viewers in remote areas. If you have an analogue TV and antenna in your rig, it may be worth buying a digital set top box to enable you to receive digital broadcasts on the road. A digital set-top box decodes the digital signals into picture and sound compatible with your existing analogue TV. At the time of writing, the Australian Government has declared 2013 as the mandatory switchover date when all analogue broadcasts will cease and viewers will depend entirely on digital broadcasts. However, there has been some discussion about network requirements and the possibility of changing that date.

It is also worth noting that although all networks are currently 'simulcasting' both a digital and an analogue broadcast of their programs in capital cities, there are still some places around the country where digital TV is not yet available. What this means for nomads is that while having the capability to view digital broadcasts may improve your TV's picture and sound, digital broadcasts are not yet available in all regions.

Satellite TV

If you take your TV viewing seriously and don't want to risk missing an episode of *Neighbours* while you're up in the Kimberley, then a satellite antenna could be the way to go. These systems, some of which can be purchased for around $1000, will give you crystal clear viewing wherever you are – unless you park under a big tree! If you want satellite TV channels above and beyond the normal free-to-air stations, you'll have to pay for them in the normal way.

TV on a laptop

It is also possible to watch TV on a laptop computer. However, you will still need to plug into an antenna and, depending on your laptop, you may also require either a USB tuner or a digital set-top box and a video capture device. Your laptop must also have adequate processing speeds, hard disk space and RAM although virtually all laptops manufactured in 2007 and later meet these minimum requirements.

TIME TO GET LOOKING

Okay, so you've thought about a few of the issues that are going to affect your rig decision. You've probably had a good look inside some vans, campervans, camper trailers, motorhomes and even tents, but now it's time for action. You've decided on your budget, you've got your finances in place, and you're ready to hit the dealerships or scan the second-hand for-sale columns in magazines and newspapers. You're about to get serious.

Make sure you:

- Visit as many sales points as you can and get inside as many rigs as possible. This is a big decision.

- Visit a few caravan parks and get chatting to some nomads. You'll be amazed how honest, open and eager they'll be to talk about their rigs. The best source of information about any product is from those who've been out there and put it through its paces. You may even get a few tips about life on the road.

- Try to visit one of the major caravan and motorhome shows. What a brilliant chance to talk to a whole host of industry experts and to see all of the various rigs and rig options up close and personal. You can often pick up a terrific deal at these events so shop around before the show so you recognise a genuine bargain when you see one. To find out when and where the caravan shows are in your state, check the Caravan RV and Accommodation Industry of Australia website at www.welovethiscountry.net.au/eventssafaris.html.

- Once you've begun to fine-tune your search, make contact with an owners' group to discuss the pros and cons of the rig. Owners' groups have sprung up for most of the major brands. These are usually independent organisations set up by real owners and they generally extol the virtues or otherwise of the relevant rig. Get on the internet and join a forum discussion.

- Don't buy your rig without giving it a good test drive or even a good test camp. Most manufacturers are happy to let you do this as long as you are genuinely serious about buying. It's essential that you know how the vehicle handles and how it feels on the road.

- Visit the factory where the vehicle is made. You're on the verge of spending tens, if not hundreds, of thousands of dollars so you're entitled to have a good look around the facility where this product is created. A surprising number of prospective grey nomads consider it prudent to fly halfway across the country in order to run their eye over the factory before committing to buy.

CARAVANS

Caravans are the most popular form of nomad dwelling. They offer a degree of comfort, privacy and security, as well as the flexibility of being able to go exploring in the tow vehicle once the caravan has been dropped. On the down side, many people don't like towing, and vans can be awkward and add to your fuel costs. See Chapter Nine for more tips on safe towing.

Caravans vary in length anywhere from about 10 feet (3m) all the way to 30 feet (9m). Most vans over about 18 feet (5.5m) have a double axle to improve stability. A fully packed van of this size will weigh in at around 1500 kilograms, and this load is best carried on four wheels rather than two.

Caravans can be divided into several different categories. They are:

Standard

While today's caravans – which may boast anything from surround sound to flat-screen TVs and 200-litre fridges – seem more luxury than standard, they are classified as standard because they have a solid roof and solid walls. Compared with their fold-down counterparts, these vans are taller and thus create greater wind resistance when towing. They are, however, easier to set up and generally provide greater storage space. The length of a standard caravan can range from about 12 feet (3.7m) up to around 30 feet (9m), and prices for a new van start around $20,000 and can go up to $100,000 or more, depending on your specifications and the luxury of the fitout.

Standard caravans can offer plenty of comfort.

Pop-top

The pop-top van is almost identical to the standard van except that its roof folds down when you're travelling and you put it up again when you set up camp. This feature offers less wind resistance on the road but requires a little extra effort to set up and pack away. Some people claim that pop-tops have better ventilation and an airy feel. These vans are generally slightly cheaper than the standard variety. Another plus is that the van can be stored in areas with low clearance when the trip is finished. Note that the pop-top part of the van can only be physically supported in vans up to roughly 17 feet (5.2m). Expect to pay around $18,000 to $70,000 for a pop-top van, depending on specifications.

Pop-top vans offer good ventilation.

Fold-down

Fold-down vans tend to be more popular with younger travellers than with long-term grey nomads. They're made of lightweight materials and pack down to look something like a big box trailer when you're travelling. When you reach camp, the roof is lifted up mechanically and canvas walls magically appear. The ends can be pulled out to make bed space. Although these rigs are extremely easy to put up and take down, most nomads shy away from the perceived difficulties. Fold-downs are generally quite small and don't provide the level of privacy and security that more solid vans do. Nonetheless, they are considerably more affordable, ranging in price from around $10,000 to $30,000, and are easy and cheap to tow.

Fold-down vans are light and relatively inexpensive.

Off-road

Older travellers are becoming increasingly adventurous, as illustrated by the surge in popularity of off-road caravans. A good off-road van allows you to get off the beaten track and take on roads that you wouldn't otherwise be game to. They boast a strengthened chassis and frame, heavy-duty suspension and increased ground clearance. Most are also geared for extended stays in the bush and include a solar panel and battery setup, extra water tanks, extra spare wheels and gas bottle holders. Be warned, though, that some vans are more off-road than others. A little extra ground clearance and a beefed-up suspension system isn't going to stop a van from shaking to pieces on corrugations. As in all areas of life, you generally get what you pay for. While a Bushtracker, Phoenix or other van of similar quality may cost in excess of $100,000, these caravans are genuinely designed to do the hard yards and negotiate tricky creek crossings. They can be seen everywhere from Cape York to the remote regions of the Kimberley. It's worth noting, however, that all of this quality makes for a heavy van and it is this weight, rather than anything else, that ultimately limits where they can be taken.

Genuine off-road vans are built to demanding specifications and you can expect to wait many months to take delivery of your new vehicle. If this is the way you want to go, then plan ahead.

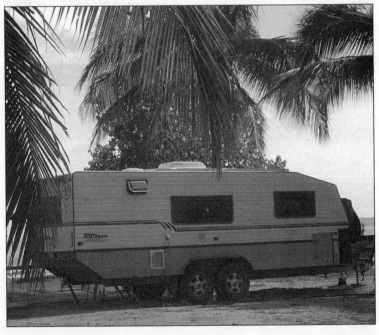

Off-road vans can open up more of the country to you.

Other caravans

As the number of people hitching up their rigs and travelling around Australia increases, so too does the level of ingenuity in the caravan manufacturing industry. More and more unique vans are being developed, in order to capture niche segments of the market.

For instance, a new motorhome has been developed in the United States that doubles as a boat so owners can choose to set up camp on dry land or to cruise down the river and stay on the water for the night.

The distinctive A-frame-shaped series of vans from A'van are almost as innovative. When set up, they provide occupants with lots of headroom and airy feel. Although popular, the Aliner, Cruiseliner, Sportsliner and Cruiser vans are extremely hard to categorise. Unusual models like these, as well as many other emerging concepts in rigs, are changing the traditional image of caravanning and are providing travellers with much more choice.

Caravans now come in all shapes and sizes.

TOWING VEHICLES

Even though normal two-wheel drive vehicles are more than capable of towing a reasonable-sized caravan, most nomads prefer to use a 4WD vehicle. A 4WD provides the opportunity to get out into remote areas, as well as giving a feeling of security. Some drivers enjoy the elevated viewing position that a 4WD offers, and the extra weight and power of these vehicles can also make towing easier.

Note that there is a limit to how much weight each type and make of vehicle can safely tow. The car manufacturer usually lists these limits in its specifications but, if the information is not included, a simple formula can be used. The weight of the loaded caravan should be no more than one-and-a-half times the unloaded weight of the towing vehicle. If the van is too heavy, there is a danger that the towing vehicle may get pushed along when it is trying to brake.

The towbar attached to your vehicle is of crucial importance. If your vehicle already has a towbar fitted, you must check it has the capability to tow your van, as some towbars are designed to only pull small trailers. Most quality towbars incorporate a plate that will show its maximum towing capacity. You must take into account the weight of your belongings as they can add some 350 kilograms to the overall weight of your van.

The mandatory separate braking system of caravans weighing more than 750 kilograms generally requires an electric brake controller to be fitted to the towing vehicle. This enables the driver to operate the brakes manually on long, slow descents and suchlike, as well as having them wired to come on automatically when the brake lights are activated.

Many people towing off-road vans or trailers choose to get a Treg hitch fitted to their vehicles. These allow for more movement both up and down and side to side than the traditional towbar.

When you are setting up your towing vehicle, remember to add some extension mirrors to offer better rear vision and side vision to the driver.

See Chapter Nine for more information and tips about towing.

Petrol or diesel

Diesel is the most common fuel in the bush but it is quite possible to travel happily right around Australia using either petrol or diesel. Diesel vehicles tend to cost a little more to buy but hold their resale value better. If you're in the market for one, the price of all second-hand 4WDs has been falling due to growing concern over their environmental impact and higher sensitivity to fuel costs, and there are some great bargains to be had.

The major advantage of diesel vehicles is that they tend to consume significantly less fuel than their petrol counterparts, and this is something you may well be grateful for as you clock up thousands upon thousands of kilometres on your trip. Diesel really is perfect for the long, steady journeys you're likely to face, especially when you are towing. On the other side of the coin, diesel engines don't normally provide the surge of power and performance of petrol engines, although the latest turbo diesels have made great strides in this department. While diesels are typically more expensive than petrol vehicles to repair, they also tend to have a significantly longer life span – if they are properly serviced.

Of course, the recent introduction of substantial government subsidies to encourage you to convert your vehicle to LPG has brought another dimension to the debate. Certainly, in pure kilometres per dollar terms, LPG is the way to go.

Availability is the key issue here, however, particularly when you get away from the major metropolitan centres. Dual conversion is, nonetheless, a possibility worth considering, depending on where you are going and the type of trip you are after.

Ultimately – like the debate over manual or automatic transmission – it is a matter of personal choice, and all fuel options have their supporters and their critics.

Equipping your towing vehicle

Once your vehicle is properly and safely set up to carry out its vital towing role, there are a number of other accessories you might consider investing in. These extras can make your time away more comfortable and enable you to get more out of your vehicle.

Later in this chapter, we look at communication and navigation items such as UHF radio, distress beacons and global positioning systems.

For many, though, the most likely extra purchase will be a standard roof rack. This relatively inexpensive addition can considerably enhance your storage options. Some of today's heavy-duty racks are so tough that their carrying capacity is limited only by the strength of the car roof itself. The main danger with roof racks is that they can encourage you to bring more possessions than you really need. They are, however, particularly useful for carrying relatively rarely used items, and can be a godsend on those occasions when you decide to drop off the van for a few days while you explore remote country in your tent. Be aware that carrying more weight up top raises your vehicle's centre of gravity. When travelling down rough tracks, this extra instability can lead to rollovers.

Storage space and organisation are both big issues when it comes to long-term trips. The frustration of unpacking the entire contents of the car to find the binoculars and compass for a spur of the moment bushwalk can spoil a potentially great day. Some travellers have found that fitting shelves and drawers into the back of the car provides a more organised space for their gear. Although it is possible to build a car storage unit yourself, certain 4WD accessory companies specialise in manufacturing and fitting vehicle storage systems. Possible additions include cargo barriers, shelves, lockable drawers, fridge slides and jerry can holders.

If you are carrying a heavy load, cargo barriers, which can seal off luggage from the people-carrying section of your station wagon, can be useful. They prevent loose items from sliding forwards and causing injury, and allow you to stack both high and safe.

Bike racks that sit on the back of the car, caravan or motorhome can be bought relatively inexpensively. They are good sturdy pieces of equipment and generally do the job well. However, some people report their bike racks don't always stand up to the rigours of heavily corrugated dirt roads. Just keep an eye on your rack and, if you see any cracks or weaknesses in the welding, take immediate remedial action. Rooftop bike racks are an alternative to the standard rear-mounted bike racks. Before you make your selection, ensure you can load and unload your bikes with ease and that your rack can withstand the types of road surface you intend to travel on.

If you plan to bring your tinny along, think carefully about how you'll transport and access it. It's no simple matter getting a tinny off a roof rack, particularly if there isn't an army of willing helpers around. A self-loading roof rack, available at many marine and boat dealerships and from roof rack suppliers, can be a sensible investment and will encourage you to use your boat more often. These devices are controlled by manual hand winch and only require one person to operate.

Bull bars are pretty much de rigueur for outback travelling. Although their value is hotly debated when they are attached to city-based vehicles, it's a different story in the bush. Wandering stock, kangaroos and even camels are a fact of life in some regions and a bull bar can be a lifesaver. Although restricting your early morning and evening driving can help to minimise the risk of an unwelcome encounter, it doesn't eliminate it altogether.

For nomads eager to get out onto the numerous 4WD-only tracks, the list of potential accessories is virtually endless. Certainly, a snorkel is a sensible insurance policy if deep-water crossings are on the agenda. A snorkel raises a vehicle's air-intake system to roof level and so allows the engine to get a steady flow of air even when the vehicle is nearly completely submerged in water.

Similarly, an electric winch mounted on the front of your vehicle could get you out of the mire – literally. If your budget is tight, a hand winch is a more affordable option. Although these can be heavy and need storing in the vehicle somewhere, they are immensely reassuring to have on board when the going gets rough. Don't forget to take along tree protectors as you will generally need to wrap the winch's steel cable around a tree to help get things moving. A hand winch enables you to pull your stranded vehicle in any direction but, be warned, can be extremely hard work to operate.

Once you have decided on your vehicle and rig, think long and hard about the best way you can set things up. As ever, talking to other nomads who have 'been there and done that' should prove your biggest inspiration.

FIFTH WHEELERS

The American phenomenon that is the fifth wheeler is gradually making its presence felt in the van parks of Australia. These are similar to caravans except they are towed by a ute or truck and the hitch is not at the back of the towing vehicle but rather inside the tray, just in front of the rear axle. This brings tremendous towing stability. Because the towing vehicle can be detached easily, fifth wheelers also offer greater flexibility than a motorhome once camp has been established. The fifth wheeler–ute combination is not as long as the caravan–towing vehicle combination and is consequently easier for other motorists to overtake safely. There is also considerable manoeuvrability with the fifth wheeler as the turning circle is far smaller than with a caravan or motorhome, making it perfect for backing into those tight spots at van parks.

Fifth wheelers offer great towing stability.

They are a lot easier to hitch up than caravans and are a single-person operation.

In general, the sleeping quarters of fifth wheelers are in the area that hangs over the ute tray, so headroom above your bed is minimal. Furthermore, most utes are only capable of carrying two people so there'll be no giving friends a ride or anything of that nature. Nonetheless, more and more people are coming to the conclusion that the advantages considerably outweigh the disadvantages, and fifth wheelers are set to make further inroads into the Australian recreational vehicle (RV) market. Fifth wheelers cost roughly between $65,000 and $150,000.

MOTORHOMES

Many of today's motorhomes are more luxurious than the average family home – and they are sometimes worth a lot more, as well. The biggest are nearly 40 feet (12m) long and can cost up to $500,000. More commonly, you would expect to pay somewhere between $100,000 and $150,000. If you've got the spare cash, are planning to travel for a long time, and like your comforts, then a motorhome could be for you. Most can be driven on a normal driver's licence but anything with a Gross Vehicle Mass (GVM) of more than 4.5 tonnes will require a Light Rigid (LR) truck licence. These can be acquired relatively easily and won't always require an actual driving test.

The top-of-the-range motorhomes will often feature all mod cons, sometimes including a dishwasher, washing machine, sound system, TV, shower, toilet, generator and air-conditioning. You may also discover a rear-vision camera in the cabin to help you know what's going on behind you, and the sort of wooden furniture, carpeting and quality finishings that you would expect to find at Buckingham Palace.

With built-in facilities like these, it's no wonder that motorhome-loving grey nomads are beginning to baulk at caravan park prices, feeling that they're paying for amenities that they don't really need or want. Some traditional caravan parks are also unable to cope with the sheer size of the new motorhomes. If you choose to buy a large motorhome, phoning ahead to check that a certain park or camping area will have sites available that can accommodate your vehicle will become imperative. There's also a growing trend for slide-out living areas, where a section actually slides out from the side of the motorhome, creating an even bigger room inside.

The living space and comfort afforded by these big motorhomes is truly mind-boggling so it is no surprise that their occupants are often happy to travel indefinitely. The all-too-familiar sting in the tail applies, however. The bigger they are, the more they cost to run and the more difficult they are to handle on the road. Always take a test drive before you buy.

The other major drawback with motorhomes is that once you've set up camp, you have to move the vehicle again every time you want to drive to the local shops or to check out that fantastic little fishing beach down the road. It somehow takes the spontaneity out of ducking out for a meal at a local restaurant when you have to take a giant motorhome with you and worry about parking. Some choose to solve this problem by towing a small 4WD vehicle behind their motorhome. The down side to this course of action, obviously, is that it will add significantly to your fuel costs, reduce your rig's manoeuvrability, and make driving more complicated. You can either flat tow your second vehicle – that is, where the towed vehicle remains on all four wheels – or you will need to buy some sort of trailer. Make sure you factor the ease of reversing into the equation when considering your options.

Some motorhomers find taking a motorbike is a less complicated solution to the mobility conundrum, and even pushbikes may be sufficient for some energetic nomads.

Motorhomes can offer both convenience and luxury.

CONVERTED BUSES

Converted buses are usually a more affordable way of enjoying the space that comes with a large motorhome. Basically, the passenger seats are taken out and replaced with a kitchen, bathroom, bedrooms, lounge room and a dining table. Unless you're particularly handy and know exactly what you want, it's far easier and cheaper to buy a bus that has already been converted and has the layout and facilities to suit a long-term trip. There is a flourishing second-hand market in these vehicles as people who've completed their 'big lap' look to offload their rig and move back into mainstream life. Just be aware that many of these vehicles are pretty old and have clocked up plenty of hard kilometres. Check out the engine thoroughly, as well as the conversion job, as you certainly don't need one of these breaking down in the outback. Also check the ventilation and air-con, as some old buses tend to get stuffy and hot when they're not in motion. That said, second-hand converted buses are often terrific buys and have a character all of their own.

Converted buses give you plenty of room to move.

CAMPERVANS

Campervans are really mini-motorhomes. They have the same basic facilities, such as kitchen, dining table, beds and sometimes even a toilet, but lack the living space. Campervans can come with a solid top or pop-top and are easy to drive. They also offer the advantages of being far more economical with fuel than a motorhome, far easier to park and they're far less conspicuous. In many ways they're ideal for single travellers or for couples, depending on how long they're travelling for and how they like to live while they're on the road. If you're travelling with a partner, you might try a campervan for a weekend before you buy. Expect to pay from $50,000 to upwards of $150,000 for a new campervan.

Campervans are generally compact but economical.

CAMPER TRAILERS

There are numerous variations on the camper trailer concept but the fundamentals are that a canvas structure folds upwards and outwards from a small lightweight trailer. A mattress, which stays on a fixed platform on top of the trailer, forms the bed and the folding canvas part creates an enclosed area above, and adjacent to, the bed. A small ladder or stool may be required to climb into bed on some models depending on the height of the trailer and how the rig has been fitted.

Camper trailers are surprisingly easy to set up, and enthusiasts say they offer a more 'genuine' camping experience than a caravan or motorhome. The kitchen generally slides out or folds out from the tailgate of the trailer and is effectively 'outside'. An annexe can usually be added for longer stays and to gain more living space. Some nomads maintain that cooking and living outside makes it easy to meet people and that they tend to spend their evenings socialising rather than watching TV or reading, as they might do if they were in a luxury, air-conditioned rig.

On the down side, you will find storage space is limited in camper trailers. This is partly because everything folds down into such a compact unit in the first place, and partly because the slide-out kitchen takes up a fair bit of space inside the trailer during travel. Manufacturers have tried to address the space issue by placing lots of specialised compartments on the outside of the trailer for things like gas cylinders, jerry cans and spare tyres. A water tank is usually installed under the trailer and innovations such as custom-made sliding drawers for the trailer and lockable storage boxes attached to the drawbar can also increase storage capacity.

Camper trailers are certainly becoming popular with the more adventurous grey nomads. Statistics from one of the leading Australian camper trailer manufacturers show that some 17 per cent of its buyers are already retired, and another 30 per cent of its customers are buying ahead of retirement, in preparation for hitting the road when their working days are over.

While many camper trailers have vinyl floors, which are attached to the canvas walls by heavy-duty stitching, others have raised solid floors that fold up to form a hard roof to the trailer when travelling. Many nomads prefer these models as it means their living space isn't directly on the ground and they are protected from saturation during heavy rains.

Camper trailers are suprisingly easy to set up.

The constant innovation in the camper trailer field is actually taking them to a whole new level of comfort, ease and functionality. The price of new camper trailers ranges from about $15,000 to $60,000.

TENTS

You won't come across them often, but every now and again you'll run into some hardy nomads doing their big trip in a tent. Before you rush out to join them, consider the pitfalls. Camping for a weekend is one thing, but living in a tent, constantly taking it down and putting it up, is quite another. It's hard work; you get hot; you get wet; you get battered by winds; and, whatever sort of bed you choose, you'll probably wish you'd chosen a different sort. Tenting, though, is cheap

Taking a tent gives you more camping options.

and it's about as close to nature as you can get, unless you want to bring your swag along instead.

Most long-term tent-dwelling travellers carry a small, easy-to-put-up tent for short stays and a larger, more luxurious tent for longer stays. Your friends might think you're crazy; your kids might think you're mad; but if you're brave enough and fit enough, it can be done!

In reality, most nomads tend to bring along a small tent as an alternative accommodation option. These tents tend to get used once in a blue moon, normally at places not generally accessible to caravans. You'll find novice tenters struggling with dome tents at spots such as the Bungle Bungles, Mitchell Falls or Cape York.

Having a tenting option opens up a lot more country to the traveller. It makes for a genuine feeling of adventure but, after a night or two under canvas, you'll almost certainly be ready to enjoy the comforts of your rig again.

Manufacturer contact information

The following are websites and telephone numbers of some of the major caravan, motorhome, campervan, fifth wheeler, and camper trailer manufacturers. The websites provide specifications of current models and can give you an idea of layout, size and weight (most of the sites don't include prices, instead providing references to local dealerships). There are also numerous independent manufacturers – check your local directory or the internet to find them. Note that this is not a comprehensive list.

Caravan manufacturers
Some of the following manufacturers also have off-road models and motorhome, campervan and even camper trailer lines.

A'van
Website: www.avan.com.au
Tel: State-by-state dealer contact numbers are on the website.

Bushtracker Caravans
Website: www.bushtracker.com
Tel: (07) 5476 5833

Coromal
Website: www.coromal.com.au
Tel: (08) 9352 0900

Jayco
Website: www.jayco.com.au
Tel: (03) 8792 2000

Phoenix Caravans
Website: www.phoenixcaravans.com.au
Tel: (07) 5495 8277

Royal Flair
Website: www.royalflair.com.au
Tel: (03) 9357 8118

Windsor Caravans
Website: www.windsorcaravans.com.au
Tel: (03) 9930 4900

Camper trailer manufacturers

Adventure Offroad Campers
Website: www.adventureoffroadtrailers.com.au
Tel: 1800 353 561

Cavalier Camper Trailers
Website: www.cavaliercampertrailers.com.au
Tel: (08) 8297 9244

Kimberley Kampers
Website: www.kimberleykampers.com
Tel: (02) 6681 6994

Tvan Camper Trailers
Website: www.tracktrailer.com
Tel: 1800 698 826

Ultimate Camper Trailers
Website: www.ultimatecampers.com.au
Tel: (02) 4474 4410

Motorhome and campervan manufacturers

ATS Motorhomes
Website: www.atsmotorhomes.com.au
Tel: (07) 5491 4829

Frontline Campervans
Website: www.frontlinecamper.com.au
Tel: (02) 9939 0600

Suncamper
Website: www.suncamper.com.au
Tel: (02) 9457 7588

Trakka
Website: www.trakka.com.au
Tel: 1800 872 552

Winnebago
Website: www.winnebago.com.au
Tel: 1800 102 201

Fifth wheelers

Fifth Wheelers Australia
Website: www.5thwheelers.com.au
Tel: (03) 5334 8158

Fifth Wheels 'R' Us
Website: www.activrv.com.au
Tel: (02) 4959 1130

Venture Fifth Wheelers
Website: www.venturevan.com.au
Tel: 1300 880 433

Bus conversions

Dick White Bus & Motorhome Sales
Website: www.busandmotorhome.com
Tel: (02) 6628 1100

The Motorhome Centre
Website: www.themotorhomecentre.com
Tel: (07) 5472 8223

Tent manufacturers

Coleman
Website: www.colemanaust.com.au
Tel: 1800 224 350

Freedom Camping
Website: www.freedomcamping.com.au
Tel: (03) 9347 7700

Oztrail Leisure Products
Website: www.oztrail.com.au
Tel: (07) 3279 1800

Tip: February/March is a good time to shop for caravans from a dealer. The new year's models are just arriving and dealers must clear space for them, often by selling off the previous year's models at discounted rates.

Caravan and motorhome clubs

A caravan or motorhome club is a great place to find heaps of useful information about caravanning and motorhoming. These clubs provide advice about a broad range of topics from maintenance and towing, to cooking and insurance. Many clubs conduct rallies where you can meet others with similar rigs or interests. Some also sponsor online forums where members can exchange advice and experiences.

Contact information

Australian RV Network (contains nationwide list of clubs for RV owners and enthusiasts; follow the links to find one in your state)
Website: www.rv.com.au

Australasian Touring Caravan, Motorhome & Camping Club, Inc.
Website: www.atcmcc.org.au

Auswide Motorhome Club
Website: www.auswide.asn.au
Tel: 1300 131 514

CMCA (Campervan and Motorhome Club of Australia)
Website: www.cmca.net.au
Tel: (02) 4978 8788

Rig power

If you're planning to stay in caravan parks virtually all of the time, you don't need to worry too much about an alternative power source. Caravans and motorhomes are wired to receive 240v power and caravan parks are set up to supply it, although you have to pay a few extra dollars per night to use it. You simply plug into the van park's power point at your site and you're ready to run your fridge, laptop, microwave, TV, DVD player and even your air-conditioning.

Things become a little more complicated, however, when you plan to do a lot of camping in the bush or in the national parks. While most van and motorhome fridges can run off gas, if you still want to use your lights, laptop, TV, air-con and recharge your mobile phone in the wilds, you'll need an alternative power source.

You'll probably find yourself becoming much more power conscious when you're travelling. Without an endless supply of power, you'll be more aware of where the next amp is coming from. Consequently, you'll turn off lights when not in use and you won't leave fridge doors open any longer than you have to – but you don't want this to become an obsession. It's far better to make a realistic assessment of what your power needs will be, and plan to meet those needs.

DEEP-CYCLE BATTERIES

The deep-cycle battery is the foundation of your alternative power system as it has the capacity to store energy and convert it into 12v electricity when required (or 240v electricity with the assistance of an inverter). These batteries are available in a large array of types, sizes and capacities.

The first step in determining what sort of battery setup best suits your needs is to assess your daily power requirements:

- Make a list of appliances that will draw electrical power, including such items as laptops, fans, lights, TVs, water pumps, microwaves and fridges (if applicable).

- Find out how many amps each appliance draws when in use. Most appliances provide information about how much power is required but this information may be detailed in terms of watts instead of amps. The formula to convert watts to amps is: watts = volts × amps. Accordingly, if you estimate that you'll use a 20-watt light for five hours a day, using 12v power, that would translate into 100 watt hours / 12v = 8.3 amp hours.

- Try to estimate how often and how long you'd need to use each appliance on a daily basis when camping in the wilds.

- Think about how often and for how long you're likely to want to be away from a caravan park. If, for example, you're planning only the odd overnighter, your power solutions will be unlike those of travellers who spend weeks at a time away from towns.

Deep-cycle battery capacity is measured in amp hours (A/H). This figure tells you how long you can draw energy from your battery using a specified number of amps per hour. Most 120 A/H batteries, for example, are designed for an optimum discharge rate of six amps per hour over 20 hours $(6 \times 20 = 120)$.

However, in practice, it is not always possible to keep your usage down to six amps per hour or under. Because deep-cycle batteries are less efficient at higher discharge rates, you will get less total A/H out of your battery if you use more than six amps per hour.

It is also important to note that once a deep-cycle battery has been run down to less than 50 per cent of its capacity, you may damage it. Nomads who find their lights dimming down as the battery reaches the end of its charge will soon find themselves shopping for a new battery. So in real terms, the 120 A/H deep-cycle battery will only provide you with around 60 amp hours of power before it requires re-charging, assuming it was fully charged in the first place.

Most modern RVs are pre-fitted with an auxiliary deep-cycle battery, which enables some appliances to be run for a limited time away from 240v power. Depending on individual power requirements, your caravan's pre-fitted battery may need to be upgraded or perhaps another battery added to it in order to meet your daily energy needs. As a very general guide, travellers who keep their fridge on gas and run a couple of lights, a TV for a few hours and use the water pump occasionally find that one 120 A/H deep-cycle battery is sufficient for stays of three to four days away from mains power. However, don't rely too much on this rough estimate – actual power usage varies a lot.

Many pre-fitted auxiliary batteries are charged via the alternator in the towing vehicle when it's running and by a mains-powered charger when the van is stopped and plugged into power. Note that deep-cycle batteries can take some time to charge up if just using the car's engine, often eight hours or more, depending on how far they have been run down. In other words, alternator charging is perfect for people who travel a fair distance, stay somewhere a night or two and then travel hundreds of kilometres again the next day but it is not the solution for most not-in-a hurry nomads.

Check with your vendor to find out more about the pre-installed auxiliary battery in your own rig, including how it's wired; what charging-up procedures are currently in place, both for travelling and staying put; and whether the battery requires any maintenance, such as topping up the water levels.

Deep-cycle batteries work best in conjunction with a regulated battery charger that draws power from solar panels, generators, an alternator, or a 240v charger. It's also important to invest in a device to measure the charge of your battery so that you can monitor whether you're dipping below the 50 per cent charge mark.

As the entire issue of choosing and installing deep-cycle batteries involves numerous considerations, including charging methods, wiring, ventilation and power requirements, it is definitely worth enlisting the help of an expert.

SOLAR POWER

The cost of solar panels has been coming down in recent years and the constantly evolving technology is dramatically increasing the viability of using sunlight as an alternative power source. In fact, quite a few travellers are upset that government subsidies available to house-dwellers who convert to solar energy are not available to them. After all, they argue, their van, motorhome or camper is their home.

Solar panels are great because once you've bought them and had them connected to the other components of your system, you can pretty much forget about them. As long as you remember not to leave them in the shade, they'll quietly and efficiently – and in a most environmentally friendly way – get on with the job of charging your batteries.

What solar panels do is convert the sun's energy into useable electricity. Although the idea is simple, setting up a system to meet your energy requirements when you're away from mains power requires detailed planning. There are several different makes of solar panels on the market. Some use a smaller panel area for the same amount of output; some are better than others at efficiently generating power when there is partial shade; and some incorporate a stronger, more durable panel.

Your solar power system will include the solar panels themselves, at least one deep-cycle battery, possibly a solar regulator, and also a dedicated battery charger to convert the power into the most efficient charge to your batteries.

The biggest issue with solar panels is that you need sun for them to work. Despite the fact that the promise of endless warm weather and constant sunshine is the reason many nomads jumped in their rigs in the first place, it can't be guaranteed – even in Australia. The height of the sun in the sky will have a direct effect on how much power your panel can generate, as will the latitude of the place that you are staying, the amount of cloud cover and any periods of shade throughout the day.

Paradoxically, extremely high temperatures may also play a part in reducing the amount of power generated. If the temperature of the panel itself – not the ambient temperature – exceeds 25°C, many units don't produce as much energy as they would at 25°C or less.

The size of the panel, or panels, you choose will obviously depend on your needs and the way in which you travel, although, budget willing, it makes sense to err on the side of too much power. As a very rough guide, a single 75W panel will normally generate some 10 to 20 amp hours per day in summer. Remember to also factor in a slight loss of energy from your system itself because batteries, wiring, chargers and inverters are not always 100 per cent efficient.

These days, panels are often fixed to the caravan or motorhome and this helps to reduce the risk of theft. Although they will perform slightly better when they are angled to face the sun, fixing the panels to the roof of your van in a horizontal position is quite a convenient option.

The entire issue of selecting and installing an effective solar power system is complex, and it is worthwhile enlisting the services of an expert to determine the most economical and reliable solution for your needs.

GENERATORS

Few subjects are likely to spark as much heated conversation around a campfire as that of generators. We either love them or we hate them. To the camping purists, they are noisy, smelly and – thanks to the rise of affordable solar power technology –

largely unnecessary. To the enthusiast, they are a convenient, inexpensive way of powering an extended stay in the outback.

Beyond doubt, generators can be noisy, and this can create bad feeling between campers. The last thing a birdwatching, watercolour-painting nature enthusiast wants to come across in a remote national park is the steady hum of a generator.

Some national parks and other camping areas are divided into generator areas and non-generator areas and this is probably the best solution all round as everyone knows exactly where they stand. Certain places ban generators full-stop. Where generators are allowed, it's prudent for users to take into account the feelings of other campers and restrict usage to sensible periods and sensible times.

Happily, technology in this field is moving along quickly and the new generation of generators are remarkably quiet. The latest Honda generators advertise themselves as 'whisper quiet' and they are certainly more camper-friendly than the cheaper two-stroke imported varieties that can be picked up in the hardware stores for as little as $100.

Besides looking at the decibel level of any generator, give some thought to its weight, as you'll be carrying it out into the bush on a regular basis. For that reason, around 25 kilograms should be the upper limit weight-wise.

A generator can be a useful addition to your camping arsenal, but you need to consider carefully what your planned usage is. The rise of solar power has meant that many people carry a generator only as a useful back-up in case of a sustained period of inclement weather. If you're considering using your generator daily as your main method of charging up your batteries, then the more expensive, more efficient, quieter four-stroke models are certainly recommended.

Most generators should only be used to charge up a battery,

which then powers your appliances. This is because the output of some models is unregulated and, when used as a direct power source, can severely damage appliances, particularly sensitive ones such as laptops. Although some of the latest 'inverter' generators on the market can power computers directly, always take extreme care and read instructions thoroughly.

Communication and navigation

UHF RADIO

Ultra High Frequency (UHF) radios are the communication must-haves for those enjoying an on-the-road lifestyle. More and more RVs have a sticker on the back announcing the occupants' names, as well as the UHF frequency they can be contacted on. In recent years, Channel 18 has become known as the caravanners' channel, although many people still monitor Channel 40 and Channel 29, which are preferred by the trucking fraternity. You can buy a UHF radio setup for your car, complete with aerial, for only a few hundred dollars, and a hand-held one costs something like $50 or $60. Some people out on a bushwalk or fishing trip like to use a hand-held to communicate with their partner back at camp via the UHF in the car.

While UHF radio is not recommended as something you should rely on in an emergency, it has certainly helped to get many travellers out of sticky situations. The UHF range is relatively limited in normal circumstances, but in the event of a crisis there's a series of repeater stations that can broadcast your message to a larger area if required. Each region has a different frequency for its repeater stations so you must do your research as you move around.

As well as emergency use, UHF radio can be used to get advice from fellow travellers about recommended camping spots, the best places to eat, cheapest places to buy beer and so on. You can also communicate with truckies and get to hear of any potential traffic hazards up ahead. Your UHF radio enables you to scan and listen to the various conversations on all of the channels as a way of passing the hours on a long and arduous journey. Be prepared to block your ears at some of the language on the truckies' channel!

HF RADIO

High Frequency (HF) radio has Australia-wide coverage and is a highly reliable way of summoning emergency assistance. Indeed, the Royal Flying Doctor Service uses HF radio and can be contacted directly through it.

HF radios also have the capacity to connect to the phone system, and users can even listen to broadcasts from such sources as Radio Australia, BBC World, School of the Air and Voice of America.

Although anyone with HF radio equipment can listen to broadcasts and transmissions without charge, you must subscribe to a network to take advantage of features such as direct dialling or operator-assisted calls to telephones, access to a message service and vehicle-to-vehicle communication. Several HF networks are on offer, and each transmits on its own frequency and specialises in different services.

VKS-737 Network

The VKS-737 Radio Network is also referred to as the Australian National 4WD Radio Network. It was established to provide radio communication and assistance for travellers and is operated as a non-profit organisation by 4WD enthusiasts and volunteers. An annual subscription fee is used to cover running costs.

The network broadcasts updates on weather and road conditions, is a point of contact in the event of emergencies and breakdowns, provides a means of communication between travellers, and can be used to request help from other users in the vicinity. VKS-737 also offers a message service facility, and members can make free urgent phone calls to family and friends. It doesn't provide full direct-dial telephone facilities, although it does offer members a limited Selcall plan to a single pre-set number for an extra charge per month. Selcall is an abbreviation for selected calling, a standard feature in most HF radios.

Radtel

The Radtel network operates as a commercial enterprise and specialises in providing users with a direct-dial telephone service through HF radio. Subscribers can choose between a number of call plans, each with a specified yearly access fee, as well as a range of pre-paid options. Radtel subscribers also receive a free messaging service and access to emergency services.

Many nomads with HF radio subscribe to both VKS-737 and Radtel to take advantage of the features offered by both networks.

HF radio equipment

The major drawback to HF radio – as with most good things – is the cost. A new HF radio setup will set you back in the region of $3000. Quality second-hand models are occasionally available from dealers for approximately half the price. It's also possible to hire the equipment for a specific period of time – useful if you plan to, for example, take the Gibb River Road. Note that not all HF radios are equipped with direct-dial capabilities, so it's worth checking with your dealer if you want this feature.

HF network contact information
VKS-737
Website: www.vks737.on.net
Tel: (08) 8287 6222

Radtel
Website: www.radtelnetwork.com.au
Tel: (02) 4943 1745

MOBILE PHONES AND SATELLITE PHONES
For more information on these vital means of on-the-road communication, see Chapter Five.

DISTRESS BEACONS (EPIRBS AND PLBS)
An Emergency Position Indicator Radio Beacon (EPIRB) or a Personal Locator Beacon (PLB) can be used to alert the authorities that someone is in dire trouble and needs emergency help. When activated, they send out a signal that's picked up by Australian Search and Rescue, which will dispatch help immediately. Obviously, these beacons should only be activated in genuine life and death situations.

EPIRBs, which are primarily designed for marine use and therefore float upright in water, transmit a signal for at least 48 hours when activated. PLBs, which are smaller, lighter and cheaper, transmit a signal for at least 24 hours after activation. PLBs are principally designed for use by bushwalkers, 4WDers, and any other adventurers embarking on a journey to a remote spot.

Some of the latest EPIRBs and PLBs are equipped with a GPS function which, when activated, transmits the GPS location of the device. Although Australian Search and Rescue can locate a signal from an EPIRB or PLB which doesn't have a GPS function, models which include them can be located more quickly.

Note that EPIRBs and PLBs must operate exclusively on the 406Mhz digital frequency; the old analogue models which used to transmit signals on the 121.5Mhz frequency were rendered obsolete in February 2009.

Prices for EPIRBs without GPS range from around $500 to upwards of $700 with GPS. There are lots of PLB models available and prices range from around $450 without GPS function to upwards of $600 with GPS. Alternatively, some companies offer EPIRBs and PLBs for hire and this option is worth considering by nomads only requiring the facility for a small segment of their trip.

If you do purchase an EPIRB or PLB, it's worth registering it with the Australian Maritime Safety Authority. Once a device is registered, the Rescue Coordination Centre can access details of ownership and emergency contacts immediately so loved ones can be alerted and possibly assist in the rescue effort.

EPIRBs and PLBs offer travellers tremendous peace of mind. Wherever you are, you'll always be able to summon assistance in the event of a crisis.

Contact information

The Australian Maritime Safety Authority website provides more detailed information about EPIRBs and PLBs as well as a link to register.

Website: http://beacons.amsa.gov.au

Tel: 1800 406 406

GPS

Global Positioning System (GPS) units are amazing pieces of equipment that tell you exactly where you are on earth in terms of longitude, latitude and altitude. The technology works in conjunction with a group of satellites orbiting the earth. Your GPS unit receives signals from at least three of the satellites, calculates how long the signals took to arrive from their positions in orbit and then, using the triangulation method of calculation, determines your exact position.

You'll find many different kinds of GPS devices on the market and they come with a range of price tags. Some units only display numbers such as the longitude and latitude coordinates of your position; some have built-in maps that display your location graphically; and others have the capacity to plot the most convenient route to a pre-determined destination or 'waypoint', direct you there by voice, and instantly plot a new course if you miss a turn along the way. Options include hand-held models, which can be taken out on the water or on bushwalks; big-screen models that can be mounted on your dash; and even a screenless alternative that plugs directly into your laptop or mobile and uses its monitor as the display.

Before you decide to purchase a particular unit, check which maps the model uses, what their scale is (for example 1:250,000 or 1:1,000,000, etc) as well as the dates they were created. If you plan to go off-road or to national parks, it is also worth checking how much detail the maps have of those places or whether other compatible maps can be purchased and installed which do cover those areas. Other important factors to consider are how to download updates or purchase upgrades to the unit's maps and how much it will cost.

In addition to telling you exactly where you are, GPS devices can be used to 'track' your journey (keep a digital record of it) and tell you how many kilometres it is to the next 'waypoint' as well as how many kilometres you have travelled. Some GPS devices can also tell you how fast you are going and even provide you with the latest traffic reports (although perhaps this is not an important feature if you're heading to Oodnadatta!).

Although many GPS devices can be installed and used directly from the box, third party software is also available which has been specifically developed for people to get more advanced functions from their GPS units or PCs. A couple of the most popular enable users to track their journeys in real time, use digital maps that have been created from a scanned paper version and enter and display their own map notes and waypoints quickly and easily.

The cost of GPS units has come down significantly in the past few years. In addition to dedicated electrical appliance shops, they are now on offer at large discount department stores and many new cars come with GPS devices pre-installed. Expect to pay $300 or less for a basic unit and around $1000 or more for a device with all the bells and whistles.

The most important consideration when selecting the best GPS system for your trip is its ease of operation and the quality of its maps of the regions you plan to visit.

3

Planning the trip

When to go

CLIMATE

The weather will have a major influence on when, and in which direction, you plan to begin your journey. One of the many reasons why the ranks of the grey nomads are growing at such a rate is, that in a country as large as Australia, it's possible to enjoy a great climate all year round. All that's needed is planning and a little bit of luck.

The far north

- *Wet season*: During the build-up, the wet season and the run-off, which normally go from about October–May, conditions are generally considered to be rather unpleasant for travellers in areas north of the Tropic of Capricorn. It's hot and humid and there are high levels of rainfall. If you are on the road, you need to be aware of the dangers of flash flooding or washouts. Nonetheless, some nomads do decide to head north in the wet season for the 'experience' and also to beat the crowds. The rains, when they come, tend to be torrential and regular, but they do clear away so there are normally lengthy bright spells each day.

- *Cyclone season*: The devastation wreaked by Cyclone Larry in Far North Queensland in March 2006 provided a timely reminder that an angry Mother Nature is not to be messed with. The region around Innisfail was nearly flattened as the category five storm swept through, delivering winds of 290 km/h. Houses lost their roofs and some were demolished, while thousands of hectares of crops were destroyed. Architects may claim to design houses that are cyclone proof but no one is making the same claims for caravans or motorhomes! The risk of cyclones is said to be highest between November and March. Cyclones don't occur every year but – when they do – they bring heavy rain and powerful winds, and are an enormously destructive force. They tend to be strongest as they make landfall and gradually peter out as they move inland.

- *Dry season*: The dry season is when grey nomads flock north in droves, colonising camping areas everywhere from Broome in the west to Cooktown in the east. The months between May and October promise pleasant temperatures, low humidity and little or no rain. And the box jellyfish risk is at its lowest. It's no wonder legions of caravanners and motorhomers choose to leave the cool southern winters behind them. Remember, though, there are no guarantees as far as the weather is concerned. Most experts agree that our weather patterns are changing and every year is different.

The Centre

- *The heat*: During the hotter months, between November and March, the temperatures in outback Australia can become unbearable. You can expect 45°C-plus days, and that is hard going for man and machine. Add to that the risk of sudden heavy rain and flash flooding and you've got a couple of good reasons to think again about the timing of your trip. Much of outback Australia has been in drought for years and it certainly doesn't rain very often – but when it does, it can rain hard, and dried-up creeks can become raging rivers in minutes; roads can disappear in seconds; and caravans can quickly become bogged.

- *The cool*: During the cooler months between April and October you can expect more reasonable and enjoyable daytime temperatures. In Alice Springs, for example, the average maximum temperature in June and July is 20°C, compared with 36°C in December and January. Many nomads are surprised by how cold it can get in the Centre overnight – the mercury often plunges down to zero in July and August – and you'll love your campfire more than ever.

The south and subtropical coastal regions

- *Summer*: In the south, you can expect the highest temperatures and the lowest rainfall in summer. In Perth, you can plan a barbecue in the near certain knowledge that it will be a perfect, sunny day. Be aware, though, that places like Adelaide and Melbourne and even Perth can become uncomfortably hot in the summer. The autumn and spring months are probably better suited for touring, offering more comfortable temperatures and still low rainfall.

- *Winter*: In some areas, particularly in Tasmania and Victoria, winters can be extremely cold and you can encounter lots of rain and even snow.

In the subtropical coastal regions of northern New South Wales, Queensland and Western Australia, the winters tend to be dry and the daytime temperatures still extremely pleasant. Coffs Harbour in New South Wales is reputed to have the most ideal year-round climate in the country, so it's magnificent to visit at any time. Similarly, on the other side of the country, towns like Exmouth have virtually no rainfall year-round and promise always pleasant temperatures.

SEASONAL FACTORS

The changing seasons and conditions in Australia's many regions bring with them a series of natural phenomena that can affect the timing of your trip. Below are some of the factors you may wish to take into consideration:

Fishing seasons

Fishing can become more than a hobby when you're travelling. It can become an effective and fun way to keep your food costs down and your diet healthy. If you're even vaguely interested in fishing, it's certainly worth bearing in mind the effect the seasons have on your target species.

Is there a fisherman alive who hasn't dreamed of catching the ultimate fighting and food fish – the barramundi? It would be almost criminal to head up north and not to have a crack at a barra. The legendary fish, which can grow to a length of 1.5 metres, inhabits areas from Mary River in Queensland, around the Top End, to Shark Bay in Western Australia. In Queensland, barra fishing is not permitted between the beginning of November and the beginning of February. All things considered, the best time to catch a barra is straight after the wet season, around April.

Always check local restrictions relating to bag limits, sizes, seasons, and fishing licence requirements. And this doesn't only apply to barra. For instance, a closed season applies to Australian bass throughout most of Queensland from 1 June to 31 August.

If trout fishing in Tassie is on your agenda, the best time to give it a go is from August until May, although the weather, water levels and food availability do have an effect. Similarly, if you're keen to take on the spectacular leaps and strong runs of an Australian salmon from the beach, head to southern Western Australia in March or April. You won't be disappointed.

In New South Wales, freshwater fishermen should be aware that the Murray cod closed season is September to November inclusive and Murray crayfish closed season is September to April inclusive.

There are many different fish and factors to consider, so research the subject properly to make sure you're in the right fishing locations at the right time.

To find out more about how fishing can help to enrich your

trip, as well as a state-by-state breakdown of fishing licence requirements, see Chapter Eight.

Wildlife migrations

- *Whale watching*: Every year, thousands of humpback whales and southern right whales can be seen migrating along the southern, east and west coasts. They can put on a spectacular show, performing tail slaps, water spouts and even breaching by launching their whole bodies out of the water. Happily, there are many top spots for viewing this amazing migration, so overcrowding isn't normally a problem. Popular places for spotting southern rights include the Head of Bight in South Australia and Warrnambool in Victoria. Hervey Bay in Queensland and Eden in New South Wales are great locations for sighting humpbacks, as are the Fleurieu Peninsula in South Australia, and Perth and Albany in Western Australia. You can see minkes in the Whitsundays in Queensland.

  Generally speaking, whales head north from around May to July on their way to their breeding grounds in warmer waters – the Great Barrier Reef in the east and off the Kimberley coast in the west. The whales tend to start heading south again from around September to November.

- *Whale sharks*: From mid-March to June each year, the world's biggest species of fish, the whale shark, appears at Ningaloo Reef on Western Australia's Coral Coast. The opportunity to see, and to swim with, these gentle giants is a huge lure for many nature-loving grey nomads. The whale sharks, which can sometimes reach more than 12 metres in length and weigh as much as 11 tonnes, swim close to the surface, so you don't have to be a scuba diver to enjoy an encounter with them.

- *Stingers*: Box jellyfish, or stingers, are found in the tropical waters of northern Australia from Gladstone in Queensland, all the way around the top, nearly to Exmouth in Western Australia. These creatures can cause serious illness or even death and the waters are best avoided when they may be present. Stings from box jellyfish have been reported in every month of the year, although there's said to be a definite season for them. This varies from region to region. Generally speaking, in southern tropical waters, the season runs from approximately December to March, while in the far north it is a little longer and runs from around October to June. Remember, though, that each area and each year is slightly different so always seek local advice before entering the water. Stingers are normally found in shallow water near creek or river mouths. They are more likely to appear after local rain, and are usually absent in rough water. Divers and snorkellers will be pleased to know they're not commonly found over deep water or coral.

Many of the popular beaches in city areas such as Cairns and Townsville are netted to protect swimmers. These nets provide protection from box jellyfish but the tiny Irukandji can still slip through the 25mm mesh and inflict an agonising, and sometimes fatal, sting.

There are also Lycra stinger swimming suits available that provide protection from stings, apart from on exposed areas such as the face, hands and feet.

It's always best to swim at beaches where lifeguards are on duty and, in stinger-prone areas, lifeguards are trained and armed with the best first-aid device for victims of a sting – vinegar.

See Chapter Seven for more information about stingers.

Wildflowers

From the coastal heathlands to the alpine slopes and from desert blooms to flowering forests, the wildflowers of Australia are an incredible spectacle. Although Western Australia is widely known as a mecca for wildflower watching, beautiful floral displays can be found in other regions as well. The following are just a few of the many places to enjoy wildflowers.

- *Wildflowers in the West*: Anyone who's witnessed the wonderful wildflowers of the west will tell you that it's a sight not to be missed. For four months or so every year, Western Australia is positively blooming with thousands and thousands of species of wildflower, bringing an amazing vibrancy and colour to the often barren landscape. The season normally starts in the north around July and gradually heads south as spring brings on the blooms, ending more or less in October in the far south of the state. Each region has its own particular attractions but the flowers are everywhere.

  Although no camping is allowed in Kalbarri National Park, some 600 kilometres north of Perth, the venue is a magnet for flower-loving nomads, and you'll see kangaroo paws, banksias, eucalypts and grevilleas. Further north you'll come across wattles, dampiera, purple peas, native fuchsias, sticky cassia and mulla mulla, while to the south you can find milkmaids, honeypots, green kangaroo paws and mountain bells.

  The Kings Park Wildflower Festival held in Perth every September is always popular, as it puts on display the best of Western Australia's wildflower species in one place.

  Wildflower season is a huge draw for travellers. You may find the roads and the camping spots slightly more crowded than at other times, but this really is something very special.

- *Wildflowers in Tasmania*: Its prolific English and French lavender farms and its abundance of wildflowers make Tasmania a popular destination for flower lovers. The following are just a few spots to view some beautiful blooms:

  - **Freycinet National Park**: In early spring the park is ablaze with a rainbow of wildflowers from pinks and purples to yellows and whites. The riot of colour continues into summer when the purple melaleuca and yellow rock orchids bloom.

  - **Granite Point Coastal Reserve, Bridport**: Located on Anderson Bay, northeast of Launceston, this coastal area is awash with wildflowers in the spring.

  - **Waldheim**: Visit in late November to see a magnificent display of red waratah along the road, myrtle trees with coppery foliage and blooming mountain rockets. At Christmastime there are scented pink boronias, yellow ground-hugging golden guinea, Christmas bells and pink trigger plants.

  - There are a number of magnificent lavender farms in Tassie that help to paint the landscape a shimmering purple in the summer months. Although not strictly 'wild' wildflowers, they are not a sight to be missed. Some plantations ask the visiting public to make a small contribution. Note that French lavender is in full bloom from mid-December to late January, and English lavender blooms from January to the end of February.

- *Wildflowers in Victoria*: The 'Garden State' is blessed with many stunning displays of colourful wildflowers, most of which can be enjoyed from late winter to early summer. The following are but a few of the many spots where you can take in Victoria's wildflowers:

- **The Grampians**: In addition to its rugged mountain ranges, this region is also well known for its display of wildflowers, mainly in the months from August to November. There are more than 900 species of flowers, and some of these are unique to the Grampians region. The colourful flowers range from white to yellow, orange, red, pink and blue. An array of regional springtime festivals and events is held to celebrate wildflower season in or near the Grampians. Halls Gap Wildflower Exhibition takes place annually in September and the Grampians Wildflower and Art Show is conducted each October.

- **Brisbane Ranges National Park**: Located 80 kilometres west of Melbourne, this park is one of Victoria's richest wildflower habitats. A few highlights of the more than 400 species of native plant are wattle, hakea, bush peas and orchids.

- **Paddy's Ranges State Park**: 170 kilometres northwest of Melbourne – More than 230 species of wildflower have been listed in this park, including some 30 orchid species. Paddy's Ranges is especially noted for its many varieties of golden wattle, which bloom in September.

- *'Tameflowers' in the Australian Capital Territory*: Each spring, Canberra becomes a kaleidoscope of colours during Floriade, a dazzling yearly floral festival. For four weeks in September and October, more than one million bulbs and annuals, selected and planted each autumn to celebrate a specific theme, bloom at this vivid extravaganza. In addition to the incredible array of flowers, Floriade features performers, activities, workshops and exhibitions as well as Australian gifts, crafts and produce.

- *Wildflowers in New South Wales*: New South Wales is positively blooming in springtime when stunning native wildflowers burst into life. The National Parks and Wildlife Service says the Glenbrook area in the lower Blue Mountains around September is a great place to find waratahs, gymea lilies and other beautiful species. Spring is said to come a little later to the upper mountains, and October is normally the best month to go on a wildflower walk around Wentworth Falls, Katoomba, Blackheath and Mount Wilson. Discovery wildflower tours, run by the NPWS, are available.

- *Wildflowers in the Northern Territory*: The Northern Territory outback is largely dry and dusty but when there is a bit of winter rain, the wildflowers spring up with a vengeance in August, September and October. Obviously, the amount and spread of rainfall varies from year to year, but areas around Alice Springs can be good places to check out some spectacular floral displays. You will see different species depending on the weather conditions of that particular year but generally there will be plenty of daisies, acacia, purple-flowered peas and a beautiful variety of eremophilas.

- *Wildflowers in Queensland*: Southern Queensland is a fantastic place to find and view some superb Australian wildflowers. Girraween National Park, 60 kilometres by road southwest of Brisbane, boasts some truly amazing wildflower experiences. Girraween is an Aboriginal word meaning 'place of flowers', and you can see how aptly the place is named when, each July, golden wattle and pea-flowers bring a splash of dramatic colour to the landscape. Later in the season, white heath bells, native bluebells, daisies, wattles, bottlebrushes, flannel flowers and others add their magic to this dazzling seasonal show. Closer to the coast, in places such as Currimundi Conservation Park, and Cooloola National Park, you can find banksias, and boronia. Other great wildflower locations can be found on the western edge of the Darling Downs in places such as Barakula and Gurulmundi.

- *Wildflowers in South Australia*: Spring also brings a riot of floral colour to South Australia, and nearly half of the state's 3000-plus plant species can be found in the Flinders Ranges, including Sturt's desert pea. The beautiful Kangaroo Island is almost as florally varied, with more than 800 native plants, and the Coorong National Park in the south and Innes National Park on the Yorke Peninsula also have quite stunning wildflower displays. And when you take into account the seasonal explosions of colour that take place in other areas such as the Eyre Peninsula and the Fleurieu Peninsula, you get a real sense of the endlessly awesome wildflower experience on offer in South Australia.

Festivals and special events

Festivals, markets and special events will play a big part in enriching your journey. Many local festivals are intertwined with nature and the seasons. For example, the 'Staircase to the Moon' is the name given to an amazing optical illusion which occurs in northwestern Western Australia from March–October when a rising full moon reflects on mudflats during extremely low tide. It gives the illusion that a staircase is actually reaching all the way up to the moon. Many nomads like to time their 'Staircase to the Moon' visit to coincide with the ten-day Shinju Matsuri Festival (festival of the pearl), which is held in Broome around August/September each year.

As you plan your trip, check the timing of the major local events. Whether or not you coincide your visit to the region to attend them, at least you'll be aware of how they may affect van park site availability and general atmosphere. Local tourist information centres are the obvious places to find the exact dates for each event.

A list of some major festivals and their approximate dates is detailed in the state-by-state breakdown later in this chapter.

Crowds

For much of the year, grey nomads have a pretty free rein in the camping spots, rest areas and caravan parks of Australia. Apart from the odd busy Saturday or long weekend, the rest of the world is by and large restricted by work and school commitments. However, the holiday periods bring the teeming masses to the camping areas and the nomads have to take their place in the queues. If you want to avoid the crowds there are a few things you need to be aware of and a few steps you can take.

School holidays and long weekends

As previously mentioned, this is when the camping experience can change dramatically. Even remote spots can fill up quickly so the best thing you can do is get in ahead of the crowd and stake out your turf. This can be a good time to go bush or to stay in a national park, as some caravan parks crank up their prices to near extortionate levels. Be aware that the states purposely stagger their school holidays to ensure key vacation destinations don't become ridiculously crowded and that the 'season' lasts longer. Buy a diary or calendar that lists all of the school holidays nationwide so you can monitor them wherever you are.

Nomad season

Don't underestimate the numbers of grey nomads doing exactly what you're doing. Certain places are heavily patronised during nomad season. The bottom line is that from mid-June to mid-August, parks in northern regions from Cairns to Kununurra cannot keep pace with burgeoning demand. And the problem, it appears, is going to get worse. The magnificent old pearling town of Broome in Western Australia is a classic example. During the dry season, it's a magnet for grey nomads from all over the country and some caravan parks take bookings years in advance. If you take pot luck getting a site in a caravan park, you may find yourself in a queue of 20 vehicles at 6am waiting for someone to leave and create a vacancy. The local councils do, however, provide overflow camping facilities to cater to those who are out of luck. This mad surge lasts only for a few months and, if you can time your visit so that you arrive in the shoulder season, you can still enjoy some magnificent weather but without the same level of crowds. Some parks in Broome go from bursting at the seams to empty in a matter of weeks.

If you plan to travel to extremely popular destinations such as Broome, Port Douglas, Mission Beach and Cooktown in the height of nomad season, be sure to book well in advance.

Calendar highlights

Apart from the weather and the beauty of a location, the other thing that brings in the crowds is a special event. That's fine if you actually want to see the event but it can be a nuisance if you don't. Birdsville when the races are on is a different place to how it is the rest of the year, and the gemfields region near Emerald changes character during Gemfest. Keep an eye on your events calendar and check with local tourist information centres, to see what's on, when and where – and plan accordingly.

Where to go

OFF THE BITUMEN?

It's possible to go all the way around Australia and have a fantastic trip without ever leaving the bitumen. However, having the capability and the will to venture onto dirt roads can add an exciting dimension to your adventure. Even the minority of people who choose to do their major trip in a conventional vehicle will find themselves able to comfortably take well-maintained dirt tracks such as those leading to many of our national parks. The same can be said for motorhomers. Nonetheless, you don't know how well maintained a road is until you travel down it, so a 4WD vehicle brings a great deal of peace of mind.

Nomads driving 4WD vehicles are only restricted in where they can go by the vehicle they're towing and by their own perceived off-road driving limitations.

Still, an amazing number of iconic tracks are accessible to conventional caravans and campers. Thousands of grey nomads tow their vans along the Oodnadatta Track and the Birdsville Track and don't encounter any trouble at all. Most of the time these tracks are well maintained and, although they can be a bit rough and stony in parts, they're certainly achievable in the dry season after the graders have been through.

As a rule, the standard of the major dirt roads is improving year on year as the number of travellers climbs. While some traditionalists may mourn the supposed loss of adventure that the graders bring, it's the grey nomads who have benefited most.

Having said that, travelling several hundred kilometres on dirt with a caravan in tow is not a task to be undertaken lightly and you should make sure your vehicle is in good order and that you're carrying sufficient spare tyres with you. It can also be reassuring to travel in convoy with another vehicle.

Those nomads who aren't comfortable taking their caravans down certain tracks can still choose to park their van somewhere and explore with a tent for a few days.

Always seek out local advice about any dirt tracks you're considering taking. Conditions change quickly and tracks that are 'highways' one week can become corrugated nightmares the next. You'll certainly find your van getting more scrapes and dents, and dust will seem to creep in everywhere. Detouring onto the dirt isn't for everybody and it's definitely not for every caravan – but travel with an open mind. If you do explore some of the many tracks that are out there, it will change the way you look at the map and it will change the way you feel about your trip – and in most cases the change will be for the better.

If you decide this off-bitumen stuff is for you, check current local road conditions; pack your belongings down well; make sure your cupboards are firmly shut, the wheel jack is handy and the spare tyre is properly inflated . . . and then hit the dirt.

Camping in the wilds

Discovering that you have the rig and the physical ability to get down some tracks – or even out into remote locations accessible by bitumen – is one thing. Enjoying the isolation and stillness of it is quite another.

Plenty of grey nomads can recall sitting in their city homes planning a trip and positively drooling over the prospect of getting out into the outback. Yet once there, they discover that the wide open spaces are really not for them. On the other hand, people who've never previously camped outside of a caravan park suddenly find the joys of 'roughing it' to be irresistible.

It's hard to prepare yourself for the vast emptiness that is the outback. In some places you might not see another vehicle all day, maybe longer. You may camp alone night after night. So think long and hard about how remote you want to go. Even bush-hardened nomads still get a bit jittery sometimes.

After a while most travellers learn to relax. Your brain tells you that there isn't another living soul within a 50-kilometre radius and, even if there were, they'd almost certainly be friendly, well-adjusted, peace-loving people.

Along the way, some nomads team up with another individual or couple they may have met at a previous camp-site, and this can make the remote travel experience a little less daunting and often a lot more enjoyable.

Ironically, those who may actively be seeking solitude find themselves frustrated by the fact that there are other people at nearly every camping spot. Grey nomads are reaching places they never used to, and even areas out in the remote Kimberley region of Western Australia can become positively 'crowded' at particular times of the year.

Whether you're travelling in a peak period or you're out there on your own, the great Australian outback is an experience not to be missed.

Relax and enjoy it.

How to soothe your outback nerves:

- Make sure your vehicle is in good shape.

- Travel with friends on your first time 'bush'.

- Have a glass of wine.

- Bring plenty of spare parts and tyres.

- Come well stocked with lighting and torches.

- Make sure you have a method of emergency communication.

- Carry lots of water and food.

- Have another glass of wine.

THE CITIES

How much time, if any, to spend in the major cities of Australia is a point of some discussion among grey nomads. To some, the population centres are places to be avoided as much as possible. The cities, they argue, are not what it's all about. A big trip should be all about wide open spaces, crowd-free campsites and starry, starry nights.

There is, of course, no right or wrong answer. It comes down to personal choice and personal preference. How long you spend in towns can also depend on how much time you've given yourself for your whole trip, how much money you have to spend, and whether or not you have friends or relatives to visit.

The good

No two cities are alike, no matter what anybody tells you. They may all have common features like the identical-looking shopping malls, the omnipresent fast-food outlets and the overcrowded city streets. But there's only one MCG and there's only one Sydney Opera House. How could you travel all the way from the east coast and not marvel at Perth's pristine city beaches and the magnificent Kings Park? How could you travel from the south to Darwin and not experience at least one or two of its many and varied markets? Each of our cities has its own unique attractions and its own unique charm. Why not discover them for yourself?

After a long haul across the country, a spell in 'civilisation' can also help you recharge your batteries and rediscover your zest for the trip. It's a chance to attend a major sporting event, to go to a nice restaurant, to do some shopping. Mostly, you'll find that prices for goods and services in the cities are a lot lower than in smaller towns. Maybe it's a convenient time to have that service done on your car, fill up the jerry cans, buy another spare tyre, or get that creaking noise in the van checked out. It can also be a good opportunity to consult the doctor, dentist or chiropractor and get both you and your rig shipshape and ready for the road again.

The bad

If you want to spend longer than a few hours in the city, you're going to have to stay in van parks and they may well be more expensive than you have grown used to. Furthermore, they're often more crowded and have a different atmosphere from those in less populated regions. You can no longer assume that every other person is a traveller like yourself, and you'll find that not everyone is now keen to spend half an hour discussing wonderful spots to visit. People will be in a rush and you may soon find yourself longing for the leisurely pace of a peaceful camp by the creek again.

The ugly

Once you hit the city, you can no longer leave your belongings scattered around outside your van. You have to suspend temporarily the trust in your fellow man that you've been building since you started travelling. Of course, it's possible to have your goods stolen anywhere, but it's far more likely to happen in the city. Get back into the habit of locking your car if you're away from it for a couple of minutes, keep your valuable items out of sight, and be more security aware.

ABORIGINAL LANDS

Often, among the things that older travellers value most from their journey around Australia is the deeper appreciation of Aboriginal culture that they gain along the way. The social problems experienced by some Aboriginal communities have been well documented and there will doubtless be times when you'll be quite shocked by the conditions in which some members of the indigenous population live. Nonetheless, the richness of the history and traditions of Australia's Aboriginal people will also become apparent, especially when you travel in more remote areas.

Aborigines have lived in harmony with nature for the past 60,000 years or so and the importance to them of the land is now being officially recognised. Some areas of the country are legally Aboriginal land and you'll need to apply for a permit if you want to travel through them. In certain cases these permits are free, in others there will be a charge. Remember, this is not Crown land; it's private land and should be treated with respect.

It's easy to underestimate the cultural differences between Aboriginal Australians and European Australians but understanding generally flows from respect. In the first instance, the best way to gain an insight into Aboriginal culture is obviously to talk to Aboriginal people. Happily, there are also an increasing number of excellent organised tours, talks, and adventures that can help to open your eyes to Australia's Aboriginal heritage. The Indigenous Tourism Australia portal offers a list of organisations that provide authentic indigenous Australian experiences for you to enjoy. Visit www.indigenoustourism.australia.com and follow the prompts to find the attractions on offer in the states and areas you will be visiting.

There are around 300 indigenous groupings throughout Australia and each has its own particular social, cultural, artistic and linguistic differences. In some communities you may be asked to avoid particular areas because of their cultural significance, and many sites have dreaming stories woven around them. It is incumbent upon you as a visitor to ensure that your presence or behaviour is not going to cause offence to anyone. If in doubt, ask.

The iconic Uluru is the classic example of a point where two cultures and two histories collide. The rock is a deeply spiritual place for the Anangu people and so visitors are asked to show respect by not climbing the monolith. However, thousands upon thousands of people choose to ignore this request and Uluru is normally swarming with climbers.

Photography is another difficult issue. Some, but not all, Aboriginal peoples dislike people photographing them or their sacred sites, and permission should always be sought before taking a picture. In tourist hotspots like Uluru, sacred areas are clearly marked and it is requested that no photographs be taken in these specific locations. The picture is not always so clear, however, in less visited places. Again, it is incumbent upon you, as a visitor, to ensure your behaviour is appropriate.

Art is the medium by which most people gain an insight into Aboriginal culture and history. The artworks that have remained on cave walls throughout Australia for thousands of years tell an amazing story of an amazing people. It's certainly worth making the effort to seek out these sites. There is so much to learn and so much to understand.

In many ways, the growing numbers of grey nomads now visiting Aboriginal lands are playing a vital role in bringing together the worlds of the ancient and the new Australia. It is an honour and a responsibility.

Contact information

Indigenous Tourism Australia, a branch of Tourism Australia, provides an insight into the indigenous culture and a list of Aboriginal-related tours and experiences.
Website: www.indigenoustourism.australia.com
Tel: (02) 9360 1111

MAPS

Road directories and maps will become your new best friends on the road and it's worthwhile having a decent and comprehensive set. Hema maps are highly regarded for their accuracy and reliability and many guidebooks and tourist brochures use Hema references as standard. A lot of nomads who don't plan to get too far off the beaten track are happy enough to save a few dollars by picking up free maps from local tourist information centres or from state motoring organisations. This is all well and good as long as you remember that the further you get from the major roads, the more detailed your chosen maps will need to be and the more you will depend on them.

Many more people are also choosing to make use of the variety of map-making websites now available on the internet. These will give you full driving directions and predicted driving times between two locations of your choice. Although these sites have different bells and whistles, they all tend to use the same basic mapping software and ultimately do the same job. Note that these sites do not provide advice about road conditions; always check with local authorities if you plan to take routes which may be affected by seasonal closures.

The growing affordability of in-car global positioning systems (see Chapter Two for full details) is also revolutionising the way many nomads navigate their way around the country. But, for all the availability of internet route planners and GPS technology, surely nothing will ever replace the simple pleasure of sitting around the campfire with a dog-eared map happily planning the next day's adventure.

Websites

Internet route planners (there are others):

www.travelmate.com.au (follow the Mapmaker link)

www.racq.com.au (go into the Travel section and follow the Trip Planner link)

STATE AND TERRITORY OVERVIEW

This book is not intended to be a comprehensive where-to-go guide. However, there are some places that definitely shouldn't be left off your itinerary, and some budget camps that are really too good to miss. Here are a select few you may wish to consider.

Australian Capital Territory

The Australian Capital Territory is 88 kilometres long and 30 kilometres wide and is the home of Canberra, the national capital. The city was established 80 years ago as a way of helping to defuse the simmering rivalry between New South Wales and Victoria. It was specifically designed to be the home of Federal Parliament and it's outstandingly neat and well ordered, although some people find it a little too sanitised. Nonetheless, Canberra is indisputably a beautiful city and it's packed with an extraordinary 12 million trees, as well as attractions such as Lake Burley Griffin. Although the city's population of around 300,000 is dwarfed by those of Melbourne and Sydney, its status as national capital is reflected in the quality of the shows, exhibitions and museums it plays host to.

Away from the pollie-filled urban streets you'll find some beautiful country areas, and the Namadgi National Park and Tidbinbilla Nature Reserve virtually back onto the New South Wales high country. There's great camping, bushwalking and fishing to be had right on the doorstep of the capital.

And when all is said and done, no circuit of Australia would truly be complete without a visit to its political heart.

Australian Capital Territory – Best budget campsites

- *Cotter Campground (Murrumbidgee River Corridor – approximately 15 kilometres west of Canberra)*: This scenic campsite is situated on the banks of Cotter River among shady native and exotic trees. It has toilets, showers, and free electric and wood barbecues. No power is available. It's a superb spot to fish, swim, walk, and relax.

- *Honeysuckle Campground (Namadgi National Park – approximately 35 kilometres south of Canberra)*: Namadgi, which occupies nearly half of the Australian Capital Territory, is the most northern of the Australian Alps national parks. It contains some fantastic walks and incredible mountain scenery. The park is well worth a visit, but the campground is only suitable for small caravans and camper trailers and you must book your campsite in advance at the Namadgi Visitor Centre.

Australian Capital Territory – Events

The list of events for the Australian Capital Territory below (and those for other states later in this chapter) is not comprehensive. The lists are designed to convey the range and flavour of the activities available. Some festivals are held at slightly different times each year, and sometimes even in different months, so please check details with the relevant tourism authority.

January
• Summernats Car Festival

February
• Royal Canberra Show

March
• Celebrate in the Park

August
• Craft & Quilt Fair

September
• Floriade Flower Festival (Sept–Oct)

October
• Oktoberfest

November
- Wine, Roses and all that Jazz
- Canberra Cup

Australian Capital Territory – Climate

Canberra	J	F	M	A	M	J	J	A	S	O	N	D
Max temp (deg C)	29	28	25	20	16	12	12	14	16	20	24	26
Min temp (deg C)	14	14	12	7	4	1	0	1	4	7	10	12
Wind speed (km/h)	12	11	11	10	10	10	11	12	13	14	12	13
Rainfall (mm)	60	51	56	49	48	38	52	48	65	62	59	46
Rain days	7	5	7	7	8	9	10	10	11	11	9	8

Further information

Website: www.visitcanberra.com.au

Tel: Australian Capital Territory Tourism on 1300 554 114

New South Wales

With a population approaching seven million, New South Wales may sound at first to be a little crowded. But this is something of an illusion as the state is vast, covering some 800,000 square kilometres. Most residents, and indeed most grey nomads, tend to spend the majority of their time close to the 2000-kilometre long coastline and there's a very good reason for that – the beaches are beautiful and the scenery top-drawer. From Sydney's Bondi to Terrigal and Nelson Bay, from Forster-Tuncurry to Coffs Harbour and Byron Bay, the sun, surf and sand is an irresistible magnet. There's enough whale watching, snorkelling, surfing, swimming, fishing and walking to satisfy the most ardent of beach lovers.

Unfortunately, the Pacific Highway, which hugs the coast, is not in the best shape and the huge trucks that thunder along it can be quite intimidating to van-towing nomads in holiday mode. For that reason, a lot of travellers are now seeking out more relaxing inland routes when it suits them to do so.

There are some magnificent national parks to enjoy in the state, and the waterfalls and sandstone escarpments of the Blue Mountains, the splendour of the Snowy Mountains, and the clay formations of Mungo National Park in the state's southwest should not be missed, no matter how tight your schedule. The same is true of the massive Kosciuszko National Park – home to Australia's highest mountain, Mt Kosciuszko – as well as Barrington Tops National Park, which sits astride the Great Dividing Range and contains some impressive rainforest areas. Then there's the outback town of Broken Hill, a legendary port of call for travellers; the country music capital of Tamworth; and the opal-fossicking mecca of Lightning Ridge. Elsewhere, the Waterfall Way between Coffs Harbour and Armidale is a drive so scenic that some argue it rivals Victoria's Great Ocean Road. And the delightful vineyards of the Hunter Valley offer another excellent reason to dally in the state.

Last but not least is Sydney itself, a colourful, vibrant city built around a beautiful harbour and with a dazzling array of natural, historical and cultural attractions. These include the Opera House, the Harbour Bridge, the Rocks district, museums, countless restaurants and world-class shows and art galleries.

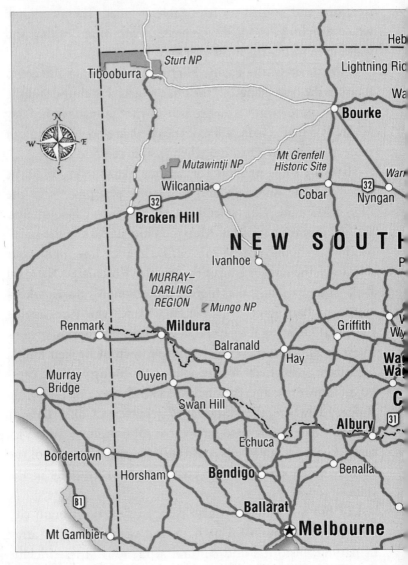

*These are intended to be general state highlight maps that include some major reference points to help with rough route planning. They are not intended to be comprehensive, and so not every lake, mountain, road or national park is included.

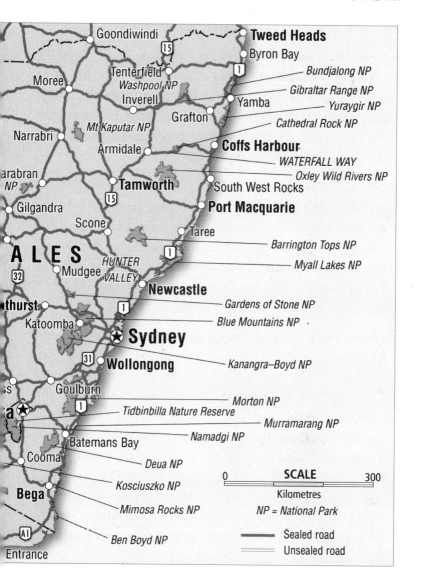

New South Wales – Best budget campsites

- *Camp Blackman (Warrumbungle National Park – approximately 35 kilometres west of Coonabarabran)*: This camp boasts excellent facilities including hot showers, toilets and power. The park itself features a range of memorable bushwalks and visitors can enjoy some unusual rock formations and lovely mountain views.

- *Gillards Campground (Mimosa Rocks National Park – approximately 250 kilometres southeast of Canberra)*: As well as long and stunning beaches, Mimosa Rocks National Park encompasses stretches of rugged coastline, breathtaking headlands and unusual volcanic formations. Take out your fishing rod to catch tea or enjoy a stroll along the beach when you stay in this lovely camp.

- *Green Gully campground (Oxley Rivers National Park – approximately 20 kilometres from Armidale on the New England Tableland)*: With lookouts over the spectacular Chandler and Wollomombi Rivers, this smallish camp is van-friendly and a real treat. Although there are only around 10 sites, facilities include picnic tables, wood barbecues, gas/electric barbecues, non-flush toilets and drinking water. Oxley Rivers is a World Heritage park with dramatic gorges and waterfalls, extensive wilderness, rainforest and (surprise, surprise) wild rivers! The highlight is Wollomombi Falls, which at 240 metres is one of Australia's highest waterfalls. Bushwalking opportunities abound.

- *Depot Beach Campground (Murramarang National Park – approximately 20 kilometres northeast of Batemans Bay)*: Visitors to this coastal park can enjoy swimming, snorkelling and fishing in crystal clear waters. The camp is near the beach and boasts showers, firewood and a population of kangaroos.

- *Main Camp (Mungo National Park – approximately 110 kilometres from Mildura or 320 kilometres from Broken Hill)*: This is very much a remote park and although its roads are generally suitable for 2WD cars, some may become impassable in wet weather. The highlight here is undoubtedly the 'Great Wall of China', an unusual landscape consisting of layers of solid sand and clay which were exposed by wind and rain erosion. You can take a fascinating 70-kilometre drive that loops through ever-changing scenery around the 'Great Wall'. The campsite itself is suitable for vans and boasts free gas barbecues, wood fireplaces and non-flush toilets. The Mungo Visitor Centre, with flush toilets and hot showers, is just two kilometres away.

- *Polblue Swamp Camping Area (Barrington Tops National Park – approximately 60 kilometres west of Gloucester)*: Spend some serious relaxation time at the top of the world in Polblue Swamp camping area where the altitude reaches a dizzying 1450 metres. Meander through snow gums and eucalypt forests on the Polblue Swamp Track and check out the incredible variety of birds and wildlife. The way in is suitable for conventional cars and caravans, although there are some sections of unsealed road.

- *Station Creek Camping Area (Yuraygir National Park – approximately 56 kilometres north of Coffs Harbour)*: This camping area has the lot – estuaries, sand dunes, a magnificent stretch of beach and a pleasant walking track to boot. Ensure you keep all your food secured as several large goannas patrol the camp. A well-maintained 18-kilometre dirt track leads from the Pacific Highway to the camping area.

New South Wales – Events

January
- Bombala – Wool and Wood Festival
- Tamworth – Country Music Festival
- Taree – Craftathon
- Tumbarumba – Rodeo

February
- Nowra Show

March
- Coffs Harbour – The Easter Fishing Classic (Easter)
- Glen Innes – Minerama Gem and Mineral Festival
- Maclean – Highland Gathering
- Narrabri – Twilight Rodeo
- Narrandera – John O'Brien Bush Festival
- Thirlmere – Steam Festival

April
- Hunter Valley Harvest Festival (Apr–May)
- Kiama – Blowhole Bigfish Classic
- Maitland – Hunter Valley Steamfest
- Tenterfield – Oracles of the Bush
- Tumut – Festival of the Falling Leaf

May
- Casino – Beef Week Festival (May–June)
- Glen Innes – Australian Celtic Festival

June
- Coonamble – Rodeo and Campdraft
- Katoomba – Winter Magic Festival

July
- Lightning Ridge – Opal and Gem Expo
- Wauchope – Timbertown Steam Festival

August
- Murwillumbah – Banana Festival (Aug–Sept)
- Narrandera – Camellia Show
- Newcastle Cathedral – Flower Festival (Aug–Sept)

September
- Batlow – Daffodil Show
- Gosford – Springtime Flora Festival
- Inverell – Celebration of the Outback
- Sydney – Festival of the Winds (kite-flying event)

October
- Booligal – Sheep races
- Cobar – Festival of the Miner's Ghost
- Coonabarabran – Warrumbungle Festival of the Stars (Oct–Nov)
- Grafton – Jacaranda Festival (Oct–Nov)
- Kundabung – Bull-riding Competition
- Tweed Heads – Rainforest Week

November
- Ballina – Rivafest
- Eden – Whale Festival
- Glen Innes – Land of the Beardies Bush Festival
- Gundagai – Dog on the Tuckerbox Festival

- Moree – Golden Grain Cotton Festival
- Wingham – Rodeo
- Young – National Cherry Festival (Nov–Dec)

December
- Abercrombie Caves – Carols in the Caves
- Hat Head – Greg Johnson – Egghead Memorial Bowls Day

New South Wales – Climate

Bourke	J	F	M	A	M	J	J	A	S	O	N	D
Max temp (deg C)	36	35	32	27	22	18	18	21	25	29	33	35
Min temp (deg C)	21	20	18	13	9	6	5	6	9	13	17	19
Wind speed (km/h)	11	11	10	9	9	9	10	12	12	13	12	12
Rainfall (mm)	42	42	35	28	30	27	23	20	20	26	29	32
Rain days	4	4	4	3	4	4	4	4	4	4	4	4

Broken Hill	J	F	M	A	M	J	J	A	S	O	N	D
Max temp (deg C)	33	32	29	24	19	16	15	17	21	25	29	31
Min temp (deg C)	18	18	16	12	9	6	5	6	9	12	15	17
Wind speed (km/h)	15	15	14	13	13	14	15	16	16	16	16	15
Rainfall (mm)	23	25	20	18	23	21	19	19	20	25	20	22
Rain days	3	3	3	3	5	5	6	5	4	5	4	3

Coffs Harbour	J	F	M	A	M	J	J	A	S	O	N	D
Max temp (deg C)	27	27	26	24	21	19	19	20	22	24	26	27
Min temp (deg C)	18	19	18	15	11	8	7	8	10	13	16	18
Wind speed (km/h)	22	21	19	17	14	15	15	18	22	23	24	22
Rainfall (mm)	170	207	232	190	138	130	94	81	68	96	104	137
Rain days	12	13	14	12	10	8	7	7	7	9	9	11

Sydney	J	F	M	A	M	J	J	A	S	O	N	D
Max temp (deg C)	26	26	25	22	19	17	16	18	20	22	24	25
Min temp (deg C)	19	19	18	15	12	9	8	9	11	14	16	18
Wind speed (km/h)	18	17	15	14	13	14	15	18	18	19	20	20
Rainfall (mm)	103	117	131	127	123	128	98	82	69	77	83	78
Rain days	12	12	13	12	12	11	10	10	10	12	11	12

Tocumwal	J	F	M	A	M	J	J	A	S	O	N	D
Max temp (deg C)	32	32	28	23	18	15	14	16	19	22	26	30
Min temp (deg C)	16	16	14	10	7	4	3	4	7	9	12	14
Wind speed (km/h)	11	10	10	10	8	9	9	11	11	12	12	13
Rainfall (mm)	32	27	34	33	42	45	43	44	40	44	33	33
Rain days	4	3	4	5	7	9	10	10	8	7	5	4

Further information
Tourism New South Wales
Website: www.visitnsw.com
Tel: 13 20 77 (to order Holiday Planner guides only)

Northern Territory

The total land area of the Northern Territory is in excess of one million square kilometres but its population is a mere 200,000 people, half of whom live in Darwin. The Northern Territory is a vast, rugged, remote and underpopulated enigma that draws grey nomads by the thousands. Whether you're interested in chasing barramundi, spotting crocs, looking at Aboriginal rock art, or simply making the most of the magnificent climate of the dry season, you'll want to linger as long as possible. The camping opportunities are as varied and as beautiful as you could imagine, and you'll forge rewarding friendships under the vast outback sky.

The rugged terrain is littered with rock canyons and dry creek beds and you can truly sense the spiritual significance the place has for Aboriginal people. The evocative white ghost gums contrasting with the endless red landscape will fill your windscreen for day after day and the red dust will probably fill every nook and cranny of your rig. In winter, the days will be warm and perfect and the nights surprisingly cool, but the campfires and abundance of animated conversation will keep you cosy.

Top of most people's must-see list is Uluru, the moody monolith that is even more stunning in reality than in the countless photographs that have been taken of it. Sunset is the best time to appreciate its unique character.

Nearly as iconic as Uluru is Kakadu National Park, which features exceptional examples of Aboriginal rock art, as well as a diverse array of wildlife and some stunning wetlands. Litchfield National Park, about 100 kilometres south of Darwin, is also gaining popularity as visitors get word of the waterfalls, swimming holes, plunge pools, shallow rapids and bushwalks.

Katherine Gorge, which has been carved through ancient sandstone by the Katherine River, is also an extremely popular destination. Visitors are able to take a cruise or hire canoes and paddle themselves through the steep-sided gorge.

Darwin has long held special appeal for nomads seeking to escape the cool winter months of the south, and the magical markets of this cosmopolitan city are wonderful entertainment. The Northern Territory also contains a number of national parks that are home to some of the greatest tropical wetlands in the world, some of the most stunning gorges on the planet, and some of the most feared hunters in history – saltwater crocodiles. Their presence means that the Northern Territory is no place for an overly adventurous fisherman or swimmer.

Full of contrasts and characters, the Northern Territory is a magical place. A trip there is an experience you'll never forget.

Northern Territory – Best budget campsites

- *Devils Marbles Camping Area (Devils Marbles Conservation Reserve – approximately 100 kilometres south of Tennant Creek)*: The unusual boulder formations at Devils Marbles provide a fantastic backdrop for this popular camping area. It's a picturesque spot to break the long journey up or down the Stuart Highway. Try to arrive early in the afternoon during the dry season as the area fills up quickly, and you won't want to miss the magnificent colours at sunset.

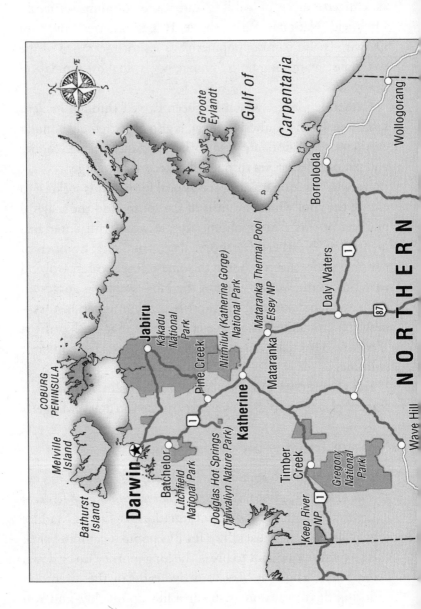

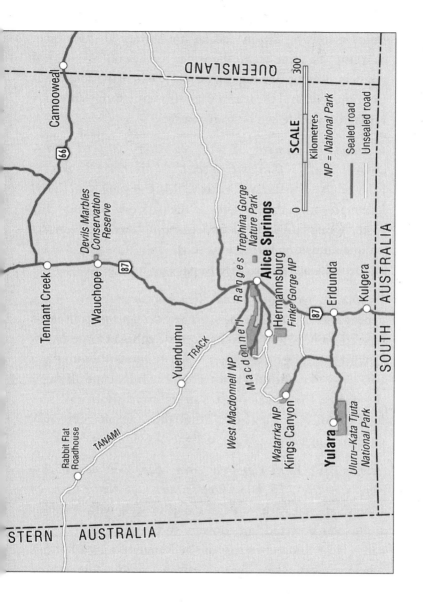

- *Douglas Hot Springs Camping Area (Tjuwaliyn Hot Springs Park – approximately 130 kilometres northwest of Katherine)*: Enjoy a relaxing dip in natural hot springs at this peaceful camp. In some areas, the water reaches 60°C but ideal temperatures for bathing can be found where the cold water from the river and the warm water from the springs meet. A variety of wildlife can be seen nearby.

- *Gurrandalng Camping Area (Keep River National Park – approximately 470 kilometres west of Katherine)*: In the far west of the Northern Territory, this camping spot is 18 kilometres from the entrance to the park down a good dirt road. A magnificent and undemanding bushwalk among unique sandstone formations starts from the campsite. It's a terrifically attractive place to park up for a few days.

- *Trephina Gorge Campground (Trephina Gorge Nature Park – approximately 70 kilometres east of Alice Springs)*: Situated in the East Macdonnell Ranges, the Trephina Gorge campground has free gas barbecues, water and toilets. From there you can strike out on a walk along the ridges and through the gorge. The Macdonnell Ranges stretch both east and west of Alice Springs and within them are magnificently coloured rugged gorges and delightful swimming holes.

- *Twelve Mile Yards Camping Area (Elsey National Park – approximately 115 kilometres southeast of Katherine)*: At Elsey National Park you can camp in style with spacious sites, solar-powered hot showers and flushing toilets. The camp is 18 kilometres east of the Mataranka Hot Springs where you can take a dip in a pristine, vividly blue natural pool.

Northern Territory – Events

February
- Darwin – Ceremonies marking the anniversary of the bombing of the city in 1942

March
- Borroloola – The Barra Classic fishing event (Easter)
- Kakadu Klash – Barramundi 'photograph and release' fishing competition at South Alligator River

April
- Alice Springs Cup Carnival – horseracing meeting
- Alice Springs – Heritage Festival, including re-enactments of historic events

May
- Alice Springs – Bangtail Muster
- Darwin – Northern Territory Orchid Spectacular
- Darwin – The Fred's Pass Rural Show
- Mataranka – Back to the Never Never Festival

June
- Finke Desert – Tattersall's Finke Desert Race
- Merrepen – Merrepen Arts Festival

July
- Alice Springs – Camel Cup Carnival
- Darwin – Beer Can Regatta
- Darwin – Darwin Cup Carnival (July–Aug)
- Katherine – Katherine and District Show
- Tennant Creek – Tennant Creek Show

August
- Alice Springs – Rodeo
- Arnhem Land – Garma Festival, a major indigenous cultural event
- Darwin – Darwin Festival
- Pine Creek – Goldrush Festival

September
- Alice Springs – Henley-on-Todd dry riverbed regatta
- Brunette Downs Campdraft, Rodeo & Gymkhana

October
- Alice Springs – Masters Games (mature-age athletes) held on even-numbered years

November
- Darwin – Christmas Craft Fair

Northern Territory – Climate

Alice Springs	J	F	M	A	M	J	J	A	S	O	N	D
Max temp (deg C)	36	35	32	28	23	20	20	23	27	31	34	36
Min temp (deg C)	21	20	17	12	8	5	4	6	10	14	18	20
Wind speed (km/h)	13	13	12	11	10	10	10	11	12	12	11	11
Rainfall (mm)	43	41	33	16	16	15	14	10	9	20	25	36
Rain days	3	3	3	2	2	2	2	1	2	3	4	4

Borroloola	J	F	M	A	M	J	J	A	S	O	N	D
Max temp (deg C)	36	35	34	34	32	30	30	32	34	37	38	37
Min temp (deg C)	24	24	23	20	16	13	12	14	16	20	23	24
Wind speed (km/h)	10	10	10	10	12	11	12	13	16	17	15	12
Rainfall (mm)	190	193	163	45	12	9	1	1	3	12	44	118
Rain days	12	11	10	3	1	1	0	0	0	1	4	8

Darwin	J	F	M	A	M	J	J	A	S	O	N	D
Max temp (deg C)	32	32	33	34	33	31	31	32	33	34	34	34
Min temp (deg C)	25	25	25	24	23	21	20	21	23	25	26	26
Wind speed (km/h)	12	11	8	8	7	7	8	10	13	12	10	10
Rainfall (mm)	393	330	258	103	14	3	1	2	13	52	124	242
Rain days	19	18	16	7	1	1	0	0	2	5	10	15

Tennant Creek	J	F	M	A	M	J	J	A	S	O	N	D
Max temp (deg C)	37	36	35	32	28	25	24	27	31	35	37	38
Min temp (deg C)	25	24	23	19	15	12	11	13	16	21	23	24
Wind speed (km/h)	12	12	12	12	11	11	11	11	11	11	11	11
Rainfall (mm)	88	90	51	15	12	7	6	3	7	15	28	51
Rain days	6	6	4	1	1	1	1	0	1	2	4	6

Further information
Tourism Northern Territory
Website: http://en.travelnt.com
Tel: 13 67 68

Queensland

There's a good reason Queensland's population has recently topped the magical four million mark and is continuing to grow apace – it's a beautiful place with a superb climate.

The tropical north is an incredibly popular grey nomad destination in the dry season and towns such as Cooktown, Port Douglas, Mission Beach and Karumba are full to bursting when the mercury starts to dip down south. Queensland has a wonderful atmosphere and the caravan parks and camping areas ring out to the sounds of clinking glasses, good-natured card game conversations, and laughter. Those who choose to head even further north up to Cape York generally drop off the van and take a tent, although a proper off-road rig will go all the way to Seisia. But that is literally the tip of this vast state, which covers more than 1.7 million square kilometres.

The national parks are second to none and Lawn Hill, Carnarvon Gorge and the Daintree are but three of the very best. There's also the outback, dotted with towns such as Birdsville, the starting point or end of the iconic Birdsville Track; Winton, where Banjo Paterson famously wrote 'Waltzing Matilda'; and Longreach, where the revered Stockman's Hall of Fame brings to life the country's pioneering past. There's no better place to get an understanding of how modern Australia was built and to learn an appreciation of the men and women who built it. Queensland lays claim to bush poets and bush balladeers aplenty and the spirit and character of the outback will never be more tangible.

But the most famous of all of Queensland's many treasures is probably the Great Barrier Reef, which can be accessed from a number of towns along the coast. Numerous large, comfortable boats are available to take you all of the way out, and you certainly don't have to be a diver to take in the magnificence of the coral and fish life. Below the surface, the visibility is tremendous, and snorkelling allows you to be a part of this magical underwater world. Glass-bottomed boats also make it easy for you to sneak a peek at what lies beneath. If you are physically capable, it's an experience that really shouldn't be missed.

While you're in the mood for a boat trip or two, you could do worse than a cruise out to the jewels of the Coral Sea, the 74 islands of the Whitsundays. A little further south, off the coast near Hervey Bay, is Fraser Island, the world's largest sand island. It's a mecca for beach lovers, anglers, 4WD enthusiasts and wildlife spotters.

Another nomad favourite is the Atherton Tableland, a lush region inland of Cairns, boasting volcanic crater lakes, spectacular views, fertile farmland and crystal clear waterfalls and streams. Lake Tinaroo, with a shoreline of more than 200 kilometres, is perhaps the centrepiece of the area and provides opportunities for fishing, swimming, boating and camping.

The state's major centres, Cairns, Townsville, Mackay and Brisbane, all have their own special appeal and history. While the capital, Brisbane, isn't actually on the coast itself, the beaches of the Sunshine Coast and the Gold Coast are within easy striking distance.

Queensland has absolutely everything a grey nomad could want and you could travel for years and not even begin to see it all.

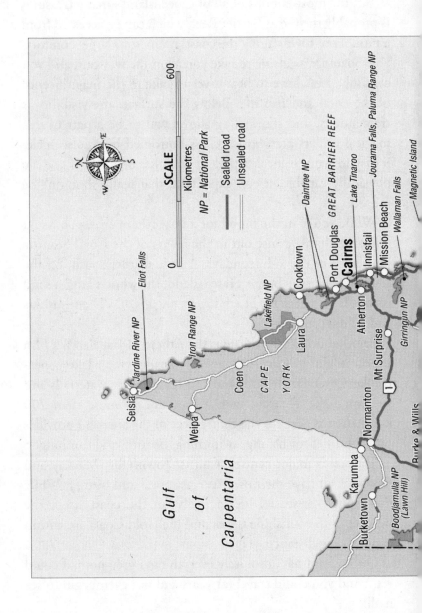

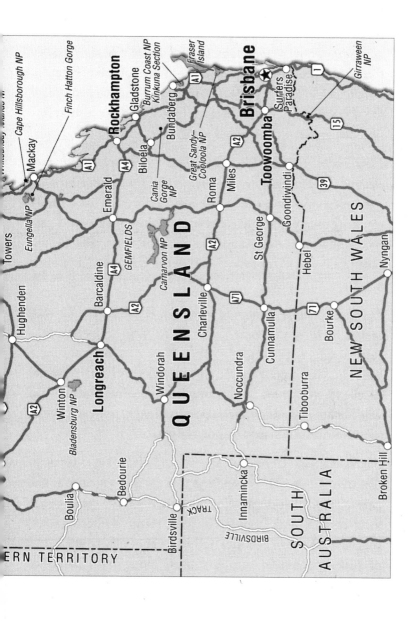

Queensland – Best budget campsites

- *Downfall Creek Camping Area (Danbulla National Park and State Forest – approximately 70 kilometres southwest of Cairns)*: A peaceful camp near the shores of Lake Tinaroo, Downfall Creek is a perfect base from which to explore all the attractions of the Atherton Tablelands. It's also accessible for conventional vehicles and caravans.

- *Eliot Falls (Jardine River National Park and Heathlands Reserve – approximately 900 kilometres northwest of Cairns on the Cape York Peninsula, 4WD only)*: Eliot Falls has a lovely camping area where several short walking tracks wind past picturesque waterways and two beautiful waterfalls: Indian Head Falls and Twin Falls. A dip in the pristine rockpools is a must.

- *Flanagan Reserve Camping Area (approximately 100 kilometres south of Brisbane)*: The Gold Coast hinterland is surprisingly scenic and this site offers a bush atmosphere with modern amenities. The nearby Logan River provides excellent swimming and fishing. Abundant birdlife and wildlife are also major attractions and you may even get to see a notoriously hard-to-spot platypus.

- *Fletcher Creek Camping Reserve (45 kilometres north of Charters Towers)*: This excellent free camping area near the entrance to Dalrymple National Park is managed by the local council and facilities include picnic shelters, tables, toilets, cold showers and wood barbecues. There are scores of superb potential camping spots along both banks of Fletcher Creek. Make the most of this winner.

- *Glenalva Gemfields (approximately 65 kilometres west of*

Emerald): Gem seekers may wish to take advantage of free camping at the Glenalva Gemfields. The interesting characters, the feeling of camaraderie and the chance to find a sapphire make this bush camp well worth a visit. Bring water, food, power and your own (or hired) fossicking equipment – there are no facilities here.

- *Jourama Falls (Paluma Range National Park, 20 kilometres south of Ingham)*: A scenic walk through the rainforest and up to the waterfall is one of the highlights of visiting this lush park. The lookout above the falls offers a splendid view down the valley and there are plenty of rapids as you explore further along the creek. Magnificent trees and plants surround the nicely planned and well maintained camping area.

- *Lawn Hill camping area (Boodjamulla National Park – 340 kilometres northwest of Mount Isa)*: Enjoy striking sandstone cliffs plunging into emerald waters, ancient fossils and memorable bushwalks at this amazing national park in the Gulf area. Paddling through the gorge in a canoe is a great way to enjoy the spectacular scenery and abundant wildlife (a canoe hire service is available). A small campground adjacent to the gorge is very popular and often full. Book well in advance if possible – but Adels Grove Caravan Park, about 15 kilometres away, is a good alternative if no space is available in the park campground.

- *Pyramid campground (Porcupine Gorge National Park – approximately 315 kilometres west of Charters Towers)*: This stunning national park encompasses dramatic sandstone cliffs, deep permanent waterholes and savannah plains. The campground has only 13 sites, ten of which are suitable for caravans so it is advisable to book ahead. The best time to visit is in the dry season, from June to August.

- *Smalleys Beach (Cape Hillsborough National Park – approximately 50 kilometres north of Mackay)*: Smalleys Beach provides campers with a lovely spot to stay in this scenic coastal national park. Take a bushwalk, fish or just relax on the beach and appreciate the views.

Queensland – Events

January
- Brisbane – Australia Day Cockroach Races

February
- Stanthorpe – Apple and Grape Harvest Festival (Feb–Mar, even-numbered years)

March
- Dalby – Cotton Week
- Emerald – Sunflower Festival (Easter)
- Gladstone – Gladstone Harbour Festival (Easter)
- Warwick – Rock Swap Meet (Easter)

April
- Calen – Wintermoon Festival (Apr–May)
- Julia Creek – Dirt and Dust Festival
- Longreach – Outback Muster and Drovers Reunion (Apr–May)

May
- Fraser Island – Bird Week
- Ingham – Australian–Italian Festival
- Richmond – Fossil Festival (even-numbered years)

June
- Gayndah – Orange Festival (odd-numbered years)
- Raglan – Old Station Fly-in and Air Show
- Laura – Dance and Cultural Festival (odd-numbered years)

July
- Cairns – Cairns Show

August
- Brisbane – Royal Queensland Show
- Cloncurry – Rodeo
- Anakie – Gemfest
- Hervey Bay – Whale Festival
- Mount Isa – Rodeo

September
- Birdsville – Birdsville Races
- Brisbane – River Festival
- Cairns – Cairns Festival
- Hughenden – Dinosaur Festival (even-numbered years)
- Mackay – Sugartime Festival
- Toowoomba – Carnival of Flowers
- Winton – Outback Festival (odd-numbered years)
- Yeppoon – Pineapple Festival

October
- Gatton – Potato Carnival
- Millmerran – Australian Camp Oven Festival (even-numbered years)
- Warwick – Rose and Rodeo Festival

November

- Airlie Beach – Whitsunday Fantasea Reef Festival
- Stanthorpe – Red November, a celebration of local red products, including poppies

December

- Rockhampton – Summer Solstice Spectacular

Queensland – Climate

Birdsville	J	F	M	A	M	J	J	A	S	O	N	D
Max temp (deg C)	39	38	35	30	25	22	21	24	28	32	35	38
Min temp (deg C)	24	24	21	16	11	8	7	8	12	16	20	23
Wind speed (km/h)	12	12	12	11	10	11	12	13	14	15	13	13
Rainfall (mm)	25	30	17	10	12	10	11	6	6	12	14	16
Rain days	3	3	2	1	2	2	2	1	1	2	2	3

Brisbane	J	F	M	A	M	J	J	A	S	O	N	D
Max temp (deg C)	29	29	28	26	23	21	20	22	24	26	28	29
Min temp (deg C)	21	21	19	17	13	11	10	10	13	16	18	20
Wind speed (km/h)	14	14	13	11	10	10	11	12	13	14	15	15
Rainfall (mm)	160	158	141	93	74	68	57	46	46	75	97	133
Rain days	13	14	15	11	10	8	7	7	7	9	10	12

Cairns	J	F	M	A	M	J	J	A	S	O	N	D
Max temp (deg C)	32	31	31	29	27	26	26	26	28	30	31	32
Min temp (deg C)	24	23	23	21	19	17	16	16	18	20	21	23
Wind speed (km/h)	8	8	8	9	8	7	8	9	8	9	9	8
Rainfall (mm)	419	422	460	264	111	73	39	42	44	50	98	203
Rain days	17	16	18	15	13	9	8	8	6	7	9	12

Longreach	J	F	M	A	M	J	J	A	S	O	N	D
Max temp (deg C)	37	36	34	31	27	24	23	26	30	34	36	38
Min temp (deg C)	23	22	20	16	11	8	7	8	12	17	20	22
Wind speed (km/h)	10	9	10	8	9	9	9	10	10	10	10	9
Rainfall (mm)	71	84	62	28	24	20	20	9	12	24	27	54
Rain days	6	6	4	2	2	2	2	1	2	3	4	5

Mackay	J	F	M	A	M	J	J	A	S	O	N	D
Max temp (deg C)	30	30	29	27	25	23	22	23	26	28	29	30
Min temp (deg C)	23	23	22	19	16	13	12	13	15	18	21	22
Wind speed (km/h)	15	14	15	14	12	11	11	13	14	14	14	14
Rainfall (mm)	335	318	308	152	94	68	41	26	40	46	74	164
Rain days	14	15	16	13	10	8	5	4	4	5	7	10

Weipa	J	F	M	A	M	J	J	A	S	O	N	D
Max temp (deg C)	32	31	32	32	32	31	31	32	34	36	36	33
Min temp (deg C)	24	24	24	23	21	20	19	19	20	22	24	24
Wind speed (km/h)	16	13	14	17	17	19	19	19	20	20	19	16
Rainfall (mm)	441	618	447	93	17	4	1	7	2	18	105	318
Rain days	24	26	22	12	5	2	1	2	1	2	9	19

Further information

Tourism Queensland

Website: www.queenslandholidays.com.au

Tel: 13 88 33

South Australia

From the cultured confines of the city of churches to the dry and dusty outback, South Australia is a state grey nomads love to explore.

As well as a staggering amount of places of worship and an incredible number of cultural and artistic festivals, Adelaide is also home to the majority of the state's 1.5 million population. But the capital's genteel character doesn't really tell the true story of South Australia. Adelaide is the starting point for the Ghan Railway, which heads north through some of the most remote country in Australia.

This is the state which houses Coober Pedy, whose tough and rugged people mostly live in underground dugouts and complete their extensions with dynamite. This is also the state through which runs the Oodnadatta Track, surely one of the most lonely and desolate drives on the continent.

Grey nomads exploring South Australia should make a point of immersing themselves in the fabulous Flinders Ranges, with its ancient landscape and towering mountains. The coastal Coorong National Park is nearly as impressive in a different way; its vast saltpans will create an almost surreal backdrop to your camping experience. And if you're into birdwatching, your field guide will alert you to the wealth of species inhabiting the area.

If you're still looking for other relaxing activities, the wineries and vineyards of the famed Barossa Valley could be your thing. Situated approximately 50 kilometres from Adelaide, South Australia's main wine region is characterised by rolling green hills dotted with pleasant small communities. Many vineyards are geared up for cellar-door tastings and purchases – an unbeatable way to increase your knowledge of winemaking and acquaint yourself with the local wines.

Also within striking distance of the state's capital is the Yorke Peninsula – more than 600 kilometres of coastline interspersed with interesting and historic seaside towns. As well as indulging in fishing, beachwalking and delving into the region's copper-mining past, nomads can view the sites of 26 shipwrecks. At the tip of the peninsula is the 9000-hectare Innes National Park, which offers fantastic scenery, bushwalking, and great camping.

The coastline of South Australia is rugged and beautiful. Places like the Eyre Peninsula and the Fleurieu Peninsula are simply must-sees, must-camps. If your budget allows, a trip across to Kangaroo Island is a very special experience, too. One-third of the island is a national park and within it are some fantastic natural attractions, ranging from a host of wildlife to extraordinary rock formations and white sand dunes. Heading west there's the Great Australian Bight and

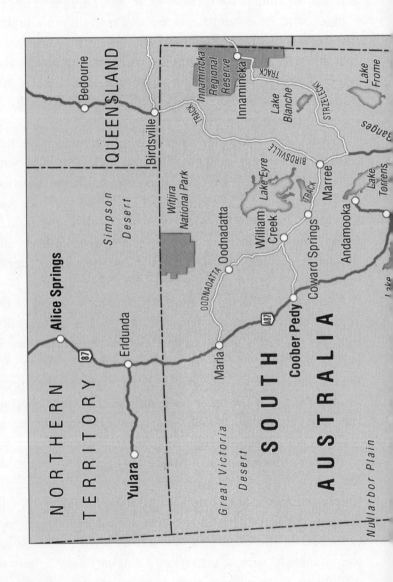

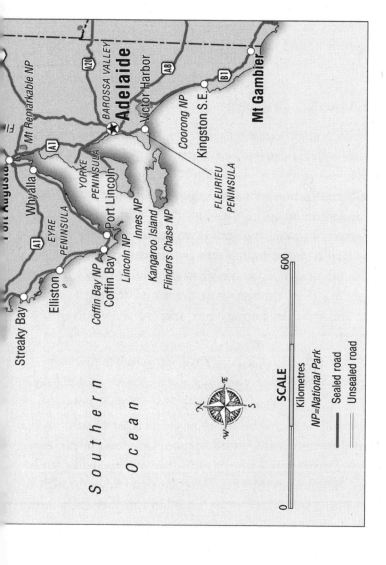

Southern Ocean

Streaky Bay
Elliston
EYRE PENINSULA
Coffin Bay NP
Coffin Bay
Port Lincoln
Lincoln NP
Innes NP
Kangaroo Island
Flinders Chase NP
YORKE PENINSULA
Whyalla
Port Augusta
Mt Remarkable NP
Fli...
BAROSSA VALLEY
Adelaide
Victor Harbor
FLEURIEU PENINSULA
Coorong NP
Kingston S.E.
Mt Gambier

A1
A1
A20
A8
B1

SCALE
Kilometres
NP=National Park
Sealed road
Unsealed road

0   600

the seemingly endless expanses of the Nullarbor Plain, where yet more adventure awaits.

Whatever you're looking for, there's every chance you'll find it somewhere in South Australia's 983,000 square kilometres. This state is bound to feature prominently among the highlights of your 'big lap' diary.

South Australia – Best budget campsites

- *Clayton Station Camping Area (on the unsealed Birdsville Track – approximately 45 kilometres north of Marree)*: What a welcome stopping place this is on the Birdsville Track. The big attraction here is a large spa, which is filled from an underground spring. It is lovely to relax in the soothing waters and exchange travel stories with fellow nomads. This facility and camping area is provided courtesy of the surrounding station, so travellers are asked to show respect by taking their rubbish with them and leaving facilities neat and tidy. An honesty box asks for a donation from campers.

- *Coward Springs Campground (on the unsealed Oodnadatta Track – approximately 130 kilometres west of Marree)*: Adventurous nomads game enough to take on the Oodnadatta Track will be struck by the mirage-like sight of palm trees on the horizon near Coward Springs. On closer inspection, Coward Springs is a true oasis in the vast desert-like landscape. Water from the Great Artesian Basin flows through a bore into a spa, where weary travellers can soak their cares away in the mineral-rich waters.

- *Forty-two Mile Crossing Camping Area (Coorong National Park – approximately 215 kilometres northwest of Mount*

Gambier): Vast saltpans and amazing birdlife abound at Coorong National Park, along the southeastern coast of South Australia. Camp facilities are basic but the unusual landscape and the birdwatching opportunities make it worth a visit.

- *Lipson Cove Camping Area (approximately 200 kilometres south of Whyalla)*: A free camp on the eastern side of the Eyre Peninsula, Lipson Cove offers captivating outlooks, good caravan access, sparkling blue waters and a lovely beach. The drop toilet is perched in an elevated position, surely offering the best view from a lavatory facility anywhere in Australia.

- *Mambray Creek Campground (Mount Remarkable National Park – approximately 55 kilometres southeast of Port Augusta)*: Dramatic gorges, a variety of bushwalks offering panoramic views, plus an abundance of birds and other wildlife, make this national park a marvellous place to camp for a few days. The campground has excellent facilities including flushing toilets, solar heated showers, water, rubbish disposal and communal fireplaces.

- *Parachilna Gorge bush camping (approximately 90 kilometres north of Hawker)*: On the Parachilna-Blinman road just outside the Flinders Ranges National Park, a gem awaits. Take advantage of free camping amongst beautiful white gum trees and ochre-coloured cliffs. The spectacular scenery of the Flinders Ranges inspired many of Hans Heysen's celebrated watercolours. Although there are no facilities here, the beautiful setting and nearby attractions make it well worth a stay.

South Australia – Events

January
- Adelaide – Tour Down Under cycling race
- Milang – Milang–Goolwa Freshwater Classic, Australia's largest freshwater yacht race
- Mount Compass – Compass Cup, Australia's only cow race
- Port Lincoln – Tunarama Festival
- Twilight Markets at the old Moonta Railway Station

February
- Adelaide – Adelaide Festival and Fringe Festival
- Adelaide – Adelaide Hills Harvest Festival
- Coonawarra – Vignerons Classic Clash Petanque Tournament
- Kangaroo Island – Cup Carnival and Street Fair

March
- Adelaide – Adelaide Cup Carnival
- Glendi – Greek Festival
- Port Lincoln – Annual Flag Raising Day

April
- Barossa Valley – Barossa Vintage Festival (odd-numbered years)
- Coober Pedy – Opal Festival (Easter)
- Laura – Laura Folk Fair

May
- Oodnadatta – Oodnadatta Races

June
- Adelaide – Adelaide Cabaret Festival

- Barmera – South Australia Country Music Festival
- McLaren Vale – Sea and Vines Festival

July
- Willunga – Almond Blossom Festival (July–Aug)

August
- Strathalbyn – Collectors', Hobbies and Antiques Fair

September
- Adelaide – Royal Adelaide Show
- Birdwood – Bay to Birdwood Run, vintage vehicle event
- Hahndorf – Heysen Festival, arts celebration (Sept–Oct)

October
- Ceduna – Oyster Fest
- Kangaroo Island – Art Feast
- Renmark – Rose Festival

November
- Lyndoch – Lavender Festival
- Tanunda – Soroptimist Craft Fair

South Australia – Climate

Adelaide	J	F	M	A	M	J	J	A	S	O	N	D
Max temp (deg C)	28	28	25	22	19	16	15	16	18	21	24	26
Min temp (deg C)	16	16	14	12	10	8	7	8	9	11	13	14
Wind speed (km/h)	23	22	21	18	17	17	19	21	21	22	22	23

Rainfall (mm)	18	19	21	35	56	57	62	50	47	40	25	24
Rain days	5	4	6	9	13	14	16	16	13	11	8	7

Mt Gambier	J	F	M	A	M	J	J	A	S	O	N	D
Max temp (deg C)	24	25	23	20	17	14	14	15	16	19	21	23
Min temp (deg C)	12	12	11	9	8	6	5	6	7	8	9	11
Wind speed (km/h)	17	16	14	13	12	12	14	15	17	18	17	17
Rainfall (mm)	32	29	36	63	84	97	107	100	77	63	46	41
Rain days	7	7	9	13	17	18	20	20	17	15	11	9

Nullarbor	J	F	M	A	M	J	J	A	S	O	N	D
Max temp (deg C)	28	28	27	25	22	19	18	19	22	24	26	26
Min temp (deg C)	15	16	14	12	9	6	5	6	8	10	12	14
Wind speed (km/h)	26	26	25	22	20	21	23	23	25	27	26	26
Rainfall (mm)	10	12	21	21	31	31	27	25	17	19	16	14
Rain days	2	2	4	6	9	9	9	8	6	5	4	5

Oondnadatta	J	F	M	A	M	J	J	A	S	O	N	D
Max temp (deg C)	38	37	34	28	23	20	20	22	26	30	34	36
Min temp (deg C)	23	22	19	14	10	7	6	7	11	15	19	21

Wind speed (km/h)	17	17	16	15	15	15	17	18	20	19	18	17
Rainfall (mm)	28	29	14	11	15	12	10	9	10	13	11	14
Rain days	3	2	2	2	3	3	2	3	3	3	3	3

Port Lincoln	J	F	M	A	M	J	J	A	S	O	N	D
Max temp (deg C)	25	26	24	22	19	17	16	17	18	20	22	24
Min temp (deg C)	15	16	15	13	11	9	8	8	9	11	12	14
Wind speed (km/h)	16	15	14	14	14	14	15	16	17	17	16	16
Rainfall (mm)	13	15	20	36	57	75	79	70	50	36	22	19
Rain days	4	4	5	10	14	16	18	17	13	11	7	6

Further information

South Australian Tourism Commission
Website: www.southaustralia.com
Tel: 1300 764 227

Tasmania

At less than 70,000 square kilometres, Tasmania is a small state, yet it's blessed with an amazing variety of landscapes, ranging from pristine beaches and wild rivers to rocky coast-lines and towering mountains. Its air is clean and fresh and its overall greenness quite breathtaking. In other words, don't make the same mistake as so many nomads in the past of not allowing sufficient time to properly explore this island state.

Tasmania has a population of 485,000, nearly half of which lives in the waterfront city of Hobart. It's an attractive place

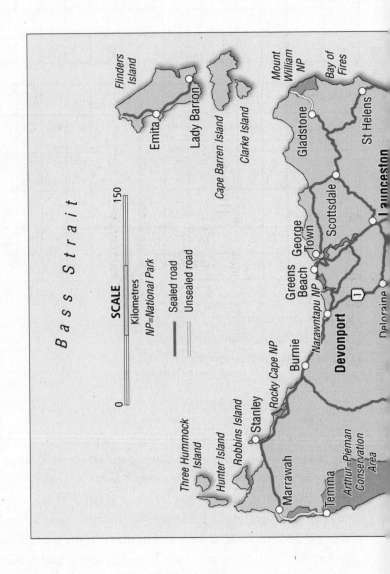

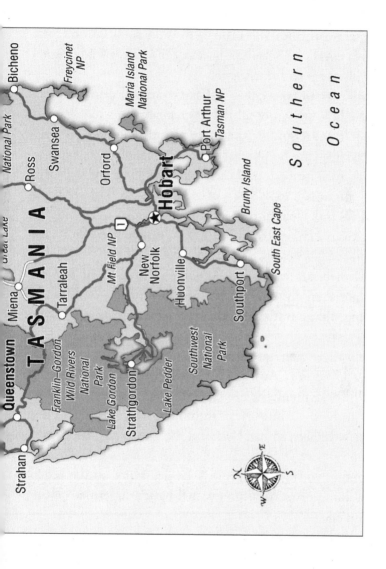

and so, too, are the other major towns of Launceston, Burnie and Devonport. They're all well worth visiting to look at and to stock up on supplies. But it's the wilderness of Tassie that is its real drawing card. The Tasmanian Wilderness World Heritage Area covers 1.38 million hectares and this is wild country that will take your breath away.

Cradle Mountain–Lake St Clair National Park is probably the best-known of all the Tasmanian parks, boasting an incredible collection of lakes, forests and mountains. Freycinet National Park on the east coast is a great place to walk and to enjoy rock formations, beaches and wildlife. The sight that greets you as you look down over Wine Glass Bay will probably live with you forever. Similarly, the Franklin–Gordon Wild Rivers National Park in the west is renowned for its rivers, mountains, gorges, and rainforests.

And there are many more memorable parks. Best of all, this state is an absolute haven for lovers of free and budget camping. Take advantage of that fact by staying as long as you possibly can.

Everywhere you go in Tasmania, you'll find something magical. The Port Arthur Historical Site is both incredibly beautiful and intensely eerie. Then there's Queenstown, which seems to be built into the surrounding rock. Both gold and copper have been mined here and the region has the scars to prove it.

Whether you're into history, wildlife, lazing on the beach, bushwalking or trout fishing, you'll have a superb adventure in Tasmania.

Oh, and the weather. Yes, it can get pretty darned cold! Go prepared with warm clothing and raincoats but keep your fingers crossed that it's the sunscreen and shorts you'll be using most often. Whatever the weather, you'll have a good time.

Tassie is far too beautiful to be spoiled by something as mundane as a cold snap.

Getting there

The *Spirit of Tasmania* sails daily from Melbourne to Devonport and from Devonport to Melbourne throughout the year. The ship offers nightly voyages only during the winter months (approx. 8pm–7am) and provides additional daytime voyages during the high season. Fares are calculated on many factors, including what time of the year you travel, whether the voyage is a night or day crossing (during the high season only), the size of your vehicle, the size of your caravan, and the number of passengers travelling. Tickets can be booked online or by phone. Book well in advance, especially for journeys during the high season.

Tel: 1800 634 906

Website: www.spiritoftasmania.com.au

Tasmania – Best budget campsites

- *Cosy Corner Campground (Bay of Fires Conservation Area – approximately 170 kilometres northeast of Launceston)*: This free campsite is one of several beauties in the Bay of Fires conservation area on the northeast coast. The region attracts lots of visitors who swim, fish and camp near its bright blue waters, startling white sands and dramatic coastline. Thankfully, this magical spot escaped the ravages of the bushfires which wreaked havoc in the surrounding area in late 2006.

- *Edgar Campground (Southwest National Park – approximately 140 kilometres west of Hobart)*: Located in Southwest National Park on the southern end of Lake Pedder, visitors to this free camp can enjoy bushwalking, fishing and boating on the pristine lake. The camp has excellent facilities including toilets, drinking water, shelters, picnic tables and firewood.

- *Fortescue Bay Campground (Tasman National Park – approximately 15 kilometres east of Port Arthur)*: The Fortescue Bay Campground is perched on a stunningly beautiful bay and is a great base from which to explore the nearby Port Arthur historical site. Facilities at this low-cost camp include toilets, showers and fireplaces.

- *Lake Macintosh (approximately 125 kilometres southwest of Devonport)*: Free camping is allowed on the shores of this picturesque lake near the town of Tullah. The lake is part of a hydro dam. Although the camping area has no facilities, the fishing, swimming and views make a stay here worthwhile.

- *Manuka Campground (Arthur-Pieman Conservation Area – approximately 145 kilometres west of Burnie)*: Situated in the 100,000-hectare Arthur-Pieman Conservation Area on Tassie's wild north-west coast, Manuka Campground has basic facilities and some spectacular scenery. It's located very close to the tiny township of Arthur River from where boat trips along the Arthur River are available. The fishing is good, too.

- *Port Sorell Lions Club Caravan Park (approximately 20 kilometres east of Devonport)*: This van park is located near the Rubicon River estuary and the beaches of the Bass Strait. It's a friendly, very reasonable, scenic park and a great place for grey nomads who want to camp near Devonport before or after a ferry crossing.

- *Springlawn Camping Area (Narawntapu National Park – approximately 40 kilometres east of Devonport)*: This is a peaceful camp in the park sometimes dubbed the 'Serengeti of Tasmania'. Spotting wildlife is the thing to do here. The park, which used to be known as Asbestos Range National Park, contains wetlands, dunes and lagoons filled with an amazing number of different plants and animals.

Tasmania – Events

January
- Hobart – Sydney–Hobart Yacht Race finishes
- Hobart – Hobart Summer Festival
- Latrobe – Henley on Mersey Pioneering Festival

February
- Evandale – National Penny Farthing Championships
- Hobart – Hobart Cup
- Launceston – Festivale

March
- Bothwell – Bothwell International Highland Spin-In (odd-numbered years)
- Sheffield – Steamfest

April
- Statewide – Targa Tasmania, rally cars compete on closed roads throughout Tasmania

May
- Carrick – Agfest, agricultural field day

June
- Hobart – Antarctic Midwinter Festival

July
- Devonport – Jazz Festival

August
- Cressy – Trout Fishing Expo

September
- Claremont – Daffodil and Spring Flower Show
- Hobart – Spring Flower Spectacular

October
- Hobart – Royal Hobart Show
- Wynyard – Bloomin' Tulips Festival

November
- Brighton – Agricultural Show
- Deloraine – Tasmanian Craft Fair
- Hobart – Fly@42 Degrees South Kite Festival
- Zeehan – Gem and Mineral Fair

Tasmania – Climate

Burnie	J	F	M	A	M	J	J	A	S	O	N	D
Max temp (deg C)	21	21	20	18	15	13	13	13	14	16	18	19
Min temp (deg C)	13	13	12	10	8	7	6	6	7	8	10	11
Wind speed (km/h)	18	17	17	16	15	15	15	17	19	19	19	19

| Rainfall (mm) | 44 | 47 | 51 | 77 | 96 | 107 | 128 | 11 | 89 | 88 | 69 | 65 |
| Rain days | 10 | 8 | 10 | 11 | 15 | 15 | 18 | 18 | 16 | 15 | 13 | 11 |

Hobart	J	F	M	A	M	J	J	A	S	O	N	D
Max temp (deg C)	23	22	21	17	14	11	11	12	15	17	19	22
Min temp (deg C)	12	12	10	8	6	4	3	5	6	7	9	11
Wind speed (km/h)	23	22	20	18	15	14	15	17	21	22	23	24
Rainfall (mm)	44	39	43	47	43	50	49	47	48	56	54	51
Rain days	9	8	10	10	11	12	13	13	13	14	12	11

Launceston	J	F	M	A	M	J	J	A	S	O	N	D
Max temp (deg C)	24	25	22	19	15	13	12	13	16	18	21	23
Min temp (deg C)	11	11	10	7	5	3	3	4	5	7	8	10
Wind speed (km/h)	20	18	17	15	12	11	12	15	20	20	21	20
Rainfall (mm)	43	38	40	58	69	78	83	76	69	69	48	50
Rain days	8	7	8	10	12	14	16	16	14	14	11	10

Queenstown	J	F	M	A	M	J	J	A	S	O	N	D
Max temp (deg C)	21	22	20	17	14	12	12	12	14	16	18	19
Min temp (deg C)	8	9	8	7	5	3	2	3	4	5	6	8

Wind speed (km/h)	16	13	12	11	9	7	9	10	13	15	16	15
Rainfall (mm)	150	99	147	211	249	220	269	268	249	210	184	168
Rain days	17	13	17	21	22	21	24	25	23	22	19	19

Further information

Tourism Tasmania

Website: www.discovertasmania.com.au

Tel: 1300 780 867

Victoria

Victoria, like Tasmania, packs masses of excitement and variety into a relatively small area – just over 220,000 square kilometres. There's the mighty Murray, the soaring peaks of the Grampians, the sensational snowfields of the alpine region, and one of the world's most spectacular coastal drives in the Great Ocean Road. And then, of course, there's the sprawling cosmopolitan metropolis of Melbourne, where the majority of Victoria's five million population lives. Visitors flock there to see Ned Kelly's gaol, iconic trams, and a dizzying array of ethnic restaurants. And Melburnians' love of sport is second to none. Even if you're not a big sports fan, try to take in an AFL match or other major event at the MCG – just for the experience.

A much-loved playground of the citizens of Melbourne is Wilsons Promontory, or the Prom as it's known locally. Its mountains, rainforest, huge granite boulders, beaches and large population of birdlife entice city folk and travellers alike. The Grampians National Park, located 260 kilometres northwest of the state capital, boasts a similarly diverse and interesting landscape.

Although the weather in Victoria is often joked about, and particularly by its larger neighbour to the north, there are few better places to be when the sun is shining than on one of Victoria's impressive beaches. Worth a mention, too, are Phillip Island, which is famed for its beach-hopping fairy penguins; the old goldmining town of Ballarat; and the elegant towns that line the banks of the mighty Murray. Sitting in a restaurant in a place like Echuca, where you can watch a giant paddle steamer idle past, is part of what being a grey nomad is all about.

The Great Ocean Road, on the state's south coast, is characterised by sheer cliffs, wild seas and dramatic views around each bend of the road.

And if all that's not enough, the high country in the northeast of the state provides visitors with the opportunity to view snow-covered mountains in the winter and wildflowers in the summer.

Victoria – Best budget campsites

- *Boar Gully Camping Area (Brisbane Ranges National Park – approximately 80 kilometres west of Melbourne)*: Wildflowers abound at this magnificent spot, an hour or so from Melbourne. Here, you can find nearly a quarter of Victoria's native flora. Not surprisingly, the birdlife and wildlife is equally varied and resplendent. Booking is recommended, especially during school holidays.

- *Lake Catani Campground (Mount Buffalo National Park – approximately 320 kilometres east of Bendigo)*: This lakeside campground is a marvellous place to camp while you explore the waterfalls, eucalypt forests and alpine scenery of the park. Booking ahead is recommended as Lake Catani

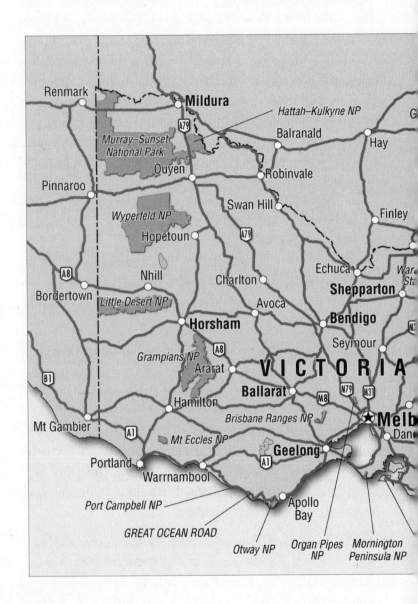

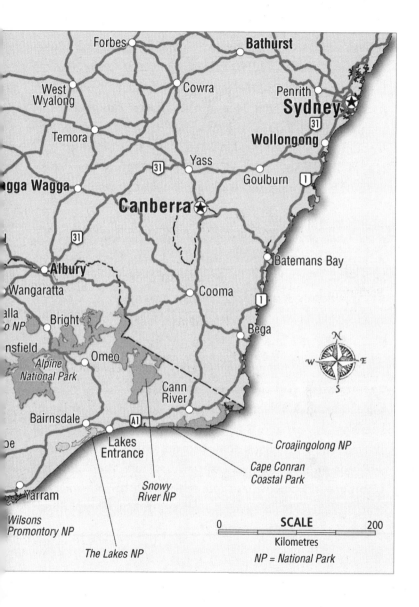

Croajingolong NP

Cape Conran
Coastal Park

SCALE

0   200

Kilometres

NP = National Park

campground is so popular during school holidays that a ballot system is in place to allocate sites months in advance.

- *Mount Eccles Camping Area (Mount Eccles National Park – approximately 250 kilometres west of Geelong)*: This fascinating spot is a vulcanologist's – and grey nomad's – paradise. Mount Eccles and the nearby landscape was formed by volcanic eruptions some 20,000 years ago. The scenic Lake Surprise, which is fed by underground springs, is actually situated on three of the main craters. The campground has 22 sites and it can get busy at peak times.

- *Pebbly Beach Camping Area (Tocumwal Regional Park – Victorian side of the river, Tocumwal)*: This free camping area, located on the banks of the mighty Murray, has basic toilets and all the facilities of Tocumwal just over the bridge. This is a terrific place to indulge in fishing, canoeing or to just relax by the river – but watch the current if you decide to take a dip.

- *Smith Mill Campground (Grampians National Park – approximately 160 kilometres west of Ballarat)*: Located near the stunning MacKenzie Falls, this camp is accessible for smaller caravans and is also quite close to the Wonderland Range. The Grampians boast breathtaking mountain views and a dazzling wildflower display in spring. The Plantation Campground nearby has more space and provides an excellent alternative for larger rigs, or if Smith Mill Campground is full.

- *Wingan Inlet Campground (Croajingolong National Park – approximately 400 kilometres east of Melbourne)*: On the far eastern coast of Victoria, Croajingolong's remote beaches, picturesque waterways and diverse population of birds and wildlife make it a photographer's delight. There are a number of good bushwalks of varying levels of difficulty, starting from or near the camping area. Wingan Inlet is popular during school holidays and booking is recommended.

Victoria – Events

January
- Beechworth – Opera in the Alps
- Cobram – Peaches and Cream Festival (odd-numbered years)
- Melbourne – Australian Open Tennis Championships

February
- Echuca-Moama Riverboats Jazz, Food & Wine Festival
- Yarra Valley – Grape Grazing Festival

March
- Bells Beach – Pro Surfing Classic (Easter)
- Buninyong – Gold King Festival
- Lara – Australian International Airshow (odd-numbered years)
- Melbourne – Moomba Festival
- Mitta Mitta – Mighty Mitta Muster
- Port Fairy – Folk Festival

April
- Adelong – Gold and Antique Fair
- Corryong – Man From Snowy River Bush Festival
- Melbourne – International Flower and Garden Show
- Stratford – Shakespeare on the River Festival

May
- Ballarat – Heritage Weekend

June

- Echuca – Steam, Horse and Vintage Rally
- Geelong – National Celtic Festival
- Rutherglen – Winery Walkabout

July

- Swan Hill – Italia Fest
- Warburton – Winterfest

August

- Beechworth – Ned Kelly Weekend

September

- Melbourne – Royal Melbourne Show
- Statewide – Numerous floral festivals across the state, including the Golden Wattle Festival at Maryborough, the Daffodil and Flora Festival at Leongatha, Daffodil and Arts Festival at Kyneton, Angair Wildflower Festival at Anglesea, and the Australian Cymbidium Orchid Festival at Ararat

October

- Bendigo – Agricultural Show
- Melbourne – International Arts Festival

November

- Mansfield – High Country Festival
- Melbourne – Melbourne Cup

December

- Lorne – Falls Music and Arts Festival
- Wandin – Cherry Festival

Victoria – Climate

Bright	J	F	M	A	M	J	J	A	S	O	N	D
Max temp (deg C)	29	30	26	21	17	13	12	14	17	20	24	27
Min temp (deg C)	11	12	9	6	4	2	2	2	4	6	8	10
Wind speed (km/h)	9	9	8	7	6	6	7	9	9	11	11	11
Rainfall (mm)	71	53	58	75	108	114	140	143	124	113	81	74
Rain days	7	6	7	8	12	14	17	18	15	13	11	8

Melbourne	J	F	M	A	M	J	J	A	S	O	N	D
Max temp (deg C)	26	27	24	20	17	14	13	14	16	19	22	24
Min temp (deg C)	14	14	13	10	8	6	5	6	7	8	10	12
Wind speed (km/h)	22	21	20	20	20	21	23	24	24	23	22	23
Rainfall (mm)	40	40	38	47	42	40	37	47	48	58	58	47
Rain days	9	7	9	10	13	14	14	16	14	14	12	9

Mildura	J	F	M	A	M	J	J	A	S	O	N	D
Max temp (deg C)	33	33	29	24	20	16	15	18	21	25	29	32
Min temp (deg C)	16	16	14	10	7	5	4	6	8	10	13	15
Wind speed (km/h)	10	9	8	9	6	8	8	10	11	10	11	11

| Rainfall (mm) | 18 | 20 | 18 | 16 | 27 | 30 | 23 | 27 | 23 | 28 | 21 | 19 |
| Rain days | 3 | 3 | 3 | 4 | 6 | 7 | 7 | 7 | 6 | 6 | 4 | 3 |

Warrnambool	J	F	M	A	M	J	J	A	S	O	N	D
Max temp (deg C)	22	22	21	19	16	14	13	14	16	17	19	21
Min temp (deg C)	13	13	12	10	9	7	6	7	8	9	10	12
Wind speed (km/h)	17	15	14	14	13	12	14	15	17	17	17	17
Rainfall (mm)	33	34	48	60	78	77	88	86	74	67	55	44
Rain days	8	8	10	13	17	17	20	19	17	15	13	11

Further information

Tourism Victoria

Website: www.visitvictoria.com

Tel: 13 28 42

Western Australia

Western Australia is a vast state covering 2.5 million square kilometres – that's one-third of the land mass of Australia. It's no surprise then that within the state are some unbelievable natural attractions and, with a population of just over two million, the place is largely empty!

The great majority of the state's inhabitants live in its south-west corner. Perth is a clean, attractive place with surely the most pristine city beaches in the world. The nearby wine region surrounding the township of Margaret River needs no introduction to anyone who enjoys a tipple – and it's a glorious part of the world to explore. Then there are the giant karri forests near Pemberton, the iconic Wave Rock, and the white sandy beaches of Cape Le Grand National Park – and still we've barely scratched the surface of this huge state.

As you head further north, the countryside becomes drier and the number of kilometres between attractions gets greater. But don't let anyone tell you there are days of mindless driving. There's always something to hold your interest. If you get your timing right, you'll be blown away by the number, colour and extent of the wildflowers which seem to sprout everywhere in the west.

The gorges of the Kimberley region, such as Bell Gorge and Windjana Gorge, are also must-sees, as is the awe-inspiring Karijini National Park. Camping areas in Karijini such as Dales Gorge and Savannah Campground are accessible to caravan-towing and motorhome-driving grey nomads. Plan your trip carefully and take as much local advice as you can. One place that certainly isn't accessible for vans or motorhomes is the Bungle Bungles but don't let that put you off getting in for a look at these unusual beehive-shaped mounds. The road is extremely rough and you may have to park your van and head in with a 4WD and a tent, but it really is worth the effort. Alternatively, organised tours are available.

The most famous of the west's beaches is the iconic Cable Beach in Broome. The old pearling town has reinvented itself as a tourist centre. If this is on your itinerary – and it should be – be prepared to jostle for pole position in the parks or else travel in the shoulder season.

And to top it all off there's Ningaloo Reef, near Exmouth, which some say rivals the Great Barrier Reef in its beauty. It's definitely more accessible – the coral starts only metres from the beach.

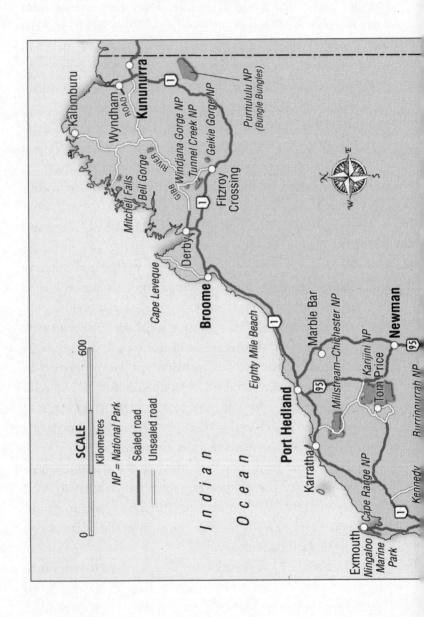

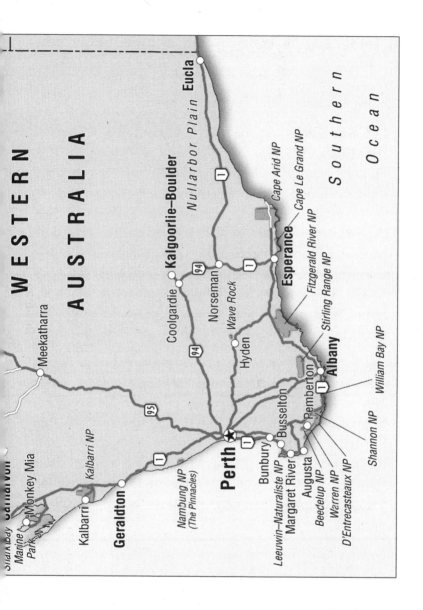

As a state, Western Australia has the lot but it is vast and you're going to spend a lot of dollars keeping your tank filled up. For the sake of your enjoyment, and your budget, take your time.

Western Australia – Best budget campsites

- *Le Grand Beach Campsite (Cape Le Grand National Park – approximately 50 kilometres southeast of Esperance)*: This stunning national park with its electric blue seas, dazzling white sands and rugged coastline is a must-see for visitors to the south of Western Australia. The park boasts two campsites – one at Le Grand Beach and one at Lucky Bay. Le Grand Beach is smaller and offers campers more privacy, while Lucky Bay has an open feel and caters for more people. Although the fees at both camps are at the upper end of Western Australia's national park fee structure, the incredible scenery makes a stay here worthwhile.

- *Conto Campground (Leeuwin-Naturaliste National Park – approximately 20 kilometres southwest of Margaret River)*: This is a popular camping area in the scenic Leeuwin-Naturaliste National Park. The site has free firewood, free barbecues and is a short drive to the spectacular Conto Beach, where you can land an Australian salmon from February to April. Other features of the park include beautiful beaches, fantastic walking tracks and giant karri trees.

- *De Grey River Rest Area (approximately 75 kilometres northwest of Port Hedland)*: A pleasant shady spot on the De Grey River, this free camp just off the Great Northern Highway is a relaxing place to break your journey. Fishermen may be tempted to throw a line in but don't be tempted to swim, as bull sharks frequent the waters.

- *Ellendale Pool (approximately 50 kilometres east of Geraldton)*: This idyllic free camp has good facilities and the scenery is superb. Relax by (or in!) the water and enjoy multi-layered cliffs towering over you and diverse birdlife around you. There are toilets, tables, gas barbecues and water.

- *King Edward River Camping Area (4WD only, Mitchell River National Park – approximately eight kilometres west of Kalumburu Road, and some 180 kilometres north of the Gibb River)*: Camp here on the way to Mitchell Falls and savour a swim – and a rest from the corrugations – in a fantastic setting complete with scenic rockpools. The camp has a drop toilet and plenty of water from the creek (boil before use).

- *Mambi Island Boat Ramp (approximately 50 kilometres north of Kununurra. Access is via a good dirt road, but the descent into the camping area is fairly steep)*: This free camp on the grassy banks of the Ord River north of Kununurra is great for fishing, birdwatching and saltwater croc spotting (be careful!). Facilities are limited to one drop toilet but the atmosphere and scenery more than make up for that.

- *Parry Beach (approximately 30 kilometres west of Denmark)*: This friendly and scenic beachside camp is a haven for swimming, boating, and fishing enthusiasts. Indeed, professional fishermen frequent this magical spot during salmon season, which runs from February to April. Don't worry, though, there's still room for grey nomads. Just be aware that it can get a little crowded during peak times.

- *Quondong Point (approximately 40 kilometres north of Broome via a reasonable dirt road)*: Enjoy the clear waters of the Indian Ocean at this lovely free campsite. There are no facilities here but the views, swimming and fishing compensate for that.

Western Australia – Events

January
- Busselton – Performing Arts Beach Festival
- Fremantle – Sardine Festival
- Perth – Perth Cup

February
- Dwellingup – Log Chop Day

March
- Donnybrook – Apple Festival (Easter) (even-numbered years)
- Mandurah – Crab Fest
- Margaret River – Leeuwin Estate Concert, Wine and Food Festival
- Wagin – Woolarama Rural Show

April
- Bunbury – Splash Festival
- Corrigin – Dog in a Ute Competition

May
- Kununurra – Ord Valley Muster
- Leonara – Golden Gift Festival
- Ningaloo Reef – Whale Shark Festival (odd-numbered years)

June
• York–Avondale Clydesdale and Vintage Day

July
• Derby – Boab Festival
• Fitzroy Crossing – Rodeo

August
• Broome – Shinju Matsuri Festival (Aug or Sept)

September
• Perth – Royal Show
• Perth – Kings Park Wildflower Festival
• Statewide – Wildflower events at many towns, including Esperance, Ravensthorpe and Walpole

October
• Kulin – Kulin Bush Races
• Kalgoorlie – Goldfields Mining Expo
• Northampton – Airing of the Quilts

November
• Broome – Mango Festival
• Margaret River – Wine Region Festival

December
• Albany – Great Southern Wine Festival

Western Australia – Climate

Albany	J	F	M	A	M	J	J	A	S	O	N	D
Max temp (deg C)	23	23	22	21	19	17	16	16	17	18	20	22
Min temp (deg C)	15	15	15	13	11	9	8	8	9	10	12	14
Wind speed (km/h)	21	20	19	16	15	15	18	18	20	20	21	21
Rainfall (mm)	24	23	68	68	120	133	145	127	102	80	43	30
Rain days	8	8	11	14	18	20	22	21	18	17	12	9

Broome	J	F	M	A	M	J	J	A	S	O	N	D
Max temp (deg C)	33	33	34	34	31	28	28	30	32	33	34	34
Min temp (deg C)	26	26	25	22	18	15	14	15	18	22	25	26
Wind speed (km/h)	14	13	11	10	9	9	9	10	13	15	17	15
Rainfall (mm)	158	144	101	30	21	23	4	3	1	1	13	76
Rain days	10	9	7	2	2	2	1	0	0	0	1	5

Carnarvon	J	F	M	A	M	J	J	A	S	O	N	D
Max temp (deg C)	31	32	32	29	26	24	23	23	25	26	28	29
Min temp (deg C)	22	22	22	18	15	11	12	14	16	18	20	17
Wind speed (km/h)	23	20	19	16	15	14	17	20	22	23	24	19

| Rainfall (mm) | 10 | 20 | 16 | 15 | 38 | 60 | 40 | 18 | 6 | 3 | 1 | 4 |
| Rain days | 1 | 2 | 2 | 2 | 5 | 7 | 7 | 5 | 2 | 1 | 0 | 0 |

Esperance	J	F	M	A	M	J	J	A	S	O	N	D
Max temp (deg C)	25	25	24	23	20	18	17	18	19	20	22	24
Min temp (deg C)	16	16	15	12	10	8	7	8	9	10	12	14
Wind speed (km/h)	19	19	17	15	14	15	17	17	18	18	19	20
Rainfall (mm)	18	20	28	45	82	100	108	97	71	55	28	23
Rain days	5	5	7	10	15	16	17	16	14	12	7	6

Kununurra	J	F	M	A	M	J	J	A	S	O	N	D
Max temp (deg C)	36	36	35	36	33	31	30	34	36	38	39	38
Min temp (deg C)	25	25	24	21	19	16	15	18	21	24	25	26
Wind speed (km/h)	6	6	6	7	7	7	7	6	6	7	7	6
Rainfall (mm)	197	213	140	21	10	1	4	0	3	26	71	105
Rain days	14	15	11	3	1	0	0	0	1	4	7	10

Marble Bar	J	F	M	A	M	J	J	A	S	O	N	D
Max temp (deg C)	41	40	39	36	31	27	27	30	34	38	41	42
Min temp (deg C)	26	26	25	21	17	13	12	13	17	20	24	26

Wind speed (km/h)	11	12	11	11	11	11	12	12	12	12	12	11
Rainfall (mm)	76	88	57	21	23	23	12	7	1	4	9	39
Rain days	7	8	5	2	2	2	2	1	0	1	2	5

Further information

Tourism Western Australia

Website: www.westernaustralia.com.au

Tel: 1300 361 351

> **Tip:** Be aware that between some states – and even between different regions within a state – there are quarantine checkpoints for fresh fruit, vegetables and organic products such as honey. You may be required to bin all fruit and vegies before you cross the border. You can check what items are prohibited and where they are prohibited at the Quarantine Domestic hotline: 1800 084 881. It's also possible to download the booklet *Traveller's Guide to Interstate Quarantine* from the Department of Agriculture, Fisheries and Forestry website: www.daff.gov.au (follow the links to publications).

Who to go with

TRAVELLING WITH DOGS

The prospect of leaving behind a beloved pooch while taking off on an extended trip is too much for many grey nomads to bear. And, after all, what could be better for a dog than running around at beautiful, open campsites, jumping into creeks and streams, and exploring rugged and interesting country?

Be warned, however, that bringing Rover along will have a profound effect on the nature of your trip. Dogs are not welcome at national parks or most wildlife reserves, and that closes off a whole lot of beautiful country to you. You'll be travelling thousands of kilometres to different parts of the country and then miss out on some of the highlights. Of course, there are those nomads who risk the wrath of the ranger and keep their canine companion hidden away in the van while they explore. Even then, the anxiety of leaving the dog alone and the fear of discovery can overshadow the pleasure of a bushwalk or waterfall swim.

The reasons why dogs and other pets aren't allowed in national parks are pretty compelling and should be obvious to all. They may chase wildlife, foul public areas, cause potentially dangerous disruptions in high-risk spots like clifftops, and they may jump up on strangers. The scent left by a dog is also said to make native animals flee from their habitat.

While state forests are more open to dogs, many of them don't allow you to camp with your pet. You also need to be aware that fox-baiting takes place in some areas and the 1080 poison used is a naturally occurring toxin that is lethal to dogs. Even in state forests where dogs are allowed, you're therefore best to keep your dog on a leash.

Give some thought also to the endless hours in the car for your dog and the sometimes less than welcoming response of certain caravan park managers and fellow travellers. Indeed, many caravan parks don't allow dogs, and those that do will often charge you for the privilege. Caravan park listing brochures make it very clear where your pet is welcome and where it is not. There are also a number of excellent books out on the subject.

Having said all this, a wide variety of camping options are

available to those travelling with dogs. Bush camps are often havens for dog owners. There are camping areas that will put you within spitting distance of dog-friendly beaches and some places will have you parked up next to a crystal clear creek where your dog can splash around happily. The occasional camp spot at the foot of hills and mountains may also allow you and your pet to roam to your heart's content. They're all out there – you just have to look harder to find them.

If you decide to leave your dog behind, only a couple of options for your pet are on offer. The best is to leave it in the care of a friend or relative. Otherwise, there's the professional 'pet hotel' route. These are not cheap, especially if you plan to be away for several months, and may not be an ideal environment for long-term placements.

The 'shall-I-take-the-dog' conundrum is a tricky one for many grey nomads. There is no right or wrong answer and there are no easy solutions. It's essential to make sure you're happy with your decision and that you're positive about it once you've made it.

Coping with dogs on long journeys

- Dogs need regular breaks as much as you do, so give them a run.

- Leave the window down a little to prevent dogs getting car sick.

- Never leave your dog alone in the vehicle for long, particularly on hot days.

- Make sure your dog can see out the window as it travels.

- Bring your registration papers along with you.

- Don't forget your pooper scooper and act responsibly.

- Keep feeding and sleeping times as regular as possible.

Books

Bush Camping with Dogs (Flat Earth Mapping). Features more than 1100 dog-friendly campsites in parks, reserves, forests and rest areas around Australia.

Holidaying with Dogs (Life Be In It). Lists more than 2000 places where you can happily stay with your dog, including B&Bs and motels, as well as caravan parks and rest areas.

Websites

www.doggyholiday.com
www.holidayingwithdogs.com.au

TRAVELLING WITH FRIENDS

For a variety of reasons, many grey nomads choose to travel in convoy with friends. That way, help and support are always at hand if someone suffers an accident or a bout of ill health, and it's reassuring to have a friendly face out there in unfamiliar conditions. And then, of course, there's the company. It's wonderful to have ready-made card-playing partners and fishing companions in the RV just ahead of you.

Often this arrangement works well, but it's not without risks. Stories proliferate about lifelong friends who return from a caravanning or motorhoming trip barely on speaking terms, or of normally easygoing holidaymakers who come to blows over whose turn it is to cook the sausages.

So why can travelling with mates go pear-shaped? Most grey nomads imagine spending happy times with people they like, but few are prepared for the challenges of spending all day, every day with them. If expectations don't match reality, it can come as quite a shock. Petty jealousies and suppressed grievances can easily bubble to the surface. This is the ultimate test of friendship.

Flexibility is important, and to keep things fresh, travelling companions should be prepared to part company for a week or two and then meet up again at a pre-determined time and place. It's sometimes hard to achieve this flexibility when you set out from home with your friends, but far easier when you make your friends on the road.

During your trip you'll doubtless meet like-minded and likeable people who are heading in the same direction and you may choose to travel together for a while. For many, this arrangement offers the best of both worlds. You have your company and your card-playing partners but only for as long as it suits you all. When one party wants to visit one particular spot and the other wants to visit another, you can part ways having enjoyed a few happy days together.

Remember also that regardless of what you say before you leave, you'll find that travelling with friends from home means you meet fewer people on the road than you other-wise would have – and that can add up to a lot of missed opportunities. You're less approachable when you're already part of a group.

Ultimately, travelling with friends is a matter of individual choice. It can bring immense rewards but it can also place an unbearable strain on friendships. When contemplating a trip, remember that the hardships of the road can bring out the worst, as well as the best, in people.

Friendship flashpoints:

- When each party wants to take a different route or to see different things.

- When one driver likes to travel faster than another.

- When something goes wrong . . . mechanical troubles or even minor illnesses can put a big strain on friendships.

- When one party wants to linger longer in a particular spot.

- When two families have a different idea of how to while away the evening hours.

- When parties are travelling on different budgets.

- When people want to stay in different caravan parks.

- When a more experienced traveller tries to take charge.

How to stay friends on the road:

- Travel with someone who has a similar rig to your own that's in similar condition – breakdown delays are bad enough when it's your own vehicle!

- Travel with like-minded individuals.

- Set out some ground rules.

- Be tolerant.

- Be honest and straightforward.

- Using a UHF radio can help you travel apart while still together.

- Mobile phone contact can help you arrange meetings further down the track.

- Make sure you find some time to spend on your own every now and again.

- If you want to stop for different lengths of time in a place, just arrange to meet again further along the road.

- Resist the urge to point out all your travelling companion's 'mistakes'.

- Don't let tensions fester . . . discuss any issues before they get out of hand.

- Be flexible.

GOING SOLO

The solo grey nomad is a significant presence on the road and these individuals thoroughly enjoy themselves. Older Australians who've lost their partner or who never married are every bit as keen to explore the country as the rest of the population – and they don't see doing it alone as a problem. In fact, many of the most sociable travellers are the lone nomads who make a point of chatting to everybody they cross paths with in the campsite, and consequently find themselves receiving lots of dinner invitations.

You may even meet someone who's travelling alone because his or her spouse didn't fancy the trip. If the grey nomad dream isn't shared by both partners, certain couples will choose to pursue their interests separately for a few weeks or a few months. This arrangement works well for some.

Travelling alone isn't for everybody. You need to be comfortable in your own company, self-reliant and confident. Even the most self-assured traveller occasionally craves the company of others, the help of others, or simply someone with whom to share a magical place or moment. On the other hand, you're free to go exactly where you want, when you want and to eat and drink what you want, and so on. You have nobody to please but yourself and it can be a liberating experience.

Even though the vast majority of solo grey nomads are men, a fair number of lone women are out there as well.

Security is a key issue for all singles, as something like tripping over a step and breaking a bone could become a potentially life-threatening situation. Some solos find travelling with a dog offers the double benefit of company and added security.

What to pack

GENERAL EQUIPMENT

What you take will depend on your rig, how long you're going for, and the level of luxury you are seeking. If you're planning a long-term trip, you'll no doubt experience a multitude of weather conditions. Bring a range of clothing to suit different climates but don't go over the top. Travelling light allows you to pack more quickly and efficiently and it'll also save you money on fuel. You can always top up cheaply on clothing and other items at op shops or local markets.

However comfortable the inside of your rig may be, don't forget to pack a folding table and campchairs for sitting outside. It's easy to underestimate the number of hours and days you'll while away sitting under your awning.

If you're taking a spare tent for occasional use when you drop your van to go exploring off-road, remember to take a portable gas cooker, too. Similarly, if camping in the wilds is going to be a significant part of your trip, don't forget to bring items such as an axe for chopping wood, firelighters and a camp oven.

Check out the ingenious camping gadgets available which may enhance your trip. A vehicle-mounted shower device powered by car battery is useful in bush camping situations if your rig doesn't have its own shower. Hammocks, Swiss army knives, portable water filters and battery-less torches are but a few other handy items to consider bringing along. Browse around a camping supply shop and keep an eye out for ideas as you travel.

COOKING EQUIPMENT

It may be tempting to bring lots of appliances from your home kitchen but try to limit yourself and take only what you envisage you'll constantly need. That cappuccino maker and grinder may make sensational cups of coffee, but can you really say they're worth the space?

STORAGE

Equipment storage

If you plan to use your saucepans and frying pan to cook over an open fire, you'll discover that they turn black on the outside and no amount of scrubbing will completely clean them up. It may be worth storing these items separately from your other cookware – perhaps in a cloth bag – to ensure that little black smudges don't appear over everything else. Some nomads find large plastic storage containers are useful for keeping together kitchen utensils and cookware.

Packing food

It's unnecessary to shop for a year's supply of everything before your trip begins, as taking hundreds of tins and other bulky items will weigh you down. However, it's handy to have a few things with you that can readily be used to make a quick meal or snack between shop-ups for fresh food. Sauces, condiments and spices can be organised before the trip begins.

Storing dry foods

Plastic containers with sealed lids are a convenient way to store food such as pasta, rice, sugar, cereal, tea, coffee and flour. These are spill-proof for when you travel over rough patches of road plus they keep out unwanted creatures. Take a few extra containers along for storing leftovers.

Storing fresh fruit and vegies

The best way to keep fruit and vegies fresh for the longest amount of time is to remove them from plastic bags, ensure they're free from moisture, and wrap them individually with something dry, such as newspaper or tea towels. If they won't all fit in your fridge, a cardboard box in a cool dry area is the next best spot.

Some fruit and vegies keep better and are more transportable than others – pumpkin, citrus fruits, potatoes and carrots, for example, travel more effectively than bananas, peaches, and eggplant.

Storing meat

If you plan to include meat on your menus, enquire into getting your meat vacuum packed at the shop. This process, known as 'Cryovac-ing', enables you to keep your meat fresh significantly longer – up to three or four weeks – than if it were kept in the normal supermarket packaging. The Cryovac process involves taking nearly all the air out of the packaging so that the meat has less chance of invasion by bacteria. Most butchers will Cryovac meat for you if you ask and you will find that meat in the more remote shops is only available in Cryovac packages. However, even meat stored in Cryovac packaging must be kept in the fridge at a temperature of 5°C or less.

SUGGESTED PACKING LIST

Ultimately, packing for your trip is a highly personal matter. Start planning what you might want to take well in advance. The old saying 'If in doubt leave it out' might have been coined for trip packing dilemmas. You can always pick up extra items on the road. The following are a few items you might want to think about:

General camping gear	
Axe	Matches
Binoculars	Portable toilet
Buckets	Saw
Campchairs	Scissors
Camp shower	Shadecloth for awning floorspace
Compass	Shovel
Fire extinguisher	Spares
Fire starters	Storage containers
Fishing gear	Tarp
Folding table	Tool kit (see Chapter Nine for more details)
Gas stove	
Jerry cans	Torch
Lantern	

Personal items	Cleaning equipment
Bedding (include some warm blankets)	Biodegradable detergents and washing-up liquid
First-aid kit (See Chapter Four for more details)	Brush and dustpan
Games	Fold-down laundry basket
Insect repellent	Garbage bags
Playing cards	Pegs
Sunscreen	Scourer
Toilet paper	Tea towels
Toiletries – soap, shampoo, etc	Washing-up bowl

Communications and high-tech equipment	Clothing
Battery charger	Selection of warm and cool clothing
Spare batteries	Fly hats
Camera	Sun hats
Distress beacon	Gardening/utility gloves
GPS	Swimwear
Laptop computer	Thongs
Mobile phone and charger	Umbrellas
UHF radio	Walking boots

Books and maps	Personal documents
Astronomy guide	Address book
Guide to Australian birds	Copy of all insurance policies
Guide to Australian flora	Diary marked with important dates and emergency contacts
Book of gems and fossils	
Book of card games	Driver's licence
Novels	Credit cards/bank cards
Maps	Seniors Card
	Motoring organisation club card
	Miscellaneous club membership cards

General cooking equipment	Campfire cooking equipment
A couple of different-sized saucepans with lids	Jaffle iron
Frying pan	Camp oven
Portable gas cooker for outdoor cooking and 4WD tenting adventures	Large wire grill or cake-cooling rack
Tongs	Billy
Spatulas	
Sharp knives	
Mixing bowl	
Aluminium foil	
Cling film	
Oven gloves or hot pads	
Toaster	
Jug	
Ladle and/or large cooking spoon	
Wooden spoon	
Food storage containers	
Plates, bowls, cutlery, drinking cups, mugs	
Tin opener	

4

Health

Keeping well on the road

Even though travelling in Australia is basically a relaxing and enjoyable thing to do, you still need to look after your health. Inevitably you'll find yourself doing things that you're not used to doing. These may include everything from driving for many hours and collecting firewood, to taking long bushwalks and spending more time in the sunshine. You need to give some thought to your health requirements while you are away.

PREPARATION

Your starting point should be a thorough check-up with your doctor. Talk to him or her about your plans and discuss how you can look after your health while you're travelling. This is especially important if you have coronary heart disease, hypertension or any other chronic condition, or if you've recently undergone surgery. Discuss any particular health concerns you may have.

As you begin serious planning for your trip, why not get into 'training' for it? Perhaps it's a good time to do a bit of extra walking at your local park or swim a few laps at the pool. With your doctor's approval, you might decide to lose a couple of kilos so you look and feel your best for the 'big lap'. The healthier you are, the more you'll get out of your trip.

As well as an awareness of your general health, you never know when you may have to cope with some sort of medical emergency. However unlikely it is, if you're camping in a remote area, you may have to deal with anything from a snake bite to a bee sting, and from an allergic reaction to heat exhaustion. It really does make sense to take a first-aid course, and there's a wide range of courses available. See 'First-aid courses' later in this chapter for details.

When it's time to actually set off, you may wish to:

- Carry your health records to make the job of any health professional you encounter on your trip that much easier.

- Take a letter from your doctor outlining your general health and any specific conditions you have, including things such as allergies.

- Make sure you have enough medication for your trip or have a plan for filling prescriptions. Sometimes you'll be in remote areas where access to pharmacies will be limited.

- Make sure you store your medications in the correct manner, particularly when in a hot climate.

- Consider taking pre-packaged daily medications so you don't forget what you're supposed to take and when.

- Consider having 'flu and pneumonia vaccinations before you depart.

- Visit your dentist for a check-up.

- Visit any other health care providers you consult with on a regular basis, such as your optometrist.

- If the medication you regularly take requires syringes (eg, if you have insulin-dependent diabetes), ensure you make provisions to have enough syringes to hand.

- Carry a good first-aid kit with you.

EXERCISE

Getting away from your old routine gives you an opportunity to fit in the exercise that you've been talking about doing for years. A change of lifestyle can mean a change to a new, healthier routine.

The most obvious and common exercise for grey nomads is walking – it's free, convenient and gentle. You'll find plenty of bushwalking opportunities in national parks and bush areas and these are generally well signposted for degrees of difficulty and length.

Alternatively, just make the effort to take a stroll around a park or along the beach for a kilometre or two. A little exercise taken regularly can be enormously beneficial.

If you're one of the thousands of grey nomads who travel with a bike rack on the back of the vehicle or van, then make sure you're not lugging that pair of mountain bikes around the country just so you can look good. Get them off the racks now and again and explore some of the country's great tracks and paths. You'll see so much more on a bike than you ever would out of a car window and you'll feel a lot better for it.

Exercise opportunities are endless and many grey nomads try Tai Chi or yoga as they aim to improve strength, balance and flexibility and general feelings of wellbeing. Swimming is also extremely popular, as it uses most muscles and is good for heart and lungs.

RELAXATION

Once all the hassles of getting ready are behind you and you're on the road, you'll gradually relax into your trip. If you have a sensible timeframe, you should have the opportunity to pursue other interests, such as reading or birdwatching, and you'll reap the therapeutic rewards of this extra relaxation time. Make sure you always get a good night's rest, as regular sleep reduces stress and gives you more energy to pursue your daytime activities. Don't get too caught up in schedules and sightseeing frenzies. Have fun . . . after all, laughter is supposed to be the best medicine.

AMBULANCE COVER

While the Medicare system caters for most emergency medical procedures, it doesn't provide cover for ambulance transport. The bill for this service can be quite hefty and prove a nasty shock to some recovering patients – particularly those taken sick in remote rural districts and transported by air.

Separate ambulance cover is available for a relatively modest price and it's something that offers considerable peace of mind.

Private ambulance cover generally pays for your ambulance costs when:

- It's medically necessary for you to be admitted to hospital.

- You need immediate medical attention at a hospital or other approved facility.

- As an admitted patient, you want to be transferred from one hospital to another, eg, to a hospital closer to home.

If you already have some sort of private health insurance, you may be covered for ambulance costs but it pays to check. Also, residents of some states – for example, Queensland and Tasmania – are eligible for free ambulance transport. Travelling Queenslanders can obtain free ambulance services anywhere in Australia, as long as they can prove they are permanent residents of the Sunshine State. Tasmanians are eligible for free ambulance services in all states except South Australia and Queensland. The situation is slightly different in each state and it is worth checking your ambulance cover status carefully as the bill for an air evacuation, for example, can run into thousands of dollars.

REGIONAL MEDICAL SERVICES

It's no secret that the standard of medical care available in the bush can be significantly lower than you'd expect to find in major metropolitan centres. Each state and territory does possess major hospitals but, depending on where you're taken sick, you may have to travel a long way to access them. In the Northern Territory, for example, there are base hospitals in Alice Springs and Darwin, with smaller hospitals in Katherine and Tennant Creek. All other areas are then covered by small health clinics and by the Royal Flying Doctor Service.

Be aware that even in towns where you do find a hospital, the full range of medical procedures may not be available,

either due to a lack of equipment or to a lack of suitably qualified medical personnel.

Contact information

Department of Health Australian Capital Territory
Website: www.health.act.gov.au
Tel: 13 22 81

New South Wales Health
Website: www.health.nsw.gov.au
Tel: (02) 9391 9000

Department of Health & Community Services Northern Territory
Website: www.health.nt.gov.au
Tel: (08) 8999 2400

Queensland Health
Website: www.health.qld.gov.au
Tel: (07) 3234 0111

Department of Health South Australia
Website: www.health.sa.gov.au
Tel: (08) 8226 6000

Department of Health & Human Services Tasmania
Website: www.dhhs.tas.gov.au
Tel: 1300 135 513

Victorian Government Health Information
Website: www.health.vic.gov.au
Tel: 1300 650 172

Department of Health Western Australia
Website: www.health.wa.gov.au
Tel: (08) 9222 4222

ROYAL FLYING DOCTOR SERVICE

As previously mentioned, doing the 'big lap' normally means visiting remote areas where medical services can be difficult to access. While not all small settlements have a medical facility or a doctor, help is never very far away, thanks to the Royal Flying Doctor Service (RFDS). This not-for-profit charitable service provides aeromedical emergency and primary health care services, together with communication and education assistance to people who live, work and travel in remote Australia.

The service was first established in 1928 and developed on a national basis in the 1930s. It operates 24 hours a day, 365 days a year.

There are a number of RFDS visitor centres located around the country which offer an excellent insight into the operations of the service. It's well worth the effort to pop in and have a look around.

In an emergency, the RFDS can be contacted via High Frequency (HF) radio. The RFDS recommends that travellers to remote areas investigate the possibility of obtaining and using an HF radio. Although HF radio equipment can be purchased, it's by no means cheap, so you may prefer to hire the equipment for a specific time.

See Chapter Two for more details about HF radio.

Chances are you won't need the RFDS, but it's still nice to know it's there.

Contact information
Website: www.flyingdoctor.net
RFDS National Office: (02) 8259 8101

First aid

Camping in remote locations, sometimes on your own, is a wonderful adventure and an unforgettable experience but it does have its down sides – particularly if you need help in a hurry. Put in place a plan in case you or your travelling companion runs into some sort of medical problem that requires emergency treatment.

Above all, keep a cool head. You'll obviously be keen to communicate news of your situation to the outside world and you may be able to do so using a mobile phone, satellite phone, UHF radio, HF radio or distress beacon.

However, the first priority is to be able to deal with the initial stages of the emergency. This will require you to have a decent first-aid kit and at least some rudimentary first-aid knowledge. Consider taking a basic first-aid course. Not only will it provide you with the official qualification to help yourself and others, but you'll gain invaluable peace of mind.

FIRST-AID COURSES

St John Ambulance

St John Ambulance conducts an extensive range of first-aid courses, ranging from a one-day emergency first-aid course covering the basics, to longer and more in-depth senior courses, which provide participants with recognised qualifications. Each state runs its own particular courses, which are slightly different from each other. To give you an idea of what is available, at the time of writing the following courses are among those run in New South Wales.

- *Senior First Aid* – This two-day course costing $165 is the flagship St John Ambulance first-aid course designed to give participants all the necessary skills to give competent care to the ill or injured until medical aid arrives.

- *Emergency First Aid* – This one-day course costing $100 teaches participants the basic life-sustaining procedures. It covers issues such as control of infection, resuscitation techniques, shock, bleeding, treatment of wounds, burns, head, neck and spinal injuries and poisoning.

- *Cardiopulmonary Resuscitation (CPR)* – This half-day course costing $65 provides participants with the skills to perform cardiopulmonary resuscitation. It looks at management of the unconscious casualty, resuscitation techniques and infection control.

- *Remote Area First Aid* – This three-day course costing $230 is perfect for grey nomads. It is designed to meet the first-aid needs of bushwalkers, climbers, 4WD enthusiasts, outdoor/adventure instructors, and anyone who gets out into remote locations. Among the topics covered are priorities in care, respiratory distress, chest pain or injury, heat- or cold-induced illness, and lifting and moving casualties.

Contact information

Website: www.stjohn.org.au
Tel: 1300 360 455

Red Cross Australia

The Red Cross also provides a range of first-aid courses across Australia. The following are just a few courses that may be of interest to grey nomads (costs vary depending on the centre):

- *CPR* – The basic cardiopulmonary resuscitation course is designed to teach the knowledge and skills necessary to maintain or restore breathing and circulation in an adult, child and infant. The course lasts approximately four hours. Successful participants receive a CPR Statement of Attainment. It's recommended that students refresh their CPR skills every 12 months.

- *Basic First Aid* – This course aims to teach you the critical skills to save life and minimise the severity of injury or sudden illness. The eight-hour course will introduce you to first aid, cardiopulmonary resuscitation (CPR), wounds, bleeding, bandaging and infection control, as well as severe allergic reactions. Successful participants receive a Statement of Attainment – Provide Basic Emergency Life Support.

- *Senior First Aid* – This more intense course is designed to teach the fundamental principles, knowledge and skills of first aid, and to prepare people to give competent emergency care until trained assistance is available. This course will last at least 15 hours. Successful participants receive a Statement of Attainment – Apply First Aid.

Contact information

Australian Red Cross has a First Aid, Health and Safety Services department in each state and territory, as well as in some regional centres.

Website: www.redcross.org.au
Tel: 1300 367 428

Private operators

There are many other organisations that offer first-aid training. Check the course content, find out whether participants receive recognised qualifications on completion, and try to get some feedback from previous students.

FIRST-AID KITS

St John Ambulance and the Red Cross produce an extensive range of superb pre-packaged first-aid kits. Prices and types vary from state to state, but expect to pay around $90 for St John Ambulance's Medium Leisure First Aid Kit and $150 for its Large Leisure First Aid Kit. The Red Cross's 4WD – Camping Kit costs $119 and its Large Backpack Kit is $149.

Alternatively, you'll find a large array of pre-packaged kits for sale at many camping shops, automotive shops and department stores or you can make up your own. Basic inclusions should be:

- 30+ SPF sunscreen

- Adhesive surgical tape

- Alcohol swabs

- Antihistamine tablets

- Antiseptic

- Bandages (roller and triangular)

- Band-Aids

- Cotton tips/wool

- Disposable gloves and plastic bags

- Eyebath and eye drops

- First-aid manual

- Insect bite lotion

- Insect repellent

- Normal saline sachets or ampoules for wound cleaning

- Pain-relief tablets

- Plain gauze squares

- Pocket torch

- Safety pins

- Scissors

- Thermometer

- Tweezers

- Variety of sterile, non-stick dressings.

PRACTICAL FIRST AID

When accidents do happen, especially in remote regions, try to keep a clear head and to act promptly. A first-aid handbook that details procedures for different kinds of injury is an invaluable part of your first-aid arsenal. Even if you haven't taken a first-aid course, it's useful to know a few basic techniques for emergencies, as well as treatments for several common injuries and conditions.

In an emergency

The DRABC ('Doctor ABC') response plan provides first aiders with a logical order for checking and responding to emergency situations:

D – Check for Danger; ensure you assess the risks to your-self and the patient before beginning any first-aid procedures.

R – Check for Response; is the patient conscious or unconscious? Shake gently and shout to see if you get any response.

A – Check the Airway; ensure it's clear of objects and open.

B – Check for Breathing; can you hear or feel air coming from the nose or mouth? Is the chest rising and falling? If not, give two initial breaths and then check for any signs of life.

C – Check for Circulation. Check the neck for a pulse.

What next?

Depending on the injuries and the condition of the victim, you may have to perform one or all of the following:

- Apply mouth-to-mouth resuscitation if the patient isn't breathing and/or begin CPR if there's no pulse (refer to a first-aid handbook or chart for exact procedures).

- Stop the bleeding – apply direct pressure to the affected area to stop the bleeding. Try to use a sterile pad or bandage if possible. Elevating the wound also helps to reduce the flow of blood.

- Reassure the patient – if the patient is conscious or regains consciousness, try to keep them calm.

Shock

Shock is a very serious condition that occurs when there's a rapid fall in blood pressure. It's often brought on by loss of blood, but it can also occur as a result of several other serious conditions or injuries. The symptoms of shock are a rapid, weak pulse; cold, clammy skin; rapid breathing; nausea; and pale face, fingernails and lips.

After DRABC has been followed and all wounds have been managed, the first-aid treatment for shock includes covering the patient to keep them warm, calming them down and moistening their lips if they're thirsty (do not provide anything to eat or drink). Try to keep them comfortable. Professional medical attention should be sought as quickly as possible.

Fractures

The symptoms to look for if fractures are suspected are severe pain, deformity or unnatural mobility, loss of power of the limb, swelling and bruising. To treat fractures, always follow the DRABC plan first. Control any bleeding and cover wounds. The basic first-aid treatment for fractures is immobilisation of joints above and below the break. Use broad bandages and place a padded splint along the injured limb if possible. Further medical attention is required and should be sought directly.

Sprains and strains

Sprains are caused by overstretching a muscle or tendon, which results in muscle soreness. This common complaint occurs when the body isn't prepared for increased or new activities, such as long bushwalks or lifting heavy items.

Strains are more serious and are caused by abnormal stretching or tearing of the supporting ligaments of any joint; the most common example is a twisted ankle. The first-aid procedure for treating both sprains and strains is spelled out in another acronym, RICE (Rest, Ice, Compression, Elevation). Ask the patient to sit or lie down, apply a cold pack to the affected area to reduce swelling and then support the joint with a firm elastic bandage. Keep the injured area elevated.

Dehydration and heat exhaustion

If you don't keep up your fluid intake during exercise or on a particularly hot or humid day, dehydration is a real threat. It can lead to rapid breathing, profuse sweating, loss of skin elasticity and pale clammy skin. Anyone suffering from dehydration should be moved into the shade to rest and given plenty of cool water to drink.

Heat exhaustion tends to happen when someone has overdone it in hot weather. Symptoms include nausea, constant headaches, rapid breathing and extreme lethargy. Again, the victim should be moved into the shade, given a cool drink and sponged with cool water. Further medical attention should be sought once the victim has recovered.

Heatstroke

Heatstroke is an extremely serious condition where the body's temperature just keeps rising, and brain damage or even death can occur. The symptoms of heatstroke include dizziness, rapid pulse, excessive fatigue, and irrational behaviour. The patient's skin will feel hot to the touch; they may have stopped sweating and may even collapse.

Move the patient into a shady area and try to cool them down, either by applying cold packs to the neck, armpits and groin or by placing a wet sheet or towel over them and fanning them. If they're conscious, give them a cool drink and ensure they rest. If they fall into unconsciousness, monitor their breathing and pulse; you may have to resuscitate them by CPR. Professional medical attention should be sought as soon as possible.

Hypothermia

People who've been overexposed to the cold or who've been immersed in cold water may show signs of hypothermia – a condition where the body temperature decreases. Although many victims don't realise they have hypothermia, symptoms include irritability and awkwardness, cramps, shivers and blurred vision.

The treatment for hypothermia is to shelter the victim from the elements and get them as warm as possible. Ensure they have dry clothes and either try putting them in a sleeping bag or provide them with blankets, additional clothes and a hat, if possible. You may also share your own body heat or apply to the chest warm compresses. Give the patient warm, but not hot, drinks.

Burns

Although burns are classified into three different degrees according to their severity, the first-aid treatment for all burns is to run cold water over the affected area as quickly as possible. Don't apply lotions or ointments. Place a sterile, non-adhesive dressing over the burn and seek further medical help if the severity of the injury merits it.

Bites and stings

See Chapter Seven for information about the treatment of bites and stings from various creatures.

Food safety

The National Food Safety Information Council has warned that many travellers inadvertently put their health at risk by incorrectly storing and cooking food when on the road.

Some 20 per cent of the 5.4 million Australians who get food poisoning each year do so due to poor food handling, so it's worth taking a few extra precautions.

STORAGE

Fridges inside caravans are generally far smaller than those in the average home, yet because grey nomads often buy up enough produce to last them several weeks, the fridges are jammed full. Giving in to the temptation to overload a fridge can stop air circulating properly and prevent it from maintaining a steady temperature.

If the temperature inside the fridge rises above 5°C, bacteria in the food can multiply and eventually make the food unsafe. Always keep a thermometer in the fridge and adjust the temperature as and when needed.

If your fridge looks like it's getting too crowded, prioritise the space. The beer and white wine can come out safely and then go back in later when space becomes available! Remember, you can always supplement your fresh foods with canned and dried products that can be safely stored outside the fridge.

WORK SPACE AND EQUIPMENT

Whether you're cooking in a caravan, motorhome or camper trailer, you'll certainly find yourselves operating in more cramped conditions than you're used to. The workbench space is smaller than in your home, you probably have less equipment, and even washing up the utensils that you do have is more awkward. There are a number of inherent risks in this situation. Cross-contamination occurs when bacteria from raw food such as meat, poultry or dirty vegetables touch or drip onto food that is ready-to-eat. Bacteria on the raw food are killed when the food is cooked, but the ready-to-eat food is eaten without further cooking – bacteria and all.

If the fridge is overcrowded, raw meat, chicken or fish are more likely to touch or drip onto ready-to-eat food and contaminate it with food-poisoning bacteria. You can minimise this risk by always storing raw foods on the lowest shelf of the fridge, below ready-to-eat and fresh foods. Make sure that the bench, chopping board and knife are carefully washed with warm water and detergent, then rinsed and thoroughly dried before you prepare ready-to-eat food.

Carry lots of leak-proof containers with you and use them for any raw food – to prevent leaks onto other foods. Ziplock plastic bags can also do the job.

Wash your hands and dry them thoroughly before preparing food and between handling raw and ready-to-eat food.

If you're using toilets in an amenities block, remember to bring soap and a towel with you, as these are often not provided.

BARBECUING

Free barbecues, as well as coin-operated ones, will feature significantly throughout the van parks, national parks and municipal and country parks that you visit. These facilities offer a great opportunity to cook in scenic locations, but sometimes a lack of general cleanliness diminishes the appeal.

Bring some cleaning utensils with you – in some cases a bit of water and a scrub will sort things out. Some nomads put a sheet of baking paper on the hotplate while cooking to avoid contact with a potentially unhygienic cooking surface.

SAFE WATER SUPPLY

If you're using an unserviced site, remember that water from natural waterways isn't necessarily safe, even if it looks like it's in perfect condition. Animal faeces and naturally occurring parasites can contaminate pristine-seeming waterways. If you're going to use the water for drinking or washing ready-to-eat food, it should be boiled for at least one minute or treated with water-purification tablets. As an alternative, you can use bottled water.

Take care with the water in your tank, as well. If it hasn't been changed for several months, it may have picked up contaminants. Ensure you empty your tank regularly to keep your water supply fresh.

DIET

There are no more excuses for an unhealthy diet now. You have the time to really enjoy your cooking and your eating. Try to eat plenty of vegetables, grains and fruit and drink lots of water. According to one old saying, you are what you eat, and a big lifestyle change offers you the chance to throw out any poor dietary habits. Depending on where you are, take advantage of the cheap fruit and vegies available from roadside stalls and fruit and vegie shops. As you move around the country you'll find your diet changing with the various regional specials. If you've brought your fishing rod and your luck is in, you should also be eating regular meals of nutritious fish.

5

Managing your affairs

How to stay in control

START PLANNING

We've already canvassed the fact that while you're travelling, there'll still be bills to pay, licences to be renewed, financial arrangements to be made, vehicles to register and unforeseen events to deal with. You need to organise ways to manage your affairs while you're on the road.

Start by making a list of all the issues you think may affect you when you are travelling and work your way through them.

Having a close friend or relative at home keeping an eye on

things for you, or even just forwarding your post, can be really useful – but it isn't essential.

Using a diary will make your life a lot simpler. It'll be useful for keeping track of important issues like vehicle re-registration dates, credit card payment deadlines, insurance schedules and birthday reminders. It's astonishing how a dramatic change to your routine can make dates that were previously seared into your consciousness completely disappear.

BANKING

Banking in the outback and in remote rural areas is becoming easier. Telephone and internet banking mean the movement of funds from one account to another is less of a drama, and the burgeoning number of places that cater to both EFTPOS and credit card customers has also helped.

Happily, post offices in most small towns have the facilities to enable you to complete some basic banking. Post offices, and businesses with post office facilities, are generally Commonwealth Bank agents. Check out www.auspost.com.au and follow the billing and financial services prompt for more information about banking in post offices.

Nonetheless, in some places, cash is still the only currency that counts. Although, for security reasons, you don't want to be carrying excessive amounts of real money, you need to carry enough to handle unexpected events.

ATMs

Automatic teller machines are reaching ever deeper into the bush and even when your bank doesn't have a presence, chances are that one of the major banks will. While these competitors' ATMs allow you to carry out your transaction, be aware that they will charge you for the privilege. Depending on your bank and the type of account, you may also be charged for using your own bank's ATM but at a significantly reduced rate.

There's also a limit on the amount of cash you're allowed to withdraw from an ATM on any given day. Check with your bank.

EFTPOS

Electronic funds transfer at point of sale machines are now a feature of even the smallest businesses and these can be used to obtain a limited amount of cash following a purchase.

Credit cards

Although some outback businesses still won't accept credit cards, they're a dying breed. You'll be amazed at some of the rough-and-ready operations that will process your plastic.

If you've never carried a credit card before, it may be worth acquiring one for the cash-free convenience it gives you. These days, it's widely assumed that everyone has a credit card and it can be difficult to book a tour or caravan park without one.

Most cards offer an interest-free period and, as long as you pay your credit off completely at the end of each billing cycle, this is brilliant news for the canny grey nomad. You can enjoy several weeks of credit, sometimes nearly eight, without paying any interest at all. While the interest rates are high on cards, if you always pay the full balance on time, it doesn't matter. You can organise a direct debit payment to ensure there are no costly oversights.

Don't use your credit card to get a cash advance unless you absolutely have to, as interest is then charged immediately.

Many credit cards attract an annual fee but this may be waived depending on your spending habits and your relationship with the bank. Credit cards also tend to run a rewards scheme whereby the more you spend using your card, the more points you earn. These points can then later be redeemed for anything from a new jug to a weekend pass to Dreamworld.

Direct debits

Direct debits, whereby you authorise your bank to make certain fixed payments at the same time each month, can be a godsend for long-term travellers. They ensure you're never late paying that credit card or mobile phone bill. If you still own a property, things such as council rates, water rates, insurance and other utilities are taken care of without you having to keep a constant eye on the calendar.

Sit down and have a good think about what regular bills you can pay by direct debit. When you're camping in the Flinders or Kakadu, you'll certainly have more pleasurable things to think about than water rates and electricity bills.

Internet banking

Internet banking has revolutionised life on the road. Grey nomads can now get instant access to account information and move finances around as and when required. And they can do it whenever and wherever they want to. All the major banks and many of the smaller credit unions offer customers internet banking facilities. All that's required is an internet connection and a little know-how.

Once you've registered for internet banking, you'll be able to go online to pay bills, transfer funds between accounts, transfer funds to different banks, and generally monitor your financial affairs.

As well as the convenience of all-hours banking from your laptop – or a computer at the library or internet café – you also save time as it's quicker to click the mouse a few times than stand in a bank queue. Fees and charges are also lower online than they are when you visit a branch.

While in the early days of the internet fear of security breaches kept people away from the service, those issues have largely been dealt with. There'll always be the occasional high-profile internet scam, but millions of Australians now conduct their banking by internet without any problems.

For those who lack confidence in this area, the major banks now run special courses to give computer novices the expertise to use internet banking.

INVESTMENTS

Thanks to the internet, a trip in the bush doesn't mean you're no longer able to monitor your investments – although maybe you should just let them look after themselves for a few weeks.

For many investing grey nomads, the most convenient way to proceed is to establish a set-and-forget portfolio with long-term investments in established companies. This fully negates the need to check investments on a daily or even a weekly basis.

It's also sensible to talk over your travel plans with your financial adviser so he or she knows that you may be 'out of the loop' for a while. Unexpected things will always crop up – in a Federal Budget, for example – that may affect your financial wellbeing and will require an adjustment to your financial approach. For that reason, ensure that your financial adviser has your mobile number and e-mail address so that he or she can at least leave a message alerting you to these changes.

Similarly, if you've rented out your home or have an investment property, check that the agent or the person you've left caring for them has your full contact details and instructions to keep you informed of major developments.

Organise your finances as well as you can before you leave, give detailed instructions to people you trust, and then relax in the knowledge that you'll be informed if anything important is happening.

LIBRARIES

Libraries will become a vital part of your trip as you seek to manage your affairs. They offer access to the internet, as well as a wealth of information about people, places and things that can help enhance your enjoyment of your surroundings.

Every state, and every council, has a different policy with regard to travellers. In some places you'll be able to take out library membership and enjoy full borrowing privileges, while in others you can only take out temporary membership with limited services available to you. Some libraries don't allow you to join at all unless you have a permanent local address.

Policies towards internet access are similarly varied. Some libraries allow to you to use their internet computing for free while others charge you for e-mails but not for internet surfing.

Libraries are terrific places to catch up with your e-mail correspondence and to examine your financial affairs. They're also the places to research roads and routes, and to check out local tourist attractions and general points of interest. Check the noticeboard for festivals and special events in the area, too.

Most libraries also have DVDs you can borrow to watch back at the van plus CDs to listen to if your collection is becoming a bit too familiar. As well as borrowing books, you can often buy cheap second-hand books from libraries.

Contact information

To find and contact a library, go to www.nla.gov.au/libraries.

Communications

MOBILE PHONES

Mobile phones can be heard everywhere these days – in restaurants, cinemas, libraries and even in churches. Their small size, relatively low cost and increasingly high-tech features provide users with a constantly evolving means of keeping in touch with loved ones. SMS, e-mails, cameras and video conferencing have revolutionised the concept of the old-fashioned phone call.

Although the phones themselves keep getting more sophisticated, travellers around Australia remain limited by the less-than-complete network coverage in remote areas. Telstra boasts that its Next G network provides coverage to 99 per cent of the Australian population, but there remain huge areas of bush, national parks and reserves which are mainly uninhabited and out of mobile range.

At the time of writing, of the mobile phone networks currently available, Telstra's Next G has the most geographically extensive coverage around Australia. However, it is important to note that to maximise coverage in regional and remote areas, specific kinds of handsets and/or antennas are recommended. Telstra has developed a rating system for its range of handsets to show whether or not they are suitable for use in rural regions. The handsets with a 'blue tick' are recommended for users who are living or travelling in areas where they need to maximise their coverage. Car kits and patch leads for the Next G network are also available to boost reception in remote areas. Telstra provides an online resource for its mobile phone users to check network coverage of any area by postcode, street or town at www.telstra.com.au/mobile/networks/coverage/maps.cfm.

Optus is in the process of expanding its 3G network and plans to continue to increase its broadband speeds. Optus provides customers with details of its network coverage at www.optus.com.au (follow links from 'About Optus' to 'Network coverage').

There are myriad options available to consumers in terms of equipment, plans and contracts. Look carefully at how often you expect to use your phone and what you'll use it for before committing to a one- or two-year contract. Some plans include a set amount of calls per month, cheap texting or discounts for calls made at a specific time of day. You can also choose to purchase a handset outright and then buy pre-paid vouchers to use as and when required. Shop around and discuss your needs with several different dealers to get a better overall perspective.

Another innovation in the mobile phone market is the GSM/Satellite dual mode handset which is the product of a partnership between Thuraya Telecommunications and Optus. The phone utilises the Optus GSM mobile phone network when it is in range and then switches to satellite coverage if the GSM network is out of range. The new phones are smaller than the traditional satellite handsets and have many more high-tech features including a camera, SMS and GPS facilities. However, at the time of writing the cost for a handset is well over $1000 and call costs are additional.

It's one thing having a mobile phone but you must also be able to keep it charged up. On the road, you can do this either via mains power while you are staying at a van park, or via the cigarette lighter plug in your vehicle (if your phone has this facility). You may also like to consider travelling with a spare phone battery.

PHONE CARDS

Although mobiles offer a convenient method of keeping in touch with loved ones, a much cheaper alternative for lengthy long-distance phone calls is to buy a discount calling card and use a public phone. The cards can be purchased at many small shops for between $10 and $30, and can be topped up by phone. They give you an access telephone number and a PIN number. Once your call has been connected, the cost per minute is quite low – some cards even advertise a price of 1 cent per minute to the UK, the USA and elsewhere. There's a wide variety of cards to choose from and some have good rates internationally while others specialise in discounted nation-wide calls. Check the rates and flagfall cost of calls you're most likely to make before weighing up your options.

Note that only specially-made Telstra cards can be used in the 'Phonecard Only' public phones.

SATELLITE PHONES

Satellite phones enjoy total geographic coverage throughout Australia. The only limitation is that you must have a clear view of the sky when you make the call.

The cost of satellite handsets has come down significantly in recent months, but a basic phone can still set you back at least $900. Once you've purchased the handset, making each phone call incurs additional costs, and these vary depending on the plan you choose.

A recent innovation in satellite phones is the launch of a handset which can access both the GSM mobile phone network and the satellite system. See the 'Mobile Phones' section above for further information.

If you plan to purchase a satellite phone or a GSM/Satellite phone, it's worth looking into the government subsidy scheme. Subsidies are available to people who work or live more than 120 days a year in areas which are not covered by a mobile or terrestrial network. For further information, go to www.dbcde.gov.au (follow links from 'Communications and technology for customers', and 'Mobile Services' to 'The Satellite Phone Subsidy Scheme').

There are also companies that offer satellite phones for hire. This is a good option if you only need the service for a short segment of your journey.

Contact information

The following are two suppliers of satellite phones for rental or purchase, although there are others; check your local directory or the internet for more:

Globalstar
Website: www.globalstar.com.au
Tel: 1300 882 448

Landwide
Website: www.landwide.com.au
Tel: 1800 454 587

POST

Keeping up with your post – or, rather, hoping your post can keep up with you – is one of the most challenging aspects of managing your affairs. Even when you've arranged for your mail to be sent on to you, your plans can change suddenly and your post will be left in limbo. Or it may take longer than expected to arrive and you're champing at the bit to leave the area.

With sound management and a little bit of luck, however, things can work out well. The good news is that Australia Post offers a free Post Restante service. Letters and packages can be re-directed to you by friends or family at home, or by a professional, to 'care of' nearly any post office in Australia. You then collect these items from the post office by showing suitable identification, such as a driver's licence or passport. The bad news is that any mail not collected within one month will be returned to sender. This Poste Restante service is absolutely perfect for travellers who are constantly on the move.

The challenge comes in correctly estimating which post office you will be nearest to at any given time. While mail delivery times will vary from place to place, you'll generally get letters within three working days. Australia Post doesn't guarantee anything, however, and in more remote areas, where mail may only be delivered two or three times a week, it can take longer. Packages and parcels normally take about twice as long to reach their destination as letters.

If for whatever reason you fail to pick up your mail from a post office before you've moved on, you must fill in a re-direction form to get it sent on or else it will be returned to sender. This re-direction will cost $6.50 if you're holding an eligible concession card and $13 otherwise.

How to get your mail sent to the Post Restante at various post offices

- If you have friends or family living in your home, simply keep in regular contact so that they can re-direct to the right place.

- If you've rented out your home, you can submit a re-direction form to Australia Post so your post goes to a friend or family member who can then send it on to you. The original re-direction costs:

One month – $13 ($6.50 concession)

Three months – $25 ($12.50 concession)

Six months – $36 ($18 concession)

Twelve months – $66.50 ($33.25 concession).

- If you no longer have a family home, you may choose to inform all likely senders, including banks, insurance companies, associates etc, to send any mail to you 'care of' the address of a family member or friend, who can then re-direct it again.

- Some travellers prefer not to 'impose' on family or friends. For this reason, a new postal re-direction industry has sprung up on the back of the grey nomad revolution. As well as re-directing mail, specialised companies will now re-direct messages, faxes and e-mails. They generally charge a registration fee of around $20 per month per surname, and a surcharge over and above normal postage costs that can be around 40 per cent.

Mail forwarding contact information
Website: www.mailaway.com.au
Tel: (07) 5428 2121

Website: www.passthepost.com.au
Tel: (07) 3351 0965

Website: www.posthasteaustralia.com.au
Tel: (07) 3801 3454

ELECTORAL ENROLMENT

You will need a residential address if you wish to stay on the electoral roll. References below apply to federal elections, not state or local. The Australian Electoral Commission (AEC) does not administer state or local elections; separate state or territory government authorities do this. The electoral roll however is one and the same for federal and state elections and is managed through a joint roll agreement between the AEC and its state and territory counterpart bodies.

No permanent address cases

People who live in Australia but have no permanent residential address can still apply for enrolment. If you have no fixed address (for example, you have sold your home to go on the road), you must enrol in the division in which you were last entitled to enrol. If you have not previously been entitled to enrolment, for example you have just returned from overseas and have let your enrolment lapse, you can enrol for the division in which your next of kin is enrolled, or, if there is no next of kin, the division in which you were born. Electors not born in Australia can enrol in the division with which they have the closest connection. The form you need to complete to apply for enrolment with no fixed address can be accessed at www.aec.gov.au (follow links from 'Enrolling to vote', to 'Special category enrolment', to 'Enrolment for persons with no fixed address').

Permanent address but temporarily living elsewhere

The 'no-fixed-address' option is not available to people who have a permanent home address but are temporarily living or travelling elsewhere. Grey nomads who have a permanent home which they intend to return to after their travels do not qualify to enrol in the manner described for those with no fixed address. People with a permanent address should remain enrolled for their home address while they are away, but are advised to notify their local Divisional Returning Officer of their length of absence to prevent their names being removed from the roll in error. You can contact your local AEC divisional office on 13 23 26 or e-mail the AEC at info@aec.gov.au to pre-advise of the length of time you will be away from your permanent address. If your trip goes for longer than expected, it is advisable to inform the AEC so your enrolment is safeguarded.

Voting

Where you are on the day of a federal election will determine the type of vote you can cast. Obviously, if you are in your own electoral division, you can cast an ordinary vote at any polling place. If you are within your enrolled state or territory, you will be able to cast an absent vote at any other polling place. If you are in any other state or territory than the one for which you are enrolled – that is, if you are interstate – then you can cast a vote at a pre-poll (early voting) centre before election day, cast a postal vote, or cast a vote in any interstate voting centre or AEC divisional office on polling day. Interstate voting centres on polling day are limited to mostly metropolitan locations. Postal vote applications are available from post offices after the announcement of the election. Early voting centre locations are advertised in major newspapers during the election or can be obtained at that time by calling the AEC national call centre on 13 23 26. For away-from-home voting arrangements for state and territory elections, contact your local state electoral authority, as it is they, and not the AEC, that conduct state and territory elections.

Other considerations for travellers

Holding a private Post Office box is not relevant to the information about enrolment provided above. Your enrolment address needs to be a residential address. For timely receipt of mail, it may be that it is better to include a postal address of a relative who will be looking after your mail while you are travelling, and therefore to be able to respond more readily to any correspondence from the AEC and other authorities.

LAPTOPS

Laptop computers used to be the exclusive domain of high-flying executives tapping away in hotel lobbies between important meetings.

Now they're much more affordable and popular – and intrinsically useful for grey nomads. They provide a handy storage solution for the thousands of digital images you'll probably take on your journey. They can also be used to access the internet, either by plugging into an online network at an internet café or by using the modem in a mobile phone or by using a wireless connection.

Some global positioning system (GPS) units can be attached directly to your laptop and you can track your progress on screen and save the paths as a digital record of your journey. You can write letters, keep a diary of your trip and even maintain records of your budget on your versatile laptop.

The most basic laptop in the shop is quite a powerful computer these days and will cope with the majority of tasks required by travellers. Normally, laptops also have built-in

CD and DVD players so you can use your computer to watch a DVD or listen to music in the bush.

If you do plan to purchase a new laptop, be aware that a recognised brand will normally come with a nationwide warranty and replacement parts will be easily identifiable and available. Find out how long the warranty is and whether you'll need to return your laptop to the manufacturer or bring it to an approved repairer if there are problems. Also check who'll cover the cost of postage. It may be worth getting an extended warranty, if available, as laptops are still delicate pieces of equipment.

Expect to pay at least $600 to purchase a decent new laptop. Most computer dealers will discuss how you plan to use your computer to determine what configuration is most appropriate for your needs. Opting for a large hard drive doesn't add much to the cost and it provides significant benefits – especially if you plan to store lots of images.

Laptops are meant to be portable and thus come with rechargeable batteries as well as the capacity to run directly from mains power. Computer batteries can be charged up via the cigarette lighter in your car – but only with the correct cabling. Normally this will come with the laptop. Be certain you're using the right equipment for your specific computer before you begin.

If you think you may be operating your laptop on battery power frequently, check how long the batteries will last and consider buying a spare or two. It can be frustrating if you're enjoying a gripping DVD at a camp on the Birdsville Track and the battery runs out. The technology is evolving quickly and the new generation of laptop batteries are lasting longer than ever.

If you haven't had much exposure to computers, now is a great time to start learning. Many public libraries and training centres offer free or discounted computer literacy courses to seniors.

WIRELESS INTERNET CONNECTIONS

The growing availability of wireless internet connections can bring a new dimension to your trip. Certainly, it can make the business of staying in touch while you are on the road much easier.

Most new laptops you can buy these days are wireless enabled. You can use your wi-fi (wireless enabled) laptop to access the internet at wireless hotspots such as those at selected McDonald's restaurants, at most internet cafés and at a growing number of other businesses such as coffee shops and caravan parks. Note that some establishments offer limited free internet access (perhaps up to two hours) if you are paying for accommodation or if you make a purchase; others may sell you a voucher valid for a set amount of time such as 30 minutes.

The other alternative for accessing the internet via a wireless connection is to sign up for a plan with an internet provider. There are lots of plans available and many come with a discounted or free mobile card which is inserted in your laptop in order to access the network. Most plans are based on a particular download limit per month and you will be charged extra if that limit is exceeded. It's worth monitoring your usage, or at least being aware of it, so you don't end up with any unpleasant surprises at the end of the month. Wireless internet connections are also available on a pre-paid basis and – although it is more costly per megabyte – you only pay for what you use. At the time of writing, the Telstra Next G network provides the most extensive wireless internet coverage geographically.

A useful resource for wireless internet users can be found at www.freewifi.com.au. This website lists hundreds of free and paid wireless hotspots throughout Australia.

Contact information
ASCCA (Australian Seniors Computer Clubs Association)
Website: www.ascca.org.au
Tel: (02) 9286 3871

Find and contact a library to enquire about possible computer courses at:
www.nla.gov.au/libraries

Insurance

In Chapter One we looked in some detail at the various costs and options for insuring your home and rig. When you are travelling and may not be receiving your post all that regularly, it is important that you make the effort to keep tabs on your policies. It cannot be stressed strongly enough just how vital it is that you keep a record of when all policies expire, so you can make arrangements to renew them before they lapse. Keep a copy of all your insurance policies with you and store the originals in a safe document storage location.

Vital documents

POWER OF ATTORNEY

Numerous grey nomads choose to give a friend or family member power of attorney over their affairs while they're away. This can be useful if something important crops up while you're in the wilds and out of contact or if you're unable to attend to a certain matter because of illness or injury. Power of attorney can be ongoing or limited to a particular timeframe or circumstance. Any decisions made by your attorney have the same legal force as if you had made them yourself, so it almost goes without saying that you want to appoint someone you trust implicitly.

DOCUMENT STORAGE

Most people have important documents they don't wish to take to the bush, store in the shed or even leave with their well-meaning but absent-minded neighbour. Papers such as deeds to the house, birth certificates and marriage certificates are worth storing in a secure location.

Many banks offer safe document storage for a nominal fee (about $30 per year). The bank provides an empty envelope and, once the customer has filled it with documents, it's sealed and locked away. The envelope is usually kept in a safe and can be accessed several times per month if required.

If you have more bulky valuables, such as jewellery, coin collections or even rare books, it may be worth considering a safety deposit box. They cost extra but provide more space and you receive your own key. Contact your bank to determine the fees and availability of the service you require.

VEHICLE REGISTRATION

Registration renewal is one of those yearly chores that must be promptly attended to in order to keep you and your rig legally on the road. If you're travelling out of your state at the time it's due, some extra planning and effort is required. Most state road authorities post out a reminder that your registration is pending about four to six weeks before it's due. Still, make a note of it for yourself, especially if your post is being forwarded to you at irregular intervals.

Every state is different when it comes to registration renewal requirements for your car and caravan. For example, in New South Wales, rego renewal seekers must produce an inspection certificate no more than 42 days old (if they have a vehicle either more than three years old, over two tonnes, or modified in any way), a compulsory third-party insurance certificate and the registration renewal form or billing number. If you qualify for a concession, you must show proof of that as well.

In the Northern Territory, the compulsory third-party insurance is included in the registration fee, so there's no need to sort that out independently. In Western Australia, some vehicles, such as buses, taxis and left-hand drives, are subject to annual checks but most other private motor vehicles aren't.

Don't forget about rego for your caravan, as in some states, the renewal process may involve an annual inspection.

Once you've organised all the necessary documents, paying the fee can be completed online, by phone or by post. Ensure that you either get a receipt number to fill in on the rego label or confirmation that a new label or certificate is being sent to you at an agreed address. Some states offer a few days' grace if you happen to miss the deadline but others don't, so it really is worth keeping on top of the whole process. Driving without up-to-date registration is an offence and may incur a fine.

Get in touch with your relevant state authority before you depart to clarify exactly what the procedure is for interstate registration.

Contact information

Australian Capital Territory
Road Transport Authority
Website: www.rego.act.gov.au
Tel: 13 22 81

New South Wales
Roads and Traffic Authority (RTA)
Website: www.rta.nsw.gov.au/registration
Tel: 13 22 13

Northern Territory
Department of Planning and Infrastructure
Website: www.nt.gov.au/transport
Tel: 1300 654 628

Queensland
Queensland Transport
Website: www.transport.qld.gov.au
Tel: 13 23 80

South Australia
Department for Transport, Energy and Infrastructure
Website: www.transport.sa.gov.au
Tel: (08) 8343 2222
Interstate: 1300 360 067

Tasmania
Department of Energy, Infrastructure and Resources
Website: www.transport.tas.gov.au
Tel: 1300 851 225

Victoria
Victoria Roads
Website: www.vicroads.vic.gov.au
Tel: 13 11 71

Western Australia
Department for Planning and Infrastructure
Website: www.dpi.wa.gov.au
Tel: 13 11 56 or (08) 9216 8484

DRIVING LICENCE RENEWALS

A valid driving licence is an essential document to bring along on any road trip, so check when your licence expires. Renewing your licence while you're away from your home state requires advance planning. Some states allow you to renew your licence a few months in advance while others don't. If you cannot renew your licence in advance, you'll have to do it remotely and this could involve completing a photo kit or providing a medical or optical certificate to comply with the requirements. If you know you'll be interstate when your licence expires, contact your relevant authority to find out what the process is and what documents and/or photos will be required.

Grey nomads in some states have special issues to consider when applying for licence renewal. The good news is that several states either waive the licence fee or provide a significant discount for seniors; the not-so-good news is that some authorities require drivers aged over 75 to provide an annual medical certificate proving they are physically fit to drive.

Below is a brief guide to each state and territory's requirements for residents to renew their drivers' licence when interstate. Please note that forms and requirements can change, so it's best to contact the relevant authority in your state or territory to verify exact procedures.

Australian Capital Territory

Australian Capital Territory driver's licences can be renewed up to three months in advance. Australian Capital Territory residents whose licences are due to expire while they're interstate must obtain, complete and return an application for renewal, a signature card, details of their new mailing address and the fee.

For more information about Australian Capital Territory driver's licence renewal, contact:

Website: www.rego.act.gov.au
Tel: 13 22 81

New South Wales

New South Wales residents whose licences are due to expire while they are interstate must obtain, complete and return a photo kit from the RTA. The photo kit contains clear instructions on how to renew your licence.

The RTA can process an application for early renewal of a licence up to six months before the expiry date of the licence.

For more information about New South Wales driver's licence renewal, contact:

Website: www.rta.nsw.gov.au/licensing
Tel: 13 22 13

Northern Territory

Northern Territory licences may be renewed at any time up to a total of five years in advance. In other words, even if your licence is valid for another year or two, you can still get it renewed for a total of five years. The Motor Vehicle Registry advises long-term travellers to ensure their licences are current for the maximum possible duration to minimise any inconvenience when interstate.

If a Northern Territory resident's licence does expire while they're outside the Territory, they should contact MVR several weeks prior to the date of licence expiry to organise a renewal.

For more information about Northern Territory driver's licence renewal, contact:

Website: www.mvr.nt.gov.au

Tel: 1300 654 628

Queensland

Queensland residents whose licences are due to expire while they're interstate must complete a driver's licence renewal kit. This kit contains instructions on how to renew your licence and includes the forms you must complete.

You may apply to renew your Queensland driver's licence up to six weeks before it expires.

For more information about Queensland driver's licence renewal, contact:

Website: www.transport.qld.gov.au

Tel: 13 23 80

South Australia

South Australia residents who are unable to attend personally a customer service centre or post office in South Australia when their licences are due for renewal should contact the customer service centre to arrange an alternative procedure.

For more information about South Australia driver's licence renewal, contact:

Website: www.transport.sa.gov.au

Tel: 1300 360 067

Within South Australia: 13 10 84

Tasmania

Tasmanian residents whose licences are due to expire while they're interstate must obtain, complete and return a photo kit from the Department of Infrastructure, Energy and Resources. The kit contains instructions on how to renew licences. Payment of fees must be by bank cheque, money order or credit card. The length of licence renewal when a resident applies interstate is limited to one year. For more information about Tasmania driver's licence renewal, contact:

Website: www.transport.tas.gov.au

Tel: 1300 135 513

Victoria

Victorian residents whose licences are due to expire while they're interstate may be able to renew their licences by BPAY, telephone or post. This is possible if VicRoads holds a recent digitised image of you and if all the details on your renewal notice are correct. Otherwise, you must complete a photo kit form and send the photos, forms and fee to VicRoads.

For more information about Victoria driver's licence renewal, contact:

Website: www.vicroads.vic.gov.au

Tel: 13 11 71

Western Australia

Western Australia residents whose licences are due to expire while they're interstate must obtain, complete and return a photo kit from the Department of Planning and Infrastructure. This kit contains instructions on how to renew a licence and includes the forms to complete.

The kits can be requested by phone or e-mail at the following numbers:

Within Western Australia: 13 11 56

Outside Western Australia: (08) 9427 6404

For more information about Western Australia driver's licence renewal, contact:

Website: www.dpi.wa.gov.au

Tel: 13 11 56

Interstate callers: (08) 9427 6404

6

Setting up camp

Which sort of camp?

Every year, more and more older Australians are taking to the road. But the idea of retirees hitching up their wagons and doing a big tour is far from a new one – people have been doing it for decades. The character of the 'big lap' is continually evolving, too. Each year there are more stretches of bitumen, more people, and many more commercial enterprises chasing the grey dollar. But perhaps the biggest change of all is in the camping experience itself.

You'd imagine that as the number of travellers grows, so too would the number of caravan parks seeking to cater to their needs. Not so. Soaring land values and land taxes have meant that many of the traditional beachside caravan parks have been sold to developers and new ones aren't springing up in sufficient numbers to fill the void. There is, however, a trend towards resort-style parks that offer more facilities than the traditional parks. Unfortunately, these can also be more expensive and don't always appeal to budget-conscious long-term grey nomads.

Another recent phenomenon is the arrival of free or cut-price council-run camping areas offering limited facilities. The thinking is that grey nomads in luxurious rigs have no real need of extras, except perhaps a dump point for the toilet waste, and so they shouldn't have to pay for them. Some small towns consider that the economic benefit of drawing extra travellers into the area, where they'll buy fuel, food and drink, makes the exercise worthwhile. Only time will tell.

Everywhere you look, there's change. Some truly devastating bushfires in recent years have highlighted the issue of camp-fires in national parks and elsewhere. More and more places are now prohibiting their use and free gas barbecue facilities are springing up in their stead.

The way you choose to camp will have a massive influence on your trip. If you've bought your rig, no doubt you've already had some ideas about the sort of places you want to stay and the level of comfort you'd like to have. Most people choose a mixture of all different sorts of camp during their trip – and enjoy every minute of it.

CARAVAN PARKS

However tight your budget might be, caravan parks will almost certainly play a big part in your trip. As we've already seen, some nomads love to check into their favourite parks in places such as Darwin or Cairns and stay there throughout the season. They like the company, the sunshine, the facilities, the familiarity, and the ease of a long stay in one caravan park and don't mind paying for the privilege. They set up their awnings, get out their TVs, their playing cards and their campchairs and invite their neighbours for a social. It's a relaxing, wonderful holiday – but it's not for everybody.

Other nomads, even those who can afford to stay wherever they want, prefer to camp in the wilds. They occasionally come into a park to get a hot shower, catch up on the laundry, do some grocery shopping in the town, and then they're off again into the bush. Whatever you're looking for, caravan parks can contribute enormously to your big trip experience.

In Chapter One, we mentioned that the nightly caravan park costs for a couple are typically around the $25 to $30 mark and sometimes higher. Those in the caravan park industry are fond of saying that the cost of caravan parks in this country is remarkably low compared with those overseas. That's undeniably true but few other countries would have so many long-term travellers. A charge of $30 per night is no big deal if you're on your annual two-week holiday, but it is a big deal if you are on the road for a year or longer! Many caravan parks provide discounts to travellers who stay a week or more, offering deals such as seven nights for the price of six. Ask the manager when you book in whether they can provide a discount – the long-stay policy may not be well advertised.

Those travelling alone may find themselves being slugged for the same fee that two people would be charged – the argument goes that they're still taking up one site. This policy encourages many solo travellers to seek out more economical alternatives, such as council-run parks, which are usually cheaper to stay in. These aren't always easy to find and are generally not as aggressively advertised and marketed as privately run caravan parks. At the local tourist information centre, ask if there are any council-run parks in the area.

The best way to find a caravan park that suits your needs is to talk to other travellers. The grey grapevine is alive and well, and you'll find no shortage of veterans eager to share their knowledge. There are also a number of excellent regional caravan park directories available and you can normally pick these up at visitor information centres.

As well as price, you'll obviously also want to consider the facilities provided. Many parks have voluntarily joined a star rating system that gives you some guide to the quality of the park and its facilities. However, many very good parks have chosen not to be part of this scheme and the stars may not reflect all aspects of a good camping spot, such as shade, location and space between sites. Depending on your own requirements and preferences, among the things to look at are:

- Does the park look clean and well run?

- Are the sites spacious and easy to access?

- Does it have good laundry facilities (you don't want to spend hours queuing to use one overworked washing machine)?

- Does it allow pets?

- Does it have internet access?

- Can you find a nice shady spot?

- Does it have ensuite facilities?

- Does it have a swimming pool?

- Are the grounds well maintained?

Security is another big issue for many travellers and in some areas it can be a problem. Commonly you'll see smart-card activated boom gates at parks to prevent would-be thieves from bringing in vehicles. Some places also have security patrols and barbed wire fences around the perimeter. Thankfully, these seemingly extreme measures aren't needed in 99 per cent of Australian parks but, where they are considered necessary, they do bring reassurance to campers.

As mentioned earlier, for those travelling in big motorhomes or even converted buses, it's always worth phoning ahead to check that a park can accommodate a large rig and that it has a suitable space available.

In several places in this book, we mention the school holiday factor. It's worth repeating because not only do prices go up sharply in these peak times but space is at a premium and the character of many parks changes. While some parks are livelier than others, most operate on a no-noise-after-10pm policy and you will find that this is a generally well-known and well-observed rule.

Always opt for a flat site with enough room to open your awning if necessary. Many parks now provide a concrete slab on each site that's suitable for campchairs, a table and other outdoor gear. Natural shade is also nice, particularly if the temperatures are high and you're planning to stay for a few nights. If you do park near or under a tree, always have a glance to check there are no perilous-looking limbs hanging over your head, particularly eucalypts – gum trees are notorious for shedding limbs. Be aware also that sap, leaves and other materials can fall onto your van and vehicle and make a right mess, especially if birds like to sit in the branches.

A spacious site is important for your comfort and also for your stress levels when you're trying to reverse the van or the motorhome into position. Some parks even offer a 'marriage-saving' service whereby they'll park your van for you. As a rule, try to approach your site so that you have vision from the driver's window. Sounds self-evident and logical, but it's incredibly easy to get in a pickle. If you can see what your van's doing, it'll be easier to manoeuvre it to the exact spot you want it.

An innovative website entitled 'Badger's Australian Caravan Park Reports' is a good resource for choosing a park, as it provides reports about van parks submitted by unbiased visitors keen to share their experiences – both good and bad. The site contains more than 3000 reports and is worth perusing for any comments about that park you've booked into for three weeks next dry season.

Badger's website: home.vicnet.net.au/~badger04

> **Tip:** Bring a set of levelling blocks to put under your van or motorhome wheels in case you find yourself on a sloping site. Chocks are also an important inclusion as they provide extra security against rolling. Both items are available commercially but you can make them yourself out of wood.

NATIONAL PARKS AND STATE FORESTS

Australia is blessed with wonderfully unspoilt scenery and our national parks are normally located in the most beautiful spots of all. If you're going to see Australia, you won't want to miss the opportunity to camp in the beachside magnificence of Cape Le Grand National Park in Western Australia or South Australia's Flinders Ranges or the wetlands of the Northern Territory's Kakadu or Queensland's lush Daintree National Park. The list goes on and on. Each and every state boasts some unique and truly spectacular parks.

Apart from the scenery, many grey nomads swear by national park camping because it helps to take the pressure off their budget. While each state has a different pricing structure (see below) the fees charged are reasonable and compare favourably with those of caravan parks.

Inevitably there's a trade-off in terms of the facilities provided. Some camping areas are simply clearings in the bush. Most national parks and state forests offer little more than a drop toilet, maybe running water and perhaps a wooden picnic table. Mostly you have to carry your rubbish out with you, bring in your own water and rely on your own power supply.

Slowly, though, things are changing and some parks now feature marked and numbered camping sites, and offer such modern facilities as hot showers, running water, gas barbecues and flush toilets.

State forests also offer great camping opportunities. Some provide space and access for caravans and motorhomes, and limited facilities are generally available.

We pointed out earlier on that, depending on your rig, access to some national parks can be an issue. You'll certainly have to travel down dirt roads, although most are reasonably well maintained. Always check ahead at local tourist information centres, national park offices and national park hotlines about the accessibility of a park and its suitability for vans or motorhomes or whatever you're travelling in. Later in this chapter, you'll find the hotlines and website addresses of the national parks authority in each state. The websites are a mine of useful information.

Some parks are listed as accessible by 4WD only. Don't be tempted to 'give it a go' with your van if you're not sufficiently equipped to take it on. Dig out that small tent we've suggested that you carry in case you want to go somewhere that your van can't. Caravan parks sometimes permit you to leave your rig for a couple of dollars a day while you strike off with your tent and your sleeping bag to some adventurous location.

National parks tend to operate a self-registration system whereby you fill out a permit and drop it, along with the required amount of cash, into an honesty box. The park ranger collects the fees from the box periodically. In well-used parks, the ranger might come around once a day to collect fees direct from campers.

Some states, notably Queensland, have introduced a booking-ahead policy for certain parks.

One of the great attractions of camping in national parks is the sense of adventure it brings. Being out in the wilds also seems to bring out the best in people and you'll find yourself meeting many like-minded travellers. This camaraderie is normally heightened in the parks where campfires are allowed and people join each other at the fireside for a drink and a chat. Some parks provide firewood while others require you to bring it in from outside the park. Crashing around in the bush with an axe and a saw is definitely not encouraged.

One of the other great attractions of national park camping is the feeling of being at one with nature. There are almost always bushwalking trails and the abundant wildlife and birdlife are a joy. Use your commonsense when interacting with wildlife and never feed the creatures.

Nearly all national parks have the same policy about pets – they're not allowed. This is quite strictly enforced and is perhaps the single biggest drawback to bringing your beloved dog with you on the big trip. State forests are a little more pet-friendly but they do require that you keep your dog on a leash at all times.

Camping in Australia's national parks and state forests is a marvellous experience and it can be addictive. Happily, many states have recognised that travellers in general, and grey nomads in particular, can have a role in helping to make the park camping experience a better one for everybody. Camp hosting programs are in place in some states, enabling volunteers to carry out basic maintenance duties in return for free camping. See the section on 'Camp hosting' in Chapter One for more details.

The following is a state and territory rundown of national park policies, including entry fees, booking requirements, fire restrictions and contact details so you can obtain more information or request brochures.

Australian Capital Territory's national parks

You'll find some terrific forest camping in the Australian Capital Territory, but only one national park, the impressive Namadgi National Park. Entry is free and camping costs around $5 per person. A three-night limit on camping applies here.

Booking policy

To camp at the national park, you must book in advance at the Namadgi Visitor Centre, either in person or by calling Canberra Connect on 13 22 81. Book early to secure a site, especially on long weekends. Campsites in some reserves and recreation areas also require booking. Again, call Canberra Connect to book.

Fire restrictions

No fires on total fire ban days. Otherwise, fires are allowed throughout the year in established campfire sites, but care should be taken.

Further information

The free brochure entitled *Get Out There!* provides visitors with an engaging and useful reference to the Australian Capital Territory's parks, forests and bushlands that are managed by the Australian Capital Territory Government. The guide also lists heritage and Aboriginal sites within parks and reserves, as well as interesting facts about fauna and places around Canberra.

The brochures can be obtained at Canberra Connect shopfronts, visitor information centres and the website below.

Contact information

Website: www.tams.act.gov.au/play
Tel: Canberra Connect on 13 22 81 (ACT and NSW only)
Interstate: (02) 6207 0494

New South Wales' national parks

There are many national parks in both inland and coastal New South Wales. Visits to these will certainly enrich your big trip experience.

Be prepared for a vehicle entry charge, normally $7, to enter some 44 of the most popular parks in the state. A number of annual pass options are available, with the most popular among grey nomads being the Country Parks Pass that gives entry to all country New South Wales parks except Kosciuszko National Park. The full price of a one-year Country Parks Pass is $45. All New South Wales Seniors Card holders are entitled to a 20 per cent discount.

Although some camping in New South Wales parks is free, charges typically range from $5 to $10 per person per night, depending on the park. Facilities are generally pretty basic but this is more than made up for by some truly spectacular camping locations.

Booking policy

Some national park campsites do require booking in advance but most operate on a first come, first served basis. Check the *Guide to New South Wales National Parks* brochure for contact details and to see whether booking ahead is necessary.

Fire restrictions

Fire danger season is October–March and this is when New South Wales often has total fire ban days. On these days, no campfires are allowed anywhere in the state. Otherwise, campfires are allowed throughout the year at some, but not all, campsites. People can phone the Rural Fire Service on 1800 679 737 to find out if a total fire ban has been declared.

Further information

The free brochure entitled *Guide to New South Wales National Parks* can be obtained from New South Wales tourist information centres, from national park visitor centres, or by phoning 1300 361 967. The brochure details locations of New South Wales national parks, conservation areas, nature reserves and historic sites and also shows what facilities are available and what charges are applicable. State forests are not included in this brochure.

Another publication of interest to travellers is the *Best Bush* map. This is a large-format, full-colour map of the forests and parks in New South Wales, covering all areas managed by the National Parks and Wildlife Service, State Forests of New South Wales and the Department of Land and Water Conservation – more than 1300 separate areas. It includes recreational and facilities listings for some 300 different parks, reserves and forests. The map costs $6.95 and can be obtained by writing to

National Parks Mail Order at PO Box 1967, Hurstville, New South Wales 2220. Alternatively, phone the New South Wales National Parks office on 1300 361 967 or visit www.bookshop.nsw.gov.au to buy the map online.

Contact information
New South Wales National Parks
Website: www.nationalparks.nsw.gov.au
Tel: 1300 361 967 (business hours)

Northern Territory's national parks
Visiting the Northern Territory's immensely varied national parks promises adventure and excitement. There are no entry fees to any Northern Territory national parks except Uluru-Kata Tjuta, and Garig Gunak Barlu National Park on the Coburg Peninsula. In parks where camping is permitted, fees vary according to the facilities provided – these are generally no higher than $6.60 per person per night.

Booking policy
Apart from Garig Gunak Barlu, no bookings are taken to camp in the national parks controlled by the Parks and Wildlife Service.

Fire restrictions
Only light fires in fireplaces provided. No fires are allowed on total fire ban days.

Further information
Call the Parks and Wildlife Service of the Northern Territory for fact sheets on individual parks.

Contact information

Parks and Wildlife Service of the Northern Territory
Website: www.nt.gov.au/nreta/parks
Tel: (08) 8999 4555

Kakadu National Park
Website: www.environment.gov.au/parks/kakadu
Tel: (08) 8938 1120

Uluru-Kata Tjuta National Park
Website: www.environment.gov.au/parks/uluru
Tel: (08) 8956 1100

Queensland's national parks

National parks in Queensland are incredibly varied. From the magnificence of Carnarvon Gorge to the sensational wilderness of Cape York, from the desolate outback to the sun-kissed islands, camping in Queensland delivers the lot. There are no entry fees to parks in the state although you will need to buy a vehicle access permit if you wish to take your car to Bribie Island, Fraser Island or Moreton Island recreation areas. Camping fees are $4.85 per person per night at all parks.

Booking policy

Many national parks and state forests in Queensland require advance booking, although some may still have a few allocated sites set aside for self-registration. Be aware that the EPA is in the process of converting all camping sites in all of the state's national parks and state forests from being self-registered to requiring advance booking.

Some popular campgrounds in the state are heavily booked,

especially in public and school holidays, so it's worth checking availability and booking early in peak times. You can book a site up to 12 months in advance, and booking at least six weeks in advance is recommended.

See contact information below for how to book a site.

Fire restrictions
Campfires are still permitted at some parks but these are gradually being discouraged. Check the rules at each park.

Further information
More information about the facilities and attractions of the state's national parks and state forests can be found at the EPA website (listed below), and the free brochure *Queensland's Parks and Forests*. The booklet is available from accredited visitor centres, park information centres, or by phoning 1300 130 372. Campsites can be booked online, by phone, or in person at Queensland Parks and Wildlife Service counters.

Contact information
Queensland National Parks
Website: www.epa.qld.gov.au
EPA Customer Service Centre: 1300 130 372

Campsite bookings
Website: www.qld.gov.au/camping
Tel: 131 304 (camp bookings)

South Australia's national parks
South Australia and its many national parks will be among the highlights of your adventure.

Locations such as the Flinders Ranges and the Eyre

Peninsula's Lincoln National Park regularly feature on the 'Top 10 spots' lists of veteran travellers.

Many parks throughout South Australia require you to pay an entry fee of around $7.50 per vehicle. However, you can buy a National Parks pass that will save you money if you plan to be in the state for a while.

A Multi-Park Pass that's valid for a year costs $67 per vehicle ($54 for concessions). A pass covering entry and camping will cost $112 per vehicle ($99 for concessions). If you're not planning to spend that long in South Australia, a Holiday Pass that's valid for two months costs $30 per vehicle ($24 for concessions). An upgraded pass that includes camping costs $50 ($40 for concessions).

If you pay for your camping per day, the cost is generally $5 or $10 per vehicle per night.

Booking policy

Campsites at Flinders Chase National Park on Kangaroo Island and Innes National Park on the Yorke Peninsula require you to book. It's also advisable to book sites during busy holiday periods at Mount Remarkable National Park and Memory Cove Wilderness Protection Area. Camping in other parks is on a first come, first served basis.

Fire restrictions

Each region and park is different. Some parks never allow fires while others permit them, except on total fire ban days. Call the Fire Bans Hotline on 1300 362 361 to see what restrictions are in force. In general, however, fires are not allowed from 1 November until 30 April. Check with the individual ranger to find out when, and if, campfires are allowed at the park you want to visit.

Further information

The DEH (Department of Environment and Heritage) publishes an excellent brochure called *South Australia's National Parks Guide*, which is a comprehensive list of South Australia's national parks, conservation parks, reserves, and recreation parks. The brochure details the facilities available in each park. These brochures can be obtained by phoning (08) 8204 1910 or can be downloaded from the website below.

Contact information

South Australia National Parks
Website: www.parks.sa.gov.au/parks
Tel: (08) 8204 1910 (DEH Information Line)

Tasmania's national parks

Tasmania is perfectly set up for camping in national parks, state forests and reserves. Despite its relatively small size, the island state encapsulates enormous contrasts in landscape, vegetation and atmosphere, and this variety is reflected in its national parks. The entry fee for Tassie's national parks is $22 per car per day. A Holiday Pass costs $56 per vehicle, offering entry to all parks for an eight week period. An Annual Pass for all parks costs $66 in the low season and $90 in peak season, which runs from 1 November to 30 April. Holders of a Seniors Card receive a 20 per cent discount.

Fortunately, national park and state forest camping in Tasmania is a pure delight and much of it is free or available for around $4 per person per night. Camping fees do vary at each park, however, so always check when you arrive.

Booking policy

A small number of campsites, such as those in Freycinet National Park, Cradle Mountain–Lake St Clair National Park and Tasman National Park, must be pre-booked in the high season.

Fire restrictions

Campfires are never allowed in listed World Heritage Areas and a few other campsites. In the camps that permit fires, they are commonly allowed all year around, except during total fire bans.

Further information

The *Caravan and Camping in Tasmania* brochure is available from visitor information centres, Service Tasmania outlets and from Tastravel on 1800 672 169. Fact sheets on individual parks are available on the Tasmania National Parks website.

Contact information

Tasmania National Parks
Website: www.parks.tas.gov.au
Tel: 1300 135 513

Victoria's national parks

The garden state is home to some of the most popular national parks in the country and areas such as the Grampians and Wilsons Promontory host thousands of visitors a year. Entry to most national parks in Victoria is free but several do charge an entry fee of between $4.40 to $14.40 per car per day. A National Parks Pass costs $72.50 and exempts, for a year, the holder from paying the entry charge to: Wilsons Promontory National Park; Mount Buffalo National Park; Mornington Peninsula National Park; Baw Baw National Park; and the

Yarra Ranges National Park. Camping fees vary but are generally around $10 per site per night.

Booking policy

Some campsites operate on a first come, first served basis; some campsites can be booked in advance; and others use a ballot system for booking ahead during peak times. There's no printed information to tell you which parks need to be booked in advance. However, tourists can phone 131 963 seven days a week from 9am–5pm to determine whether booking is necessary.

Fire restrictions

Some parks allow campfires throughout the year and some parks never allow fires. Fire danger season is November–April and tourists should be aware of the possibility of total fire bans during that time.

Further information

The free *Parks Discovery* booklet and *Camping in Victoria* guide are available at Victorian visitor information centres, park offices and by calling Parks Victoria's information centre on 13 19 63.

Contact information

Parks Victoria
Website: www.parkweb.vic.gov.au
Tel: 13 19 63

Western Australia's national parks

Western Australia has some of the most incredible national parks in the country. The gorges of Karijini National Park, the white beaches and turquoise waters of Cape Le Grand

National Park, the uniqueness of the Bungle Bungles and the wonder of Mitchell Falls in the Kimberley could be the highlights of an entire continent, yet they are but a few of the attractions of a single state.

Entry to many Western Australia national parks costs $10 or $5 for concessions per day per vehicle. However, an Annual All Parks Pass providing unlimited access to the parks for one year is available for $75 or $50 for concessions. Concessions are valid for drivers holding Australian issued Seniors, Aged Pension, Department of Veterans' Affairs, Disability Support, Carer Payment, Carer Allowance and Companion cards. Alternatively a four-week Holiday Pass is available for $35.

Selected areas managed by the Department of Environment and Conservation are free for campers, but in national parks the average charge is $6.50 per person per night for areas with basic facilities or $4.50 for concession card holders. Campsites with upgraded facilities such as hot showers, flush toilets and camp kitchens command a slightly higher fee. At the upper end of the scale, camping costs may be as much as $10 per person at parks such as Windjana Gorge and Purnululu (Bungle Bungles). The Department of Environment and Conservation say that all fees collected are used to assist in conservation and park management, including the improvement of visitor services and facilities.

Booking policy
There are currently no advance bookings at any locations for stays in Western Australia national parks. Sites are secured on a first come, first served basis.

Fire restrictions
Campfires are permitted in some parks but only when a

total fire ban is not in force. Depending on the conditions of the particular year, a total fire ban is often in place between November and March. The Department of Environment and Conservation asks visitors to help reduce the potential for a bushfire by using portable fuel stoves at all times.

Further information

A comprehensive listing of all Western Australia national parks and details of their facilities can be found in the 64-page *National, Marine and Regional Parks in Western Australia – A Visitor's Guide to the State*. The publication *Fees and Charges – A Visitor's Guide* is designed to answer all your questions on the specific fees. More information and additional brochures on areas managed by the Department of Environment and Conservation can be downloaded from the website www.dec.wa.gov.au or by phoning the information line on (08) 9219 8000.

Contact information

Department of Environment and Conservation
Website: www.dec.wa.gov.au
Tel: (08) 9219 8000

BUSH CAMPING

For a good percentage of the population, camping in the great Australian bush is what a big trip is all about. You're out there in the heart of some fantastic country, you're self-sufficient, and you're surrounded by wonderful wildlife under some of the biggest skies in the world. When the stars are out, the campfire's roaring and the billy's boiling, there's surely no better place to be.

Bush camping, for some people, means ducking up a dirt track and looking around for a suitable spot to park up for a night or two, often a place where nobody has previously camped. For others, it means camping pretty much any place where the camping is free. This may include some established camping spots with basic facilities like a drop toilet or a make-shift fireplace.

Bush camping is a part of our Australian heritage but one that is under threat, thanks to the ignorance and carelessness of a minority of travellers. Sadly, in their trail they've left some beautiful bush camping spots looking like rubbish tips. Remember that virtually all of the land in Australia's vast outback is under someone's management, which means access to almost any area could be withdrawn, if needs be. Always take care of your environment and try to leave no trace of your visit.

- Either use bins if provided or take your rubbish out with you.

- Leave your campsite as you found it; don't dig trenches or cut branches.

- Don't use detergents in creeks or rivers.

- Don't interfere with fences, bores or any equipment you come across.

- If you light a campfire, be sensible and extinguish it properly.

- The still outback air carries sound a remarkably long way. Don't make excessive noise, even when you think you're alone.

Going bush camping often means doing without facilities, and that will test your resourcefulness. Unless you're camping near a creek, you'll have to carry in with you sufficient water – and other provisions – for your stay. Remember always to boil water from a creek before drinking.

Living without a toilet is perhaps the biggest challenge of all when bush camping. While you may have a toilet of sorts in your setup, they're not generally adequate for long stays in the wild. Carry a small shovel with you when you're heading into the bush and be ready to dig some holes. Always bury your waste and toilet paper deep enough that it won't be dug up by creatures. Portable toilets should be emptied in official dump points.

Books

There are a number of excellent books that list and describe some of the many top spots to bush camp around the country. Among them are:

Priceless Camps and Rest Areas in the Northern Territory (Priceless Publishing, Western Australia, 2003)

Priceless Camps and Rest Areas in the South of Western Australia (Priceless Publishing, Western Australia, 2003)

Priceless Camps and Rest Areas in the North of Western Australia (Priceless Publishing, Western Australia, 2005)

Camps Australia Wide 5 (Philip & Cathryn Fennell, Queensland, 2009)

Camping in Australia (Explore Australia Publishing, Victoria, 2007)

ROADSIDE STOPS AND REST AREAS

Growing evidence of the role fatigue plays in many accidents on our roads has given rise to a marked improvement in the number and standard of rest areas.

In a country as vast as Australia, their purpose is to give weary travellers an opportunity to break their journey and to move on refreshed and revived. Each state has its own policy with regard to overnight stays at rest areas and most have produced free maps showing where the rest areas are and what facilities are available. Picnic tables, rubbish bins and toilets are generally provided at sites where 24-hour stops are permitted, and many places also offer shade.

Inevitably, these rest areas are quite close to the road, but they are commonly down a short access track that offers some protection from traffic noise. You'll find that the more attractive roadside stops prove quite popular, and by 4pm a cluster of grey nomad caravans has normally gathered. Given that it is never ideal to camp near big roads where anyone might pull in during the night, amazingly few security problems are reported.

Just be aware of your surroundings and your neighbours.

Overview of state and territory rest area policies and maps

- *New South Wales*: Overnight stops are permitted at numerous rest areas in the state. The Roads and Traffic Authority (RTA) New South Wales has brought out a guide entitled *Stop, Revive, Survive; New South Wales Road Map with Rest Areas & Driver Reviver Stops*. Phone 13 17 82 to get a free copy or call into any Motor Vehicle Registry in New South Wales to pick one up. It can also be downloaded from www. rta.nsw.gov.au (follow the 'Rest area maps' link).

- *Northern Territory*: Travellers are permitted to stay overnight at many rest areas throughout the Northern Territory. A highly detailed and comprehensive rest area map is available online at www.nt.gov.au/transport/ntroads/ roadside/restareas. This site maps out exactly where each rest area is, what facilities are available and it even includes a photo so visitors know exactly what to expect when they arrive. A clear indication of whether camping is allowed or not is also provided.

- *Queensland*: Overnight stays are permitted in a number of Queensland's rest areas. The Queensland Department of Main Roads has developed a thorough guide to roadside stops in the state entitled *Guide to Queensland Roads*. Call (07) 3306 7254 to receive a free copy, or download one from the internet at www.mainroads.qld.gov.au (following the links under the heading 'Plan your trip').

- *South Australia*: Rest areas in South Australia are a place for drivers to park safely off the main road while they take a break from their journeys. Camping overnight at rest areas is not encouraged although drivers should ensure they feel refreshed and revived before they continue their journey. The Department of Transport, Energy and Infrastructure publishes a guide to roadside stops and rest areas entitled *Roadside Rest Area Guide*. Call 1300 360 067 to obtain a free copy or download one from the internet at www.transport.sa.gov.au/publications/safety.asp.

- *Tasmania*: Each local council controls the rest areas in its own municipality in Tasmania. Policies regarding overnight stays are also determined by local authorities and no comprehensive, statewide map of rest areas has been compiled. Travellers who want to find out more about rest areas in a particular region should either contact the relevant authorities when they arrive, or contact the council in advance

through the local government website at www.lgat.tas.gov.
au (follow the links from 'Tasmanian Councils' to 'Maps
and Contacts').

- *Victoria*: Drivers in Victoria are encouraged to take a break
from the road at rest areas when necessary and revive themselves before resuming their journey. The use of rest areas as
camping grounds/caravan parks is discouraged. VicRoads
has produced a brochure entitled *Drivers' Guide to Rural
Victoria* which provides details of rest areas and other interesting information for travellers. Copies are free and can be
obtained at VicRoads outlets or by phoning the VicRoads
bookshop at (03) 9854 2782. It can also be downloaded
from www.vicroads.vic.gov.au (follow the links from 'Roads
and Projects').

- *Western Australia*: Travellers in Western Australia are
allowed to stay overnight in designated rest areas throughout the state. Main Roads Western Australia offers travellers
a choice of two brochures that detail roadside amenities and
rest areas, as well as indicating which sites permit overnight
stays. The brochures cover the north and the south. Call
138 138 to obtain free copies or download them from the
internet at www.mainroads.wa.gov.au (follow the links from
'Touring WA and Maps').

OVERFLOW CAMPING

We've mentioned several times the rapidly increasing cost
of staying in some caravan parks, which may be a direct
consequence of soaring land rates. Steep charges are a bone
of contention for many grey nomads, particularly those who
pride themselves on their self-sufficiency. You end up with a
Mexican standoff between park owners trying to maintain a

profitable business and grey nomads who'd prefer to camp for free or for very little in camping areas just outside town.

At the heart of the problem lies the fact that – although most parks are full to bursting during peak times, particularly in popular dry season destinations such as Broome and Port Douglas – average year-round occupancy in Australian caravan parks is barely 40 per cent.

Nonetheless, caravanners and motorhomers who can't get into caravan parks in peak periods need to be catered for elsewhere and overflow arrangements have had to be put in place in some towns.

The success of these experiments has led some councils to provide permanent, cut-price camping facilities at showgrounds and racecourses near towns – in some cases within spitting distance of caravan parks. The initiative has been particularly welcomed by the drivers of large motorhomes or converted buses, who find many traditional parks cannot cope with rigs of their size.

The Campervan and Motorhome Club – which boasts a membership of more than 50,000 – has become involved and is negotiating with a number of local councils, encouraging them to provide places for travellers to stay. They say their members are self-contained and don't need full facilities, yet still bring money into small communities via the provisions and the fuel they buy.

In the Queensland town of Thuringowa, just west of Townsville, for example, the local council provides free camping areas close to town that can accommodate caravans and motorhomes. The council says the facilities will stop people leaving town and going elsewhere and some will be able to cater to the big rigs that may be 60 feet (18m) long.

Not surprisingly, the caravan parks industry is less than

impressed by this trend and feels many parks are being placed in an impossible situation where they're unable to compete on a level playing field.

Some places are following the example of Karumba on the Gulf of Carpentaria. To solve the problem, visitors can buy vouchers to camp at the local sportsground when caravan parks are at capacity. When space does become available, they are then obliged to move into a caravan park.

This whole issue is changing rapidly as various parties lobby for their point of view. Just be aware that some towns may provide low-price camping with limited facilities, particularly in the peak seasons. Contact the relevant tourist information centres and ask them directly what council-sanctioned camping areas are available.

Dump points

Dump points are special facilities designed to take the waste from your portable toilets. More of these are popping up as the number of travellers increases. They're most commonly found in caravan parks but many local councils are now providing special disposal spots, as well.

Formaldehyde-free chemicals for your toilet are best as they minimise the potential damage to the environment in the event of spills or inappropriate dumping. Always try to leave the dump point clean after use as there are few things worse than arriving at such a facility to find the previous user has left a mess. If you are caught short – inasmuch as you need to dump your toilet waste in a hurry – you can always check with local visitor information centres and or other travellers to find the nearest location.

Safety and security

ACCIDENTS

Camping should be a relaxing and enjoyable experience for everybody but, unfortunately, accidents can and do happen. Even a simple mishap can turn into something far more serious when you're camping in remote locations. Having good communications is vital to your safety, and a satellite phone, distress beacon, HF radio or even a UHF radio can be a lifesaver. If you do have these items, make sure you and any travelling companions know how to use them properly. The first few minutes after a snake bite is not a good time to be getting out the instructions book!

We've recommended two potential lifesavers – a well-stocked first-aid kit and some basic first-aid training. Both issues are covered in more detail in Chapter Four of this book.

RIG FIRES

It's amazing how quickly caravans, campervans and motorhomes can burn once fire takes hold. Always be very careful. While camping you'll often find yourself in the proximity of gas bottles, open fires, cramped cooking conditions, jerry cans full of fuel and limited supplies of water. It's a potentially explosive combination.

Limiting the risks of fire

- Never leave cooking food unattended.

- Always switch off gas bottles when you're travelling and always turn off gas appliances after use.

- Equip your rig with a fire extinguisher that works and make sure you know where to find it and how to use it.

- Never join together two power leads as the connection point will not be waterproof.

- Always use extreme caution when lighting a campfire. Don't leave obstructions or pieces of firewood laying around where someone may trip over them and topple into the fire.

- Always properly extinguish your campfire and take care when coming across an old one. Fires that have had sand rather than water thrown on them can stay dangerously hot for days afterwards. Every year, dozens of people end up in hospital as a result of campfire burns.

BUSHFIRES

Bushfires are an ever-present danger in a hot and dry country such as Australia. Searing hot temperatures, huge expanses of untamed bushland, powder-dry spinifex and occasional gusting winds can turn large areas of this country into a veritable tinderbox. Every year people die, property is destroyed and lives are shattered.

None of us will ever forget the devastating bushfires that swept through Victoria in early 2009, claiming more than 200 lives, destroying 1800 homes, and leaving 7000 people homeless. The worst natural disaster to hit this country in a century was a horrific wake-up call to us all, and underlined once again the potency of the danger we face and the need for constant vigilance. Grey nomads are often drawn to the beautiful country most at risk from bushfire, so a thorough awareness and understanding of the threat is absolutely critical.

When a total fire ban is declared, it means the conditions

are ripe for a bushfire. Never light a fire in these times and think carefully about taking a bushwalk or doing any remote activity. Bushfires spread quickly and are highly unpredictable. If you do see smoke, however far away it is, try to get into an open area that will have less material for the fire to burn. If you can, move your rig into an open space, and clear away any flammable material.

If you're caught in a bushfire while you're out on foot, remember that most victims aren't burned to death, they're overwhelmed by radiant heat as the fire front passes over them. The temperature at the face of a low-intensity fire is around 1000°C. Do whatever is possible to protect yourself from radiant heat – cover yourself in flame-retardant blankets, roll in the mud, cover yourself in dirt – anything you can think of that might help. If you can, hide behind some sort of raised object that can also offer a measure of protection.

In Victoria in 2009, many victims died in their cars while trying to flee the bushfires. Obviously, if you can safely leave the area in your vehicle you should do so, but trying to flee can sometimes be at lease as dangerous as staying put. When the fire moves as quickly as it did on Victoria, however, there really are no good options. Nonetheless, the Queensland Rural Fire Service recommends that people do not attempt to drive through heavy smoke; lack of visibility makes it inadvisable.

If the fire front is about to pass over you while you're in your vehicle, get yourself lower down than the windscreen, cover yourself with blankets or something similar, and make sure the windows are rolled up and that the air-conditioning and fans are turned off.

If you are caught in a bushfire, here's your wisest course of action:

- Keep calm.

- Protect yourself from radiant heat.

- Keep low and stay in cleared areas.

Whenever you're anywhere near a bushfire, drink lots of water to prevent dehydration.

A shovel is perhaps the most important piece of fire-fighting equipment in the bush, where there may be limited water supplies. It will enable you to clear away flammable debris and to shovel sand or earth on top of a small grass fire that might otherwise spread.

Don't become paranoid about the bushfire threat but always be aware and alert and listen to local advice.

What will a bushfire do? Fire patterns are influenced by three main factors:

- *Fuel* – the intensity and rate of spread of a fire is determined to some extent by the type and amount of fuel available to it. For example, in forest land a fire burns with high intensity, but moves slowly, whereas in grassland the fire is less intense, but moves quickly.

- *Weather* – the intensity of fires will be increased on hot, dry days as opposed to cool, humid days. The wind can also dramatically affect fire behaviour and a blaze will obviously spread more quickly on a windy day.

- *Topography* – the way a fire travels will also be affected by the topography. A blaze will move more quickly uphill because of the preheating effect.

Do your best to understand these factors, predict how they'll interact, and take appropriate actions.

Safety summary

• Don't park on or near flammable undergrowth.

• Don't park too close to another caravan.

• Close off your gas cylinders when not in use.

• Act sooner rather than later.

• Take advice before you set up camp.

• Put in place a bushfire action plan.

• Keep an eye out for smoke.

• Listen to the local radio station.

• Keep water handy.

WILD WEATHER

In a land of scorching sun, surging creeks and seasonal cyclones, the weather demands respect from campers. Devote careful attention to the timing and direction of your trip as in many areas there are distinct seasons for cyclones and other violent storms.

Severe storms can strike anywhere in Australia and are responsible for more damage (as measured by insurance costs) than tropical cyclones, earthquakes, floods or bushfires. Severe thunderstorms are rare in the north during the dry season and tend to strike there between September and March. Conversely, in the south, extreme winds tend to occur in winter and spring.

If you're travelling at a time when you think severe weather is a possibility, monitor your radio closely. To help minimise injury and damage, the Bureau of Meteorology provides warnings of dangerous weather. Check its website regularly for local and national forecasts at www.bom.gov.au.

Wild weather poses a number of particularly serious dangers for campers. Camping under trees, particularly gums, can be extremely perilous. Large limbs can fall off trees at any time but they're more likely to do so during storms and in high winds. In the past few years, falling trees have killed campers in both Queensland and Western Australia and it can happen anywhere. Fatalities also occur when small boats capsize in storms, and when unsecured items turn into lethal projectiles in high winds.

High winds

From November to April, the Australian coast north from Perth, all the way around the Top End and tropical Queensland down to northern New South Wales, faces the threat of cyclone. Other types of storm, even tornadoes, can strike any part of Australia at almost any time of the year. These winds can be incredibly destructive, and caravans, with their lightweight construction and generally flat sides, are vulnerable.

Wherever possible, seek out natural windbreaks, as long as you're not placing yourself in greater peril from falling trees or flying debris. It can also help to park your van in such a way that its smallest side is facing the prevailing wind. If possible, your van should be tied down securely, the parking brake applied and the wheels chocked. Caravan parks in high wind areas can sometimes provide ground anchor points for you to tie down your caravan chassis.

If high winds are expected, you may consider these measures:

- Tape the van door and all windows.

- Turn off electricity and water supplies.

- Lower the van jacks to the ground to provide additional stability.

- Move away from trees.

- Remove loose items from outside the van that could become wind-borne missiles.

- Take down the annexe and fold away and secure the awning.

- Listen to local radio for storm advice.

- Disconnect outside TV/radio aerials.

Flash floods

Rainstorms can reach intensities of greater than 200 millimetres per hour so, not surprisingly, flash flooding can, and does, occur regularly.

Surfaces that may not have seen rain for months, or even years, are hard and impenetrable. Consequently, mini lakes and rivers spring up in a matter of minutes. If you're camping in remote country, make sure you have plenty of food and water in case flooding does cut you off. Remember that conditions can change rapidly, so listen to weather forecasts and be prepared to adapt your plans.

To reduce the risks of being caught out by flash floods:

- Don't camp next to creek beds when heavy rain is expected. You'll be amazed at how quickly even dried-up creeks can turn into torrents of raging water.

- Be prepared to blow the budget and head for a caravan park in town if you know the weather is going to turn particularly nasty.

- Avoid low-lying areas that may be cut off during heavy rain or flooding.

- Take plenty of food and water with you into remote areas.

Lightning

It's somewhat surprising to learn that lightning poses a greater threat to individuals than almost any other natural hazard in Australia. Statistics show that each year lightning kills ten people and injures more than 100.

The longer you travel, the more likely you are to encounter some pretty spectacular light shows. These awesome displays of nature's power are an amazing spectacle but they do pack a powerful punch. Just be careful and exercise commonsense.

During a lightning storm:

- Take shelter in your vehicle or, if possible, a building. If you are in your vehicle, don't touch the metal framework because lightning passes through this.

- Before the storm arrives, disconnect external aerial and power leads to radios, televisions and computers. Stay away from electrical appliances.

- Keep clear of windows.

- Don't handle long or metallic objects, such as fishing rods and umbrellas.

- If you're driving, slow down or park well clear of trees and power lines.

- If you're caught out on the water, get ashore as quickly as you can.

- If you're caught out on, for example, a bushwalk, drop as low to the ground as possible.

- Mountain summits are dangerous places to be during a thunderstorm. Try to descend so that you're not at the highest point of the landscape.

- Stay away from metal fences and water.

- Don't shelter under trees or other tall objects, and remain as low to the ground as you can.

PERSONAL SAFETY

Statistically, grey nomads are far more likely to be involved in a road accident than face problems at a camping area – but personal safety remains a real issue for many, as previously mentioned.

Police report no significant issues relating to the security of travellers at remote campsites, and indeed, there's an argument that the more remote the campsite, the more secure you are.

For that reason, most people try not to camp too near to towns, especially on Friday or Saturday nights. This is when you may be joined by local youths looking to party. Nine times out of ten, this is little more than a slight nuisance but any group of people drinking heavily should be treated with caution.

Once again, it's comforting to have some form of communication with you, and a UHF radio, HF radio, satellite phone or, in some areas, a mobile phone can provide a measure of reassurance.

Before you stop each night, it's also prudent to orientate yourself as to where the nearest place of refuge may be if you get in trouble. This could be a ranger headquarters, road construction camp, or other camp area nearby.

You'll normally get a feel for a camp as soon as you pull up, and if the place is littered with discarded wine casks and crushed beer cans it should ring a few alarm bells. Similarly, if there are other campers around, it's always good to say hello and to check them out. Chances are you'll feel better knowing who they are and they'll feel better knowing who you are. If you do feel uneasy for any reason, don't be afraid to move on as long as you have the time to do so and know where you're heading.

It can be reassuring to camp near others and, with more and more grey nomads on the road, you'll normally be doing exactly that.

Statistics show that you're more likely to suffer theft or disturbance at a caravan park than in the bush, although obviously some parks have a higher incident rate than others. Again, the best way of learning about the character of the various parks is to talk to other travellers.

Most parks have a 10pm-no-more-noise policy. Take any problems you have to the management. Remember, though, that such problems really are extremely rare.

THEFT

By their very nature, campsites are not particularly secure environments. Things cannot be locked up as effectively as they can be in houses, and in caravan parks there are hundreds of 'strangers' wandering about at all times of the day and night.

Nonetheless, if you visit any caravan park or camping area in Australia, you're likely to see plenty of valuables left lying around. There'll be fishing rods, barbecues, fridges and even the odd laptop computer – and all may be left unattended for extended periods.

Things are much the same after dark. A midnight visitor will probably see camping chairs, fluoro lights, gas cookers, tables and other assorted goodies left outside the van.

As the number of long-term travellers surges, it's almost certain there will be more theft from campgrounds. Grey nomads are bringing with them a lot more creature comforts as they travel for longer periods. Mobile phones, digital cameras, laptop computers and DVD players are standard accessories for many – and they're valuable enough to make them a target for thieves.

Nonetheless, there's no evidence to suggest that criminals are deliberately targeting caravan parks and camping areas – most thefts are opportunistic, which means you can reduce the risks by taking a few commonsense precautions. A simple thing like placing any valuable items out of view in a locked vehicle would probably prevent the vast majority of stealing offences. Thieves usually try to avoid confrontation and will endeavour to get in and out of your vehicle within seconds. They tend to check the obvious hiding spots for valuables – the centre console, the glove box, under the driver's seat, under the sun visor – and then they grab any bag that's handy. Don't make it easy for thieves.

Don't leave your belongings lying around outside your rig when you're away from your camp. Store any valuables you're not taking with you in the boot of your car, or in a secure and inaccessible area of your camper trailer, motorhome or van.

Thieves don't usually vet the stuff they steal until they're well away from the scene of the crime, so another thing to remember is that even if an item isn't valuable, it may look like it is.

An apparently full plastic 'Harvey Norman' bag containing medicines or toiletries will just as easily appear to a thief as a bag full of valuable electronic gear. They may not steal anything of significant worth, but any robbery leaves you feeling violated.

You can also reduce the chance of theft by getting to know your campsite neighbours. Once you've established that they're decent people, you can implement your own mini-neighbourhood watch scheme.

Some parks will have a number of security measures in place, often including boom gates, locked toilet facilities and even barbed wire perimeter fencing and security patrols.

Security tips

- Don't leave valuable items out in the open. Even fishing rods can disappear.

- Phone the police if you see anyone behaving suspiciously.

- Keep a pen and paper handy so you can record registration and car details if you need to.

- Make sure you leave your caravan or motorhome locked when you are out and about.

- Leaving loose change visible in your car is a bad habit. Don't do it.

- Mark your accessories and valuables with your driving licence number.

- Always take your mobile phone when you are out walking.

- Don't hide your valuables when you arrive somewhere – thieves could be watching – place items such as handbags out of sight prior to parking.

7

Wildlife

The key to enjoying the wildlife you will come across on your trip is to remember that it should be exactly that – wild. Don't feed the creatures; it's not good for them and it's not good for you. Possums, kangaroos, goannas and dingoes that have been fed by previous campers will come back to your camp looking for more of the same. Don't encourage them.

Then, of course, there are the crocodiles, the snakes, the mozzies and the ants – there's never a dull moment when you're out camping!

Threatening creatures

SNAKES

Snakes are high on the fear list of nearly all grey nomads moving out into the unknown. Statistics tell us, though, that snake bites are relatively uncommon, and fatalities from snake bites are rarer still. Nonetheless, there are plenty of snakes out there and you may well come into contact with them. As recently as March 2008, author Val Plumwood – who famously survived a crocodile attack in 1985 – was killed by a bite from an unknown snake species at a bush retreat near Canberra. Be careful.

The bad news is that Australia is home to 21 of the 25 deadliest snakes in the world. The most dangerous snakes found here include brown snakes, copperheads, death adders, black snakes, taipans, mulgas and tiger snakes.

Now, the good news. Snakes are more scared of you than you are of them and will do all they can to get out of your way. Normally, snakes will only bite when people either try to kill them or disturb them accidentally, so go carefully. Try not to camp near long grass, wood piles or rocks.

The vast majority of snake bites occur below the ankle or on the hand, so you can substantially reduce your risks by wearing sturdy boots when out walking and by exercising extreme caution when picking up things such as rocks or pieces of wood.

It also pays to keep your camp as clean and tidy as possible. Dropping crumbs and bits of food around outside can attract mice or rats, and mice or rats attract snakes. Always keep your annexe as thoroughly sealed as possible at night and just be aware of the places snakes like to hide.

One of the spookiest walks is the middle-of-the-night trip to the drop toilet. Keep your boots handy and pull them on. Always take a powerful torch with you and have a good look around before you get too comfortable. If nothing else, it'll make you feel a little better.

You'll probably encounter most snakes while you're out bushwalking and this is where appropriate clothing and footwear are vital. Many people like to carry a snake identification book with them, but don't get too close or too curious.

Knowing your snakes might enable you to help the doctor pick the right anti-venene if you do ever get bitten. Try not to panic and misidentify the culprit, as getting the wrong anti-venene can be extremely serious.

The latest first-aid advice is that you shouldn't apply a tourniquet to snake-bite victims. Instead, apply a pressure bandage over the wound, starting from the bite and strapping up the limb in the direction of the body. Sterile crepe bandages from a first-aid kit are best, but clothing or towels torn into strips could also be used. The bandage should be firm but not so tight that it hurts. The resulting dressing restricts movement of the limb and also limits movement of the venom through the bloodstream. Try to keep the patient calm, and immobilised if possible, until medical help arrives. Any movement, such as walking, can speed up the spread of the venom through the bloodstream.

If you haven't been able to identify the species of snake that inflicted the bite, a medical expert may be able to do so from the venom left, so don't wash the skin.

Above all, you must act quickly and calmly to get the victim professional medical care. The potential outcome of an encounter with these lethal creatures is well known.

SPIDERS

Australian spiders deserve to be treated with respect. A bite from certain among them, such as the infamous funnel web, can be extremely painful and even fatal. Luckily, not all of Australia's 2000 spider species are quite as menacing. Most have venom which, while it may be able to paralyse the spider's prey, is quite harmless to humans.

Spiders are found all over the country in a wide range of habitats so train yourself to be spider-aware. As a general rule, don't leave shoes, socks, hats, gloves or any other items of clothing lying around outside the van or in the annexe. If items have been left outside, always check before putting them on. You need to be especially careful when collecting firewood and it's probably sensible to wear gloves when doing so. Rotten logs are a common habitat of spiders and other insects.

The world's most deadly spider, the **funnel web**, is found in quite a small geographic location around Sydney and in northeastern New South Wales and southeastern Queensland. Funnel webs live in burrows that have a distinctive silk-lined entrance. As well as its unusual web, the intense black of the funnel web spider, its large fangs and its overall menacing appearance will help you quickly identify this killer.

Out in the bush, the funnel web's burrows are hidden under clumps of grass, in logs, near tree roots and under rocks. While both the male and female funnel webs give a painful bite, only the male's bite is dangerous to humans. Victims become disorientated, sweat profusely, vomit and struggle to draw breath. Those who are not given an anti-venene will die within days, if not hours.

The **redback** spider can be found in most coastal areas around Australia. It's the female redback that's dangerous and she can be easily identified by the red stripe on her body. While the redback is well known for lurking in the roofs and floorboards of houses, it also likes to hang out in logs, shrubs and under rocks. A redback bite is extremely painful and can cause weakness, headaches, sweating and high blood pressure. An anti-venene is available.

Wolf spiders are found in every area of Australia and their bite can cause serious skin damage and extreme pain. The **white-tailed spider** is also capable of inflicting serious skin damage and immediate medical attention is needed if a person is bitten. They can also be found all over the country and like to live under bark or under leaves.

Mouse spiders are found everywhere in Australia apart from Tasmania and can be extremely aggressive. They live in burrows and wait near the entrance at night to capture their prey. A bite from a mouse spider can cause vomiting, breathing difficulties and even induce a coma.

Although the above spiders are among those considered the biggest threat to humans, they are by no means the only ones. The **barking spider** and the **sac spider** are just two others that give a painful and unpleasant bite.

The first-aid treatment for snake bites applies to spider bites, too. Apply a pressure bandage and try to keep the victim calm. Don't wash the skin where the bite has occurred; a medical expert can identify the venom from a swab. Seek further medical help.

DINGOES

Unless you're planning to spend your entire trip tucked up in urban caravan parks, the eerie howl of the dingo will probably become a familiar sound to you. Dingoes, which are now considered native to Australia, are found in every region of the country except Tasmania. In recent years, the number of pure-bred dingoes has been in decline and some believe that inbreeding with domestic dogs could make the pure dingo extinct within a couple of decades. Around

90 per cent of dingoes found along the east coast are now a mix of pure dingo and wild dog and they can form packs. It is these hybrids that are generally blamed for attacks on people and on sheep.

According to many experts, the practice some campers have of feeding dingoes has led to increased incidences of aggression. This problem was put in the spotlight in dramatic fashion when a nine-year-old boy was killed by a pack of dingoes on Fraser Island in 2001. Dingo attacks on people, however, remain extremely rare, so don't become paranoid. You will long remember your nights sitting around a crackling campfire with the spine-chilling sound of dingoes howling in the distance. Just be sensible.

Coping with dingoes

- Never leave food lying around in your camp.

- Never feed a dingo.

- If you come across a dingo, don't harass it in any way.

- Don't run away from a dingo. If you fall down, you become a smaller and more vulnerable quarry.

- Don't leave your shoes outside your van at night. Dingoes are notorious shoe thieves.

CROCODILES

The number of saltwater crocodiles in Australia is surging and the prehistoric creatures are now venturing into new areas. Anecdotal evidence suggests that attacks on humans are on the increase and travellers need to be more croc-aware than ever before.

The estuarine crocodile is far larger and far more aggressive than the relatively harmless freshwater crocodile. It's found in coastal streams and estuaries in areas north of the Tropic of Capricorn, with the greatest populations in Cape York, the Gulf of Carpentaria and the Northern Territory. In the 1960s, the reptiles were heavily hunted and their numbers massively reduced, but commercial croc hunting has been banned for decades now and crocodile numbers are booming. Some experts estimate that there are around 75,000 salties in the Northern Territory alone.

Saltwater crocodiles are top of the food chain and have no natural enemies, other than man. They can grow to be around five metres long and view humans merely as another source of food. If you encroach on their territory, you can expect to be treated as dinner. A crocodile grabs its victim in its powerful jaws, drags it into the water and goes into a death roll, drowning its prey. It will then store the carcass underwater, where it rots and is consumed at the beast's leisure.

Fishermen are clearly among the most at-risk members of the travelling population. The lure of catching a big fish should never be enough for you to suspend your commonsense and risk life and limb.

In September 2008, a 62-year-old grey nomad man was taken by a 4.3 metre saltwater crocodile while checking his crab pots at Endeavour River near Cooktown in Far North Queensland. Despite this incident and all the publicity and debate it generated, if you travel into tropical regions, you'll still see fellow travellers wading into croc-infested waters to fish.

And it's not just those crazy enough to venture into the water who are at risk. Crocodiles can, and do, travel great distances over land. There was widespread concern surrounding an incident in Cape York in 2004 when a 4.2 metre-crocodile dragged a 34-year-old man out of his tent in the middle of the night. The tent had been pitchèd about 30 metres from the water's edge. Another camper, a very brave 60-year-old woman, then jumped on the croc's back, whereupon it released the man and grabbed her instead. Happily, her son rushed to the scene and shot the croc dead. And everyone lived to tell a quite extraordinary tale. Unfortunately, most croc attack stories don't have happy endings.

Crocodile safety tips

- Don't camp at the edge of crocodile-infested waterways. Don't be lulled into a false sense of security by other people parking their van close to the water's edge. Just because they're taking a risk, it doesn't mean you have to. There's no recommended safe distance to camp from the water. Use your own judgement.

- Don't clean fish at the water's edge or leave food scraps in camps where crocodiles can be attracted by the smell.

- Don't make a habit of washing or gathering water at the same time every day. Crocs watch for patterns and seize their opportunities after patiently observing a potential meal for the best time to strike.

- Always obey swimming warning signs and be aware that some croc-filled waterways may not have a crocodile hazard sign. Always check with local authorities before taking a dip in croc country.

- Don't dangle arms or legs over the side of a boat.

- Don't think because you can't see a crocodile it's not there. They can stay underwater for a considerable period of time and may remain completely motionless for hours on end.

SHARKS

Shark attacks have been the stuff of nightmares since well before the movie *Jaws* took the fear factor to a new level. More than 160 of the world's 370 known shark species can be found in Australian waters but, hearteningly, the vast majority of them are considered harmless to humans.

Nonetheless, the Australian Shark Attack File records that 65 people were killed by sharks in the 54 years up to 2008. Of these, 23 were in Queensland, 17 in South Australia, ten in New South Wales, eight in Western Australia, four in Tasmania and three in Victoria. No fatal attacks were recorded in the Northern Territory in that time period.

It's certainly worth being aware of sharks. They can be found in the waters right around the coast of Australia and in estuary mouths and they can swim in surprisingly shallow waters. A surfer even came across a great white in waters off Sydney's Bondi Beach in early 2006.

The most dangerous types of shark are generally considered to be the white shark, the tiger shark and the family of whalers which contains both the bronze whaler and the bull shark. The bull shark is particularly feared because it's aggressive and it likes shallow waters. It also inhabits fresh water and has been known to attack people in canal estates in places such as Queensland's Gold Coast.

Most experts agree that shark-attack victims are generally just very unlucky and that sharks don't normally attack humans for food. Remember, although a shark attack is very nasty, it really is rare, particularly if you follow some commonsense rules.

Shark safety tips

- Don't swim at dusk, dawn or at night.

- Don't swim if there are large schools of fish moving about.

- Don't swim in murky water and near river mouths (especially after heavy rain), channels, or steep dropoffs.

- Don't splash around excessively as this can attract sharks.

- Don't wear jewellery or shiny objects that could be mistaken for fish.

- Don't enter the water if you have open wounds or are bleeding. Sharks can detect even small amounts of blood.

- Don't swim with pets.

- If a shark is sighted, leave the water quickly and calmly.

BOX JELLYFISH

In 2006, a seven-year-old girl on the Cape York Peninsula became the 70th person to die from a box jellyfish sting in Australia since records were started in 1884. Although box jellyfish stings have been reported in every month of the year, the peak season generally runs from October to April. Box jellyfish are found in tropical waters and are more common after rain, especially near river and creek outlets. They are usually absent when seas are rough. Box jellyfish are pale blue and transparent and their tentacles can be up to three metres long. Apparently a sting is so painful that you may go into shock and drown unless you're rescued straight away. Immediate treatment is required if you are to survive.

Box jellyfish safety tips

- Don't swim in tropical waters during box jellyfish season.

- Take local advice about recent sightings or stings before entering the water.

- Always take vinegar to the beach with you. Vinegar can neutralise the stinging cells of tentacles.

- Swim in stinger enclosures where available.

- If you simply have to swim when box jellyfish are present, wear a specially designed stinger swimming suit.

IRUKANDJI

Irukandji jellyfish are usually less than three centimetres long but their sting can result in severe lower-back pain, excruciating muscle spasms, vomiting, headaches and occasionally cardiac arrest. Irukandji are found mostly in the deeper coastal waters of northern Australia, although they may be swept inshore by the current. Every year around 60 people are hospitalised after stings.

First aid

The first-aid treatment for both box jellyfish and irukandji stings is to douse the affected area liberally with vinegar. Then, with a vinegar-soaked bandage, apply the pressure immobilisation technique to the affected area. Seek medical help immediately.

CONE SHELLS

Cone shells are a deadly Australian secret. They are actually marine snails, living inside striped or speckled cone-shaped shells. They lay in sand flats and shallow reef waters, and can be found in Australia's temperate and subtropical waters, although most species live in tropical regions. The snail can extend its long proboscis and use the small harpoon-shaped teeth on the end to inject venom into its prey. This poison can result in death or, if not, neurological symptoms, pain, swelling and numbness. Be mindful of the existence of cone shells and don't pick them up.

First aid

First-aid treatment of cone shell bites involves the same pressure immobilisation technique used for snake and spider bites. Try to keep the victim calm. Seek medical assistance immediately, as a bite from this creature can be fatal.

STONE FISH

The stone fish is mottled brown–green and fiendishly hard to spot. It likes to hang out on coral reefs, near rocks and in muddy or sandy banks above the Tropic of Capricorn. This potentially lethal creature boasts venomous spines along its back which can cause extreme pain and a great deal of swelling if trodden on. The venom causes muscle weakness and temporary paralysis, which may result in death if not treated. Don't walk around danger areas without shoes on and always wear sandshoes in stone-fish habitats when swimming.

First aid

First-aid treatment consists of immersing the affected area in hot water. Don't bandage or try to restrict movement of the area that's been penetrated by the spine. Seek further medical treatment.

Pests and pains

FLIES

Flies in the outback will drive you crazy. At certain places at certain times you'll find your clothing almost black with the annoying insects. Picnics will become impossible and it may be hard to breathe without swallowing a mouthful of them. They're a fact of life in some places at some times of the year, so prepare for what's to come. A fly hat with a mesh that comes down to cover your face can be a lifesaver, although it isn't going to help you while eating. You can also buy fly-proof screen gazebos which will enable you at least to sit outside your van in comfort. Roll-on or spray-on insect repellent is also effective up to a point. Mercifully, flies disappear at dusk, but that is also when the mozzies make their appearance!

MOSQUITOES

The high-pitched buzz of a mosquito strikes fear and loathing into the heart of any camp-loving grey nomad. In some places the mozzies can be so fierce that they'll make it impossible for you to enjoy sitting outside once dusk has arrived. In these instances, about the only thing you can do is get in your rig and be thankful that you're able to close the door on them. Under no circumstances should you leave your van or motorhome door open around dusk or you'll find yourself in for a dreadfully long night. Pick your campsite carefully and remember these buzzing nightmares love marshy areas, standing water and swamps.

Avoiding mosquitoes

- There are a number of excellent insect repellents on the market going all the way up to tropical strength. These can be an astute investment.

- Wearing long-sleeved shirts, long trousers, socks and shoes offers a measure of protection.

- If you're sitting outside, a screen tent keeps mosquitoes at bay and the traditional mosquito coils can also help.

- Mosquitoes aren't big fans of smoke but if the only way you can enjoy sitting outside is to sit on top of your campfire exposing yourself to the risk of severe smoke inhalation, then maybe it's better just to grab an early night. Of course, as well as being a major irritant, mosquitoes are renowned carriers of diseases such as Ross River fever and encephalitis, so do everything you can to minimise your exposure to their bites.

ANTS

Ants can drive the most patient of campers to distraction. They can get into anything and everything. Before setting up camp, have a look around, particularly if you're near trees, and check for ants' nests and mounds. Many grey nomads travel with an ant spray in a very handy location and deal with the pest ruthlessly. It can be smart to put ant kill around your jockey wheel and wheels to stop ants entering your van.

If you've camped in a spot with no obvious ant problem, you'll want to keep it that way; you certainly don't want to encourage them. Never leave scraps of food around and make sure all items such as sugar or jam are stored in airtight containers.

The bites of bull ants and even some of the smaller ants are extremely painful and can cause swelling, redness and discomfort.

It's always worth carrying with you some sort of sting and bite treatment, such as Stingose or calamine lotion or even baking soda. Ants can also bite holes in your awnings and have been known to eat wiring inside cars.

WASPS AND BEES

Even the least experienced of grey nomads knows that bees and wasps should be left well alone. Keep an eye out for hanging nests or nests in the hollows of trees. In the vast majority of cases a sting is little more than a painful and unpleasant experience. Mild reactions can be treated with antihistamine medication but things aren't always that simple. Extreme allergic reactions to a bee sting can result in respiratory failure, cardiac arrest and death.

There've been a number of examples of travellers discovering in the worst possible way that they're allergic to these stings. If you know you require medication for allergic reactions, make sure you carry it with you at all times. For bee-sting allergies, an adrenaline pen, or EpiPen, is quite possibly a lifesaving piece of equipment. Keep it close and ensure you and your partner know how to use it correctly.

SANDFLIES

Sandflies, or biting midges as they are sometimes known, are a nightmare. These tiny fly-like insects are only between 1.5mm and 4mm long, but their bites itch like crazy and can lead to infection. Unfortunately, they can be present in large numbers in seaside caravan parks and they love grassy areas near the coast. Sandflies are generally only a nuisance at dawn and dusk. Again, it makes sense to wear long clothes and to coat yourself with insect repellent. An old-fashioned mixture used by many experienced grey nomads in severely sandfly-infested locations is eight parts baby oil to one part Dettol. It both helps to deter sandflies and to soothe the discomfort of existing bites.

TICKS

Although some ticks can make children sick and kill small dogs, they're not normally a serious threat to adults. However, if an extreme allergic reaction occurs, ticks can cause lethargy, muscle weakness, double vision and breathing difficulties. Check for them regularly, particularly if you've been out on a bushwalk. Wear insect repellent; stay to the middle of marked paths; wear long clothing; and tuck your trousers into your boots. There is some debate about the best way to remove a tick. However, one recommended option is to remove it with tweezers, preferably with a curved end. Try to grasp the tick as close as possible to the skin so you don't leave the head behind. The biting parts of the head have barbs on them that can be difficult to remove. Put antiseptic cream on the area.

SCORPIONS

While Australian scorpions aren't as deadly as their American counterparts, they still pack an uncomfortable punch. As a general rule, the bigger the scorpion, the more it's going to hurt, so keep your eyes peeled. Don't go carelessly picking up stones and rocks or you may just get a nasty surprise. Scorpion bites are normally no more than a painful experience that gradually eases after an hour or so. Nonetheless, always be mindful of, and vigilant for, any more serious reaction to a sting.

LEECHES

Ever been bushwalking and taken off your boots to find a leech or two clinging to your foot? They're unpleasant things but no more than that. They love damp areas and can mysteriously attach themselves when you're passing through their favoured habitat. Note that they don't like insect repellent.

Leeches are best removed by sliding a fingernail or other flat object under the leech's head to break the suction and then flicking it away as quickly as possible. Old methods such as using salt and matches may cause the leech to vomit into the wound possibly causing infection. Leeches have an anticoagulant so wash this off your skin to reduce bleeding. Finally, apply a bandage.

CENTIPEDES

Despite their fearsome appearance, most Australian centipedes are harmless to humans. However, some can, and do, give a painful bite that causes localised swelling and irritation – and most likely very little else. Despite the fact that some species are extremely large – *Ethmostigmus rubripes*, for instance, grows up to 14 centimetres – there've been no recorded deaths from centipede bites in Australia. Centipedes tend to live in moist areas such as rock crevices, in litter or under bark, and come out at night to hunt.

Wonderful wildlife

KANGAROOS AND WALLABIES

There are several different types of kangaroo and wallaby and, as your journey unfolds, you may learn to distinguish between them.

The red kangaroo keeps to flat open plains but both the eastern grey and the western grey prefer denser scrubs and forests. As their name suggests, rock-wallabies live among piles of boulders and rocky hills, while tree-kangaroos make their homes in the dense rainforests of north Queensland.

Although some species are considered to be under threat, many others have thrived in recent years. European settlement led to the establishment of bores and ground tanks in arid regions that would otherwise have been uninhabitable for kangaroos, which like to stay close to a water source.

When you camp out in the bush, particularly in national parks, you may well find your camp visited by these sometimes overly friendly Australian natives. Kangaroos aren't considered aggressive but they are large and don't like to be cornered. Enjoy watching them and keep your distance.

LIZARDS

From tiny skinks to the giant two-metre goannas, you'll often come across cold-blooded lizards trying to warm themselves in the sun. Lizards are thought of as harmless creatures but they're best left alone, particularly the larger varieties.

You won't have been at many national park camps before the goanna makes itself known to you, lumbering through the undergrowth and sniffing around your camp. These large lizards can move pretty quickly when they want to and can be aggressive when provoked, so keep yourself – and your food – out of their way.

The blue-tongued lizard announces its identity by flicking out its startlingly blue tongue, while the thorny devil is even more striking in appearance, due to the fact its entire body is covered in spikes. The thorny devil can be observed in the heat of the day in the deserts of central Australia and the desert regions of Western Australia and South Australia.

If anything, the frill-necked lizard is even more distinctive. Found in the wooded areas of the northern regions of Australia, this reddish-brown lizard erects its brightly coloured frill when it wants to intimidate potential enemies. Spotting this extraordinary creature is an experience made all the more memorable if it runs along on its hind legs for you.

BANDICOOTS

The nocturnal bandicoot is a small, omnivorous marsupial that can be found throughout Australia. There are a number of different species living in a wide variety of habitats, ranging from rainforests to heathland. They've had a tough time at the hands of imported species such as cats and foxes but can still be seen, with luck and patience. At night, the rat-sized creature likes to scratch around on the ground in search of insects to eat so listen out for it.

Bilbies are actually a type of bandicoot and are sometimes referred to as rabbit-eared bandicoots. This small marsupial is famed for the large ears which give it superb hearing. However, this hearing has not been enough to prevent a dramatic decline in bilby numbers and they can now only be found in very small areas in Western Australia, the Northern Territory, South Australia and Queensland.

ECHIDNAS

This gentle creature with its mass of dramatically long spikes, is a monotreme – one of the few mammals that lays eggs – and eats termites and ants. You could well come across one by the side of the road or walking track. When it's threatened, the echidna curls up into a tight, protective ball. While the echidna can be found anywhere from seaside dunes to central arid regions, its habitat is being slowly eroded by urban sprawl. For that reason, you're more likely to see one of them in a national park, state forest, or remote bushland. Echidnas live in every state of Australia.

WOMBATS

Wombats live in underground burrows and are not often seen by campers. These sturdy creatures can grow to about 1.3 metres in length and are powerful diggers. Wombats inhabit wooded areas and generally stay in their burrows during the day, emerging at night to graze on native grasses and the roots of trees.

TASMANIAN DEVILS

This meat-eating marsupial is active at night, when it searches for food. It will eat any small creature, as well as any carrion it can find. The Tasmanian devil now lives exclusively in the island state but archaeologists say it once lived on the mainland.

KOALAS

They're cuddly and cute and an Australia icon – but koalas are fiendishly difficult to spot. As we all know, the koala bear isn't actually a bear at all but rather an arboreal marsupial. It lives almost exclusively on eucalyptus leaves and inhabits the eucalypt woodlands of eastern Australia.

Sadly, the koala habitat has been rapidly eroded by the relentless march of humans. Much prime koala land has now been taken over by the farmer and the house-dweller, and the koala has been left clinging to an uncertain future in increasingly isolated patches of land. Attacks by dogs have also been blamed for reducing numbers to dangerously low levels.

Nonetheless, koalas are still out there in the wild and eagle-eyed grey nomads can spot these less-than-energetic creatures. So keep scanning the forks of the trees and you may catch a sleeping koala taking a break from its busy schedule.

PLATYPUS

If you're on the lookout for a platypus – best of luck! These egg-laying mammals come out from their burrows in the river bank in the evening to look for food in the water. One of the best places to spot these elusive creatures is in Eungella National Park near Mackay – and the camping there is great, too.

POSSUMS

The brushtail possum will become a regular visitor to your camp when you're out in the bush or in national parks. It likes wooded areas but is extremely adaptable and can pop up almost anywhere in eastern Australia and in the southwestern corner of Western Australia. It likes to eat a variety of plants, insects and anything you leave lying around. It's cheeky and persistent, so if you don't want to be woken up by the sound of clanging pots or rustling paper, make sure you store all of your belongings securely at night. Possums have sharp claws and know how to use them.

CAMELS

It comes as a surprise to many people to learn that there are hundreds of thousands of feral camels wandering the Australian outback. Some estimates even put the figure closer to a million – and their numbers climb all the time. They were initially brought to this country in the 19th century to carry supplies to remote stations but were released to roam the bush once a rail and road system was established. The long-term impact that camels will have on Australia's delicate environment has yet to be established, although they have extremely large appetites.

It's quite a thrill to see your first wild camel and the whole experience can be slightly surreal. Remember, though, these are massive creatures and they can cause quite a dent in your vehicle, so keep an eye out for these ships of the desert when you're cruising the outback.

Collisions between caravan-towing vehicles and camels are certainly not unknown.

DOLPHINS

Watching dolphins cavorting around the ocean in pods of a dozen or more is a wonderful sight and one you're likely to witness a number of times. Many of the world's 33 different dolphin species can be found in waters around Australia, often close enough to the shore to be observed and enjoyed.

The most frequently sighted dolphin is the bottlenose dolphin, which is playful, entertaining and seems genuinely to enjoy being in close proximity to people. For this reason, they're often seen close inshore and it's the bottlenose dolphin which visits the fabled Monkey Mia in Shark Bay, Western Australia, a couple of times a day. Whereas close human interaction with these dolphins at Monkey Mia was once actively encouraged, nowadays the feeding exercise is closely controlled by guides. Sadly, it seems, some people previously abused the privilege, with one visitor apparently even attempting to put a lighted cigarette into a dolphin's blowhole.

The bottlenose, which can grow up to four metres in length, is a warm-blooded mammal that breathes air. Nonetheless, dolphins can swim under the water for about 15 minutes, and, thanks to their collapsible ribs, can swim to depths of more than 100 metres. They are truly remarkable creatures.

WHALES

As mentioned in Chapter Three when we discussed the best time and places to see migrating whales, these giants of the sea can put on a spectacular show.

As you wend your way along the coast, you may wish to look out for species such as the humpback whale, which is about 15 metres in length and often performs aerial leaps. Each year, these magnificent creatures head from Antarctica to the subtropical waters of Australia to give birth and to mate.

The southern right whale, which can grow up to about 18 metres in length, heads to the southern coasts of Australia each year. It likes to come into shallow water with its calves, so is easily seen from the shore.

The minke whale, which measures some eight to ten metres, is another species that is commonly sighted in Australian waters. These relatively speedy whales flourished back in the days when their larger relatives were hunted.

Other whales such as the giant blue whale, which can grow up to 30 metres in length, prefer to stay in the open ocean and so are rarely sighted near the coast.

FAIRY PENGUINS

The fairy penguin, or little penguin, which is found all along the southern coast of Australia, is an amazing creature. Standing less than 50 centimetres tall and weighing around one kilogram, it's a terrific swimmer and a great entertainer. No wonder thousands of tourists flock to see colonies of these waddling, lovable birds go about their daily business in places as far afield as Tasmania and Penguin Island in Western Australia.

The most famous colony of fairy penguins in the country is, of course, the one at Phillip Island in Victoria, where huge crowds gather at dusk to watch the penguins emerge from the ocean and waddle to their burrows.

BIRDLIFE

With more than 700 species to look out for, you'll need to study hard to recognise all the birds you'll come across during your travels. For more information on some of the more striking bird species, see the Birdwatching section in Chapter Eight. There, you'll also find some advice on how to get started in this rewarding and pleasurable pursuit, and how to get the most out of it.

8

An exciting new lifestyle

Nothing – apart from life on the road – can prepare you for life on the road. Superb scenery, wonderful new companions, near limitless time to relax and enjoy yourself – it's all out there waiting for you. Amazingly, though, this dream life can take a while to adjust to. Here are a few pointers to help you make the most of your carefree existence.

Relationships

After 30, 40, or even 50 years of marriage, you'll know your spouse almost as well as you know yourself. Even so, you'll suddenly find yourself living in close proximity to your nearest and dearest for 24 hours a day, seven days a week and the results are not always pretty. Conversely, the trip can bring you closer than you've been in years as you spend quality time together without the distractions of your old house-dwelling lifestyle.

The following are a few tips on how to deal with the culture shock:

- Be patient. This is a different experience for both of you, so make allowances for your partner. Don't say things in the heat of the moment that you might live to regret. If you think the van's small now, just wait until you've had a falling out!

- Make the most of the time you have together but don't stop doing things just for yourself. Take a break from each other and get away on your own for a walk, to read a book, or to organise your rock collection.

- Take the opportunity to learn something new together. You can both take up T'ai Chi, or jewellery design, or painting. Growing together into a new hobby will help to keep things fresh.

- Keep talking to each other. You're in uncharted territory now so it's vital you let your partner know what you're thinking and feeling. If you think the trip isn't going well, or you think you should take a different route, or you're upset because he or she keeps leaving their shoes in the caravan doorway, then tell them – in the nicest possible way. Don't let things fester.

- If the kitchen has been the longtime domain of your partner, then don't try to take over just because you're living right on top of it now.

- Don't take your partner for granted.

- Develop a new hobby or interest for yourself. It'll be good for you and might help to make you more mysterious and interesting to your partner. After all these years, who says you're not still full of surprises?

Socialising

As well as the impressive country you'll see, the hobbies you'll develop, and the nearly infinite time you'll have, one of the greatest things about the trip will be the people you'll meet.

Grey nomads are on the rise and you'll find no shortage of like-minded travellers in campsites and caravan parks. And the best news of all is that they're pretty much all as relaxed, friendly, happy and interesting as you are.

Try to make a point of introducing yourself to your neighbours in the campsite. At worst, you'll find out who's camping around you and at best you'll make a friend for life. Most people will be more than happy to share tips on everything from the best places to camp and the cheapest places to buy fuel, to how you know when your fire is in exactly the right state to make damper and how to rig the line to catch a trout.

Make sure you've got a couple of spare campchairs and a couple of spare mugs, wine glasses or stubby holders with you, and enjoy this endless supply of new friends.

Occasionally, you may fall in with people you've met following the same route and then arrange to meet up a few weeks or a few months later. Slowly, as the days pass, you'll find your address book filling up. Make sure you write people's names down in full, and maybe where you met them and what you did with them, as it's incredible how the memories fade. You might scratch your head for hours trying to figure out who Bob Smith is and then remember he was the guy who entertained you for hours with his Indiana Jones impersonations on the Carnarvon Gorge bushwalk last July. Gosh, what a long day that was, and what a character!

The longer you travel, the more addresses you'll accumulate and you'll eventually find that some of these nomads have become ex-nomads who are happy to have you park your rig in their backyard for a day or two. It's a great way to break up your trip, catch up with old friends, and keep the budget down.

And you'll need to keep the budget down, as you'll be spending an absolute fortune on cards and stamps at Christmas time.

Keeping in touch

Homesickness is one of the most widespread afflictions suffered by grey nomads – particularly those with young grandchildren. Even though your trip can offer you adventure, excitement and loads of new company, it can't offer you proximity to your family and friends. Depending on how remote the regions you travel to are, even keeping in phone and e-mail contact can prove difficult.

There is no easy answer. Unfortunately, you can't have your cake and eat it and, if you want to travel for a few years, you have to make some sacrifices. You can't be in Darwin for the Beer Can Regatta and also watch your youngest granddaughter blow out her birthday candles in Sydney in mid-July.

Your best option is to try to anticipate how difficult it will be for you to be away from your loved ones and to make arrangements that will help you deal with that. If your financial situation allows, why not fly home for a short visit every now and again and then resume your trip; some grey nomads do precisely that. For most, though, budgetary constraints mean this is not really an option.

The advent of mobile phones has made staying in regular touch that much easier and it's reassuring to know your family can try to contact you any time, day or night. Even if you're out of mobile range, they'll be able to leave a message that you'll receive as soon as you're back in range.

The internet has been another massive plus for long-term grey nomads and it's great to travel with a laptop on which you can compose e-mails to those at home. It's also possible to receive and to send photos quite easily from internet cafés and wireless hotspots, and this can help to make you feel that much closer to home.

Webcams enable you to see your family members on a computer monitor as you talk to or message them, and this is an easy and affordable thing to organise. It can help to make the whole internet contact experience a lot more personal.

Keeping in regular contact is probably the best way to ease the symptoms of homesickness but you have to try to get the balance right. Often you'll be thousands of kilometres away from your family and you can no longer live with them through every up and down of their lives.

Cooking

Meals are often a much-anticipated event – whether you've just completed a long day's driving, an arduous bushwalk, or merely a day relaxing at camp. It's a time to discuss the day's activities, the plans for tomorrow or simply to hash over the true meaning of the latest book you've been reading. Food is the element that brings it all together and keeping your menus interesting, nutritious and fun will definitely improve the quality of your trip.

Most caravans and motorhomes contain well-equipped kitchens that have at least two – and often four – stovetop burners, a microwave and sometimes even an oven. You'll be able to cook most things in your RV that you could at home, but why not take the opportunity, when possible, to shake things up a bit?

Variety, flexibility, simplicity and forward planning are the keys to successful cooking on the road. Take advantage of cheap local produce and organise the menu around it. There are plenty of good recipes that don't require delicate procedures, exact timing and state-of-the-art food processors. Look around for an interesting cookbook and keep an eye out for new recipes in women's magazines, which often litter the laundries of van parks. Herbs and spices don't take up too much space in the van and they can add a lot of diversity and interest to your cooking.

CAMPFIRE CUISINE

Grilling steaks or fish over a campfire for a sunset dinner, making damper in the hot coals for breakfast, and even toasting cheese sandwiches in the jaffle iron, evokes images of adventure and an outdoor lifestyle. Campfire cooking is cheap, it gives food a great flavour, and the fire itself provides a wonderful atmosphere for the meal and a focal point for the evening. If you think you may be spending some time in national parks or in bush camps where campfires are permitted, investing in a few specialised items such as jaffle irons, a metal grill and a camp oven will provide you with all the tools required to create a huge variety of tasty meals.

Cooking over a campfire is not really much different from cooking on a burner, although getting the fire just right is often a bit tricky. Fillets of meat or fish can be grilled directly over the coals and food such as fish and potatoes can be wrapped in foil and buried in hot ashes for an oven-baked effect. Try putting leftovers between a couple of slices of bread in a jaffle iron for a light meal.

A camp oven is an incredibly versatile piece of equipment that can be used to cook a wide range of dishes from roast joints to quiche and from Irish stew to chocolate cake.

A trivet in the base of your camp oven acts as a buffer between the hot coals of the fire and your baking dish, so the bottom of your cake, pie, quiche, or whatever you're baking, won't burn.

Once the meal is finished, you can build up the fire and have a good chat about the day's adventures.

Instructions for making damper

Damper is traditional campfire fare which is both easy to make and delicious to eat. There are many variations on the theme but the basic recipe is as follows:

2 cups self-raising flour; ¾ cup water; ½ teaspoon salt. The dough can be cooked in several different ways: in a greased camp oven placed in a bed of hot ashes for 40–60 minutes; in aluminium foil parcels buried in hot ash or wrapped around a stick and roasted slowly over the fire.

Damper is best eaten fresh with butter and honey or golden syrup. Enjoy.

New hobbies and interests

FISHING

Fishing is far and away the most popular hobby among grey nomads. Very few of the vans and motorhomes you see plying the highways don't have a rod and tackle box stashed somewhere. It's a pursuit tailor-made for people with time, patience and a desire to save a few dollars.

The good news is that even a complete novice can quickly learn the basic techniques required and start to catch edible fish straightaway. You're heading into areas containing some of the world's most beautiful and well-stocked fishing waters, so take advantage.

Obviously, if you're travelling with a tinny, a lot more fishing opportunities are going to open up to you, but there's still plenty of good sport to be had from the beach or the bank.

Fishing in places with unfamiliar weather patterns and currents, however, does require extra caution. Grey nomads are not immune from crocodile attack, drowning, or slipping off wet rocks, so be careful.

Fishing authorities offer the following advice to anglers:

• Stay alert at all times.

• Avoid fishing in exposed areas during rough weather or big swells.

• Spend time watching the sea before starting to fish.

• Always wear suitable clothes and shoes.

• Don't turn your back on the sea.

• Check weather and sea reports before starting to fish.

- Let someone know where you're fishing and when you expect to be back.

- Don't fish off rocks if you can't swim.

- Never fish from rocks when you're on your own.

- Never fish off rocks that are wet.

Putting out in unfamiliar waters in a small boat carries enormous safety responsibilities. Fishers are urged to check the seaworthiness of the boat regularly, and to carry the correct safety gear. Depending on the boat and where you're heading, this might include life jackets, oars, buckets, electronic positioning indicator radio beacon (EPIRB), anchor, flares, first-aid kits, rope, fresh water, tool kit, waterproof torch, signalling mirror and a spare motor.

What not to eat

Not everything you pull out of the water is safe to eat, particularly so if you're in tropical waters. In Queensland alone, for example, puffer fish, toadfish, trigger fish, red bass, paddle-tail and Chinaman fish should definitely be off your menu. Large reef fish are also known to occasionally have harmful levels of toxic organisms in their flesh. Get a good book to identify your catch and don't be afraid to ask advice from a local. The golden rule is: if in doubt, throw it back. Baked beans on toast – again – is infinitely preferable to a hospital trip.

The various states and territories all have their own rules and regulations governing such things as fish size, seasons and bag limits and, in some states, you'll be required to purchase a fishing licence.

New South Wales

Whether you fish off a New South Wales beach or in one of the state's myriad rivers, streams or lakes, you're unlikely to get back to the van empty-handed . . . too often!

Saltwater fishers relish the opportunity to have a crack at bream, flathead, tailor, kingfish, snapper, whiting and luderick, while their freshwater-loving counterparts covet Murray cod, trout and golden perch.

Always bear in mind seasonal restrictions governing when you can fish for species such as Murray cod, trout, Murray crayfish, Australian bass and estuary perch. There are also some specific local restrictions so check these out before you cast a line.

Licences

Fishing licences are required in New South Wales, although holders of a Commonwealth Pensioner Concession Card issued by Centrelink or the Department of Veterans' Affairs are exempt. You're also exempt if you have a Veterans' Affairs Gold Treatment Card endorsed 'Totally and Permanently Incapacitated' or 'Extreme Disablement Adjustment'. Seniors Cards do not exempt you from buying a fishing licence.

Licence costs are $6 for three days, $12 for one month, $30 for one year and $75 for three years.

Further information

Copies of New South Wales *Saltwater Fishing Guide and Freshwater Fishing Guide* and rules and regulations summary brochures are available from the Department of Primary Industries (DPI) Fisheries. These publications can be obtained by calling the Fisheries Information Line on 1300 550 474. Publications can also be found at DPI Fisheries Offices throughout the state.

Website: www.dpi.nsw.gov.au/fisheries

Northern Territory

Fishing in the Northern Territory is a thrill that shouldn't be missed. It's basically got the lot, with inviting billabongs, massive rivers, spectacular coastlines and fish-filled estuaries.

Local anglers talk of four distinct fishing seasons in the Top End – there's the wet, the run-off, the dry and the build-up. The run-off between March and April, when the rain eases and the floodplains drift back into the sea, is reckoned to be the best time to catch barramundi, so time your visit carefully and get ready for a battle.

Besides the barra, though, there's still plenty to keep even the greediest fisherman happy. There's the jewfish, cobia, queenfish, giant trevally, red emperor, saratoga, threadfin salmon, golden snapper and, of course, the giant mud crabs. Oh, and if you're unsure about the legal fish sizes, they say in the Northern Territory that if it fits in your Esky, it's probably undersized!

Licences

Following a recent Federal Court ruling, people now wishing to fish in tidal waters overlying Aboriginal land require a licence and a permit from the Northern Land Council. This applies to approximately 80 per cent of the Northern Territory coastline and tidal rivers, and includes popular fishing spots such as parts of the Daly River, Finniss River and Roper River. However, permits are not required to fish in Darwin Harbour. At the time of writing, these permits are issued free of charge but this is expected to change. For up-to-date information call the Northern Land Council on 1800 645 299 or visit www.nlc.org.au.

Further information

Several types of fishing publications are available free of charge from the Department of Regional Development, Primary Industry,

Fisheries and Resources. These include the authoritative *Fish Notes* series of pamphlets, which cover everything from throwing a cast net to catching a barramundi. For more information on recreational fishing matters, contact the Department on (08) 8999 2144. Website: www.nt.gov.au/d/Fisheries

Queensland

Queensland's rich fishing waters are renowned throughout the world – and with good reason. From the teeming waters of remote Cape York and the Gulf country to the well-stocked lakes of the Atherton Tableland and the dams of the southeast, there is virtually no limit to what's available. If you can't stock up your freezer here, then you might as well take up stamp collecting as a hobby instead.

Each year, more than 700,000 fish are caught for recreation in Queensland, with anglers taking home around 8500 tonnes of finfish, crabs and prawns.

Anglers can treat themselves to a variety of fishing challenges, including seeking out the mighty barramundi or the highly prized freshwater Australian bass. Other species, such as coral trout, bream, estuary cod, flathead, kingfish, mangrove jack, mulloway, pearl perch, whiting, tailor, giant trevally and snapper, are also on a lot of line-throwing nomads' wish-lists.

When not out looking to land the big one with rod and reel, many nomads choose to while away their carefree hours in Queensland's temperate climes by laying traps for the state's delicious crab specimens.

Mud crabs that are found along the length of the Queensland coast – inhabiting estuaries, tidal flats and mangrove-fringed areas – can grow to more than 25 centimetres in breadth and specimens have been recorded at over 2.4 kilograms! They're taken in crab pots and dillies, using fish frames as bait. Mud crabs are prized for their eating qualities and are keenly sought after by recreational anglers. Watch out for the pincers, as they're capable of inflicting immense pain and serious injury.

Blue swimmer crabs, which are said to have a more delicate taste than 'Muddies', are best targeted in the warmer months. They grow to about 19 centimetres across the shell and, although they inhabit the whole of the Australian coast, in Queensland they are most commonly caught in the southern half of the state.

Licences

No licence is required to fish in the coastal waters and rivers of Queensland, but you may need a permit to fish in a stocked dam. There are 30 dams in the state for which a stocked impoundment permit is required, so check before you start fishing. Permits cost $7 per week or $35 per year. You are, however, entitled to a ten per cent discount if you have a Queensland Government Seniors Card, Pensioner Concession Card, Health Care Card or Repatriation Health Care Card (Gold Card). One permit covers all 30 dams.

Further information

A free brochure called *Recreational Fishing Rules and Regulations for Queensland* is available. To receive a copy, call the Queensland Department of Primary Industries and Fisheries on 13 25 23 (in Queensland) or (07) 3404 6999.
Website: www.dpi.qld.gov.au/fishweb

South Australia

Fishing in South Australia is quite an experience. Trying to land a feed of the state's iconic King George whiting off the beach is an enjoyable challenge, while chasing yellowbelly and barcoo grunter near Innamincka in the heart of real outback is magical – particularly if you succeed.

Elsewhere, there's plenty to keep the angler occupied, with cuttlefish, garfish, mulloway, snapper, flathead, Australian herring, silver trevally, yellowtail kingfish and samson fish being just a few of the target species. If you're throwing a line in the Murray River, you'll certainly be hoping to pull in a Murray cod or even a trout or two. Then, of course, there are the sand crabs, giant crabs, blue crabs, abalone, southern rock lobster and the easy-to-catch razor fish. These shellfish can be found at low tide poking up out of the sand and can be collected and prised open with a sharp knife. The scallop within can be fried or you may prefer to soak it in vinegar and eat it with a little chilli sauce – many nomads swear by this simple recipe. Alternatively, you may opt to use the scallop as bait to catch a different meal.

Licences
No fishing licence is required in South Australia.

Further information
Obtain the free South Australian *Recreational Fishing Guide* by calling the FISHWATCH hotline on 1800 065 522.
Website: www.pir.sa.gov.au

Tasmania
Tasmania's pristine waterways are a magnet for fishermen of all abilities and ambitions. Between August and May, grey nomads are among the thousands of anglers who fish the small streams, rivers and lakes for the prized brown trout. Despite the popularity of trout fishing, however, a recent survey in Tasmania showed that nearly two-thirds of people

who fished recreationally fished only in salt water. Luckily, the oceans around Tassie are as well stocked as its rivers and streams. Flathead, Australian salmon, pike, trevally, striped trumpeter, morwong, bream, cod, and various reef fish are all popular targets. And that's not all. If you're ready to splash out on a game fishing expedition, Tasmania isn't a bad place to do it. Southern bluefin tuna, yellowfin tuna, stripey tuna and striped marlin are all distinct possibilities.

As with the other states and territories, there are regulations governing minimum legal sizes, bag limits and closed seasons, so check out locally what they are before you cast your line.

Licences

You don't need a licence for marine/sea fishing with a rod and line in Tassie but licences are required when fishing recreationally for abalone (taken by any legal method); doing rock lobster diving; using rock lobster pots, rock lobster rings, gra-ball nets, mullet nets, or beach seine nets; or doing scallop dredging and scallop diving. Licences for these activities are available for $44.80, although Commonwealth Pension Card holders and Seniors Card holders will pay just $25.60.

For inland and freshwater fishing, a special angling licence is required. The full charge is $62.50 for a season, although Senior and Pensioner Card holders need pay only $34.50. Inland fishing licences are available from the Inland Fisheries Service and special marine fishing licences from the Department of Primary Industries and Water.

Further information

Department of Primary Industries and Water
Website: www.dpiw.tas.gov.au
Tel: 1300 368 550

Inland Fisheries Service
Website: www.ifs.tas.gov.au

Victoria

Whether you're into freshwater fishing in Victoria's many rivers and lakes or saltwater fishing along the spectacular and often rugged coastline, the garden state is an angler's paradise.

The most popular inland fishing targets are trout, redfin, golden perch, Murray cod, river blackfish, Australian bass and the Macquarie perch that can only be legally fished from Lake Dartmouth, the Yarra River and the Upper Coliban Reservoir and their tributaries. As usual, certain restrictions relating to bag size, fish size and seasons do apply. For example, between early June and early September, anglers may not take or possess trout or salmon in rivers and streams or in some lakes. Always check local restrictions and regulations.

When they want to take a break from the rod and reel, fishers may also pick up yabbies and spiny freshwater crayfish.

In the ocean, King George whiting, flathead, bream, Australian salmon, flounder, snapper, tailor and silver trevally are the main attractions. You truly are spoilt for choice.

Licences

A recreational fishing licence is required in Victoria. It covers all forms of recreational fishing in all of the state's marine, estuarine and fresh waters.

You are exempt if you're 70 years of age or over, a holder of a Victorian Seniors Card, Veterans' Affairs Pensioner Card, or certain Commonwealth Pensioner Concession Cards. A 28-day licence costs $12; a one-year licence costs $24.50; and a three-year licence costs $66. These are available from the Victorian Department of Primary Industries.

Further information

Websites: VRFish, the Victorian recreational fishing peak body, www.vrfish.com.au

Department of Primary Industries, www.dpi.vic.gov.au

Tel: Department of Primary Industries, 13 61 86

Western Australia

Western Australia is a vast state with a vast coastline, offering an enormous range of exciting fishing opportunities. The west coast attracts about 79 per cent of the state's recreational fishers, some 474,000 anglers a year, who target around 1000 species of estuarine, inshore and demersal marine finfish.

For fishing purposes, the state has effectively been divided into four regions – the west coast, Gascoyne, the south coast and Pilbara/Kimberley. Each area has its own specific fishing rules that were developed to suit its ecology, mix of fish species, and particular fishing pressures.

For an angler, there can be no greater thrill than standing at an awe-inspiring spot such as Eighty Mile Beach in Western Australia's north, pitting your wits against the ocean's myriad fish life. Or, perhaps, fighting barramundi on the River Ord near Kununurra or chasing Australian salmon off the beach in the south.

For those with the inclination, a different dinner awaits every night of your trip. Start off with herring, blue swimmer crabs, skipjack trevally, squid, tailor and dhufish, and then perhaps move on to coral trout, emperors, Australian salmon and golden trevally.

If freshwater fishing is more your thing, both rainbow and brown trout, as well as freshwater cobbler and redfin perch await. The trout season in Western Australia generally runs from 1 September to 30 April the following year.

Licences

You do need a licence for certain types of fishing in Western Australia.

The annual costs are:

Rock lobster licence	$35
Abalone licence	$41
Marron	$24
Freshwater angling	$24
Net fishing	$29

A licence covering all of the types of fishing will cost $81 per year.

A discount of 50 per cent is available if you're receiving an age pension or hold a Seniors Card issued by the Office of Seniors Interests.

Licences are available from the Department of Fisheries.

Further information

Western Australia Department of Fisheries

Website: www.fish.wa.gov.au

Tel: (08) 9482 7333

There are some brilliant publications that show you the best fishing techniques for certain species, the best places to fish for them, and provide a guide to help you identify your catch. These are normally a sound investment, particularly for beginners. Check out the wide choice of fishing-related publications at tackle stores, bookshops and libraries.

> **Tip:** After cleaning your catch, you might want to get rid of your fishy smell before going back into the van. Try rubbing your hands in the juice of half a lemon before washing them with soap and water as usual.

4WDING

For grey nomads travelling in a 4WD, or towing a 4WD behind a motorhome or bus, the lure of the dirt tracks will probably prove irresistible. There's so much of Australia that can only be accessed if you're prepared to get your wheels a little muddy. As you travel and as you gain more confidence and experience, you'll find yourself eager to learn more and to do more.

4WDing is about learning what your vehicle is capable of and – every bit as importantly – what it's not capable of. These vehicles are designed to go over rough tracks and water crossings, so don't be afraid to have a go – just be confident that your insurance policy covers your 4WD and your van (if applicable) for going off-road.

Basically, a 4WD vehicle will give you:

- Better traction when you're driving in mud or sand or when one or more of your wheels leave the ground on bumpy tracks.

- Better ground clearance when travelling on rough or rocky roads or through water.

- Stronger construction so your vehicle won't shake apart on corrugated roads.

The best way to learn how to get the most out of your 4WD is to do a 4WD course or join a 4WD club before you leave. Here you can learn the fundamental techniques and better understand the capabilities of your chosen vehicle.

A course will give you basic skills and teach you things such as:

- How to drive in sandy or muddy conditions.

- How to tackle creek crossings.

- How to recover your bogged vehicle.

- How to cope with steep ascents and deep descents.

- How to use a winch.

Whatever your level of 4WD expertise, you'll quickly accumulate more knowledge once you're out there in the dirt and the dust. There'll be no shortage of fellow travellers willing to talk to you about their experiences. As you walk through the camping areas, keep an eye out for muddy vehicles or vehicles with winches or rugged tyres, then drop by for a chat.

There's been a fair bit of debate in recent years about areas of beach and bush being closed off to 4WDers. While this is happening to some extent because of a growing awareness of the need to protect our environment, it's also partly due to the irresponsible behaviour of some 4WDers. Although no one would say that grey nomads are the worst offenders in this regard, it would be ridiculous to claim that they're totally innocent, either. Grey nomads are now becoming a major presence on the dirt roads of this land and have certain responsibilities.

Try to:

- Stick to marked tracks.

- Don't drive after rain as this will cause rutting when the road dries out.

- Keep it steady. A pothole full of bulldust is as impossible to detect at 60km/h as it is at 100km/h – but the consequences may well be a lot less severe.

- Show courtesy towards other drivers and respect towards the environment.

For more on 4WDing, see Chapter Nine.

Contact information

Australian National Four Wheel Drive Council

This organisation provides information about 4WD training courses, equipment, specialised insurance policies, remote driving advice and lots of other interesting material.

Website: www.anfwdc.asn.au

STARGAZING

The magnificence of the southern sky will never be more vivid than when you're travelling in the outback. For many grey nomads, there comes a time – as they sit there staring up into the twinkling infinity of our universe and beyond – when they want to learn more. Most people can pick out the Southern Cross and Orion's Belt, but the grey nomad is in the perfect position to take things a step further. Even without a telescope – which, incidentally, can be surprisingly inexpensive and easy to transport in the van – there are an awful lot of things to see and learn. There are more than 30 amateur astronomical societies in Australia and these organisations are happy to do what they can to encourage the enthusiastic beginner. They often hold skywatching meetings to discuss astronomical events, and guide members and guests on a tour of the stars and planets. Log on to the Australian Astronomy website (listed below) to find and contact the group closest to you.

There are also more than 30 public observatories, visitor centres or planetariums. In addition to their powerful telescopes, many of these centres offer educational planetarium shows about aspects of the universe.

If you're keen to learn more, another good way to start is to pick up a monthly or yearly guide to the night sky. The *Australian Sky Guide* is published every year and includes a calendar of the sky for the following 12 months. It provides easy calculations for wherever you are in Australia to determine local rise and set times of the sun, moon and the planets, as well as lots of tidal information. The guide is produced by the Sydney Observatory.

Another good guide to the night sky that details monthly astral phenomena and events is *Astronomy Australia – Your Guide to the Night Sky*, produced by Quasar Publishing.

If you're only interested in finding a few highlights to look out for, note that local and regional newspapers often include a special astronomy section alerting readers to rising or visible planets, comets or unusual astronomical phenomena.

So while you may find some magnificent lonely camping spot in the farthest reaches of the remote outback, as you look skywards at night, you'll most certainly realise . . . you are not alone.

Contact information

The Australian Astronomy website is a mine of helpful information for budding amateur astronomers.
Website: www.astronomy.org.au

Publications

Astronomy Australia – Your Guide to the Night Sky, published annually by Quasar Publishing.
Website: www.quasarastronomy.com.au

Free monthly downloads of evening skymaps.
Website: www.skymaps.com

Australian Sky Guide (Sydney Observatory). Check good bookshops or call (02) 9217 0129

BUSHWALKING

The mere mention of the word 'bushwalking' may send shivers down your spine. Maybe it conjures up images of fit young people striking off at an alarming pace with a big stick and an even bigger backpack. Well, forget all that. The fact is that 99.9 per cent of grey nomads – who, after all, are fit enough to take on an extended journey around the country – are more than capable of enjoying some quite stunning bushwalks. Nonetheless, a few rules of commonsense do apply and you should always learn as much as you can about the walk you're planning to take, including the distance and the degree of difficulty. There are many wonderful walks that don't require strenuous climbing or rock hopping or navigation skills.

Most established walking trails in national parks and other tourist attractions are clearly marked and graded on a scale from one to six. The categories are:

1 – Similar to urban footpath with disabled wheelchair access.

2 – Similar to urban footpath suitable for able-bodied walkers.

3 – Typical walking trail suitable for new walkers.

4 – Walking trail for experienced, skilled walkers.

5 – Trails with indistinct marking, requiring navigation skills, advanced bush skills, and self-sufficiency.

6 – Trackless areas requiring walkers to be highly skilled, extremely fit, and totally self-sufficient.

It goes without saying that you should never take on tracks that may be out of your comfort zone. If in doubt, err on the side of caution. It's one thing challenging yourself; it's quite another exposing yourself to genuine danger. The Australian bush should never be underestimated. The temperatures are often extreme and conditions can change quickly. A simple accident can quickly become a tragedy in remote country.

Once you've selected a walk that you think is suited to your levels of fitness and bush skills, let someone know where you're going and when you expect to be back.

Don't forget to:

- Make sure you have plenty of time to complete your walk in daylight.

- Keep to established tracks and trails.

- Carry sufficient food and water.

- Wear sunscreen and a broad-brimmed hat.

- Wear decent walking boots and thick socks.

- Take a first-aid kit.

- If there's the remotest possibility of rain, take some protective clothing.

- Take your time. If you feel the need to rest, then rest.

Bushwalking is a terrific activity that helps to keep you fit and helps you to better understand and appreciate the countryside. Be sensible, be careful and be ready to get out and enjoy it.

BIRDWATCHING

Given the diversity in colour, shape and song of Australian birdlife it comes as no surprise that many grey nomads either extend their birdwatching hobby or begin from scratch. A trip around Australia is just the ticket for a pursuit such as this.

Birdwatching is a relatively cheap pastime that you can do anywhere. It's a means of meeting people and learning more about the natural environment. The best way for a complete novice to start is to purchase a field guide of Australian birds, invest in a pair of binoculars, and contact birding clubs in the areas in which they're travelling. These clubs are dedicated to educating people about wild Australian birds and the environment in which they live.

When you go bush, here are some hints for better birdwatching:

- Take your binoculars and a bird identification book, or field guide.

- Look for birds in the early morning and late afternoon, when they're usually most active.

- If you're in a national park, ask the ranger about the best places for birdwatching.

- Go birdwatching with an expert.

- Be quiet and you'll see more birds.

- Leave your pets behind and you'll see more birds.

- Never feed any birds. Let them find their own food!

Even if you're new to birdwatching, you might still recognise a few of the more striking species immediately. These could include:

The **wedge-tailed eagle**, which is the largest bird of prey in Australia, is a fairly common sight in the outback. You're most likely to see it picking at roadkill on the more remote highways. These birds won't be difficult to recognise, as they're simply huge, with a wingspan of some two metres. As their name suggests, their tails are wedge-shaped.

Black cockatoos are also huge and are difficult to miss in flight. They have black feathers and a distinctive call. They are found in a number of locations across the country and always make for a spectacular sight. You'll also enjoy keeping an eye out for the **rainbow lorikeet**, which is recognised by its blue head, orange breast and green body; the equally brightly coloured **rosella**; and the impressive and startlingly white **sulphur-crested cockatoo**.

One bird that you'll certainly recognise the instant you see it is the **cassowary**, which is found in Far North Queensland, most famously around the grey nomad hotspot of Mission Beach. Although these large birds are normally quite shy, they can also be aggressive and are best left alone. Despite all the warning road signs in cassowary country, you can count yourself especially lucky if you do spot one.

Another feathered Australian icon you won't need your binoculars to spot and identify is the **emu**, which can grow to be some two metres tall and is therefore also best left to its own devices. You may see the flightless bird running through the bush or occasionally knocking around in your camping area.

You've no doubt seen the cute **kookaburra** before but you'll be seeing – and hearing – an awful lot more of it now you're on the road. Be sure to keep a close eye on your snags when you're barbecuing! Although the **kookaburra** is present all around the Australian coast, the blue-winged variety is only found in the north.

Among our more famous long-legged birds is the red-headed **brolga**, which lives in the wetlands of northern Australia. Like the iconic **jabiru**, which has thin orange legs and a black-and-white body, the brolga grows to be about one metre tall.

As you're about to discover for yourself, the diversity and beauty of Australian birdlife is simply staggering.

The more you learn about birds, the more you'll appreciate this hobby.

You can find out more about birdwatching and about the various clubs around the country by contacting the Bird Observers Club of Australia.

Contact information
Bird Observers Club of Australia
Website: www.birdobservers.org.au
Tel: (03) 9877 5342 or 1300 305 342

WILDLIFE SPOTTING

As you camp in national parks, in the bush or even in some of the more natural caravan parks, you'll find yourself coming into close contact with a number of our friendly native wild animals. Okay, so you might not always appreciate a possum creeping around your picnic table in the evening or the presence of an inquisitive and hungry dingo near your camp, but you'll gain an appreciation for them that you could never have got from a book or television documentary. Many grey nomads like to keep a list of the animals they see and perhaps write a little bit about what the creatures looked like and their behaviour. You'd be surprised how quickly such a list and observations can fill up the pages.

Australia's geographic isolation has blessed it with an extraordinary number of creatures that are unique to these shores. Take your binoculars and keep your eyes open.

The more people learn about our native animals, the more determined they tend to become to help protect them for future generations to enjoy.

For that reason, take note of these recommendations:

- Avoid feeding animals.

- Leave the habitat as you found it.

- Don't disturb the animals as they go about their business.

- Make sure your pets are properly secured if you are leaving them alone at camp.

- Don't use detergents in or near natural waterways.

- Store rubbish where animals won't find it.

See Chapter Seven for more details on the wildlife you may encounter.

SWIMMING

A good swim, whether it's in a rock pool, lake, river or the ocean, will be something you'll savour – particularly after a long and dusty drive. Rich treasures await you, as the country has countless truly awesome swimming spots and you'll long remember your dips under cascading waterfalls or perhaps in the warm turquoise waters of the Indian Ocean.

Swimming is fantastic exercise and requires the use of virtually every muscle in the body. It also offers the advantage of not being a high-impact exercise such as jogging.

For all the good points, however, there are certain dangers in swimming in unfamiliar waters and you need to use your commonsense.

Safe swimming

- Don't swim in waters that may be occupied by crocodiles or stingers.

- Always heed warning signs.

- Don't swim alone.

- Be extremely wary of possible rips and strong currents.

- Always swim between the flags, where possible.

- Be careful when swimming in extremely cold water and don't stay in too long.

- Don't dive or jump into murky waters that may be hiding submerged obstacles.

- Don't dive or jump into waters until you've established their depth.

- Don't attempt to swim 'challenging' distances across open water.

WINE TASTING

When travelling in the southern half of the country, many grey nomads take more than a passing interest in the great wine regions of Australia. After years of quaffing liquid from bottles with labels reading 'Hunter Valley', 'Margaret River', or 'Barossa Valley', now could well be the time to take your hobby to the next level and actually visit these places. With nearly 100 different grape varieties, Australia's wine industry has been establishing a formidable reputation in the field and its products are earning respect the world over. For the wine-loving nomad eager to research this area further, a number of pleasant days, weeks, or longer beckon. There's no better way to while away a summer's day than by moving from winery to winery sampling the local tipple and discussing the merits of each label.

There are one or two wine-producing areas in southern Queensland and Tasmania, but most are found in New South Wales, Victoria, South Australia and Western Australia. These regions typically contain dozens of small and not-so-small wineries with tasting facilities established for visitors. Some also offer tours and explanations of how the wines are produced.

Even if you're not crazy about wine, many of Australia's wine-producing regions lie in beautiful countryside dotted with scenic small towns that are well developed for tourism and offer some great places to eat.

If you or your partner fancy a drink and therefore don't fancy driving, check with local tourist information centres about bus tours. Or make friends with that couple in the 22-foot Jayco on Site 16 and see if they may like to check out the wineries with you – in their vehicle, of course!

Websites

The following are a few of the many websites dedicated to providing information about the major wine-producing regions in Australia. Also contact the local tourist information centre in the area you wish to visit.

www.barossa.com

www.margaretriver.com

www.winecountry.com.au

FLORA

Just as the landscape and climatic conditions of Australia are rich in contrasts, so is its flora (as also discussed in Chapter Three). This may be one of the driest continents on earth but it's more than capable of growing some remarkably beautiful plants and flowers. Of course, things have changed greatly in the 200 plus years of white settlement. Vast areas have been cleared for pasture and in some areas native plants have given way to imported varieties, yet there is still much to appreciate and much to marvel at. If your exposure to Australian flora has been restricted to a spot of suburban gardening or an annual stroll through the botanical gardens, a decent book of Australian trees and plants will probably bring you considerable pleasure as you travel.

The wildflowers of Western Australia, which draw nomads by the thousands, are perhaps the most spectacular celebration of our native flora. Up and down the coast, from July to October, you'll see kangaroo paws, banksias, grevilleas, wattles, dampiera, purple peas, native fuchsias, sticky cassia and mountain bells. See the 'Wildflowers' section in Chapter Three for more information.

Every state and territory of Australia has its own unique and equally interesting flora, and each has its own floral emblem. They are:

- Australian Capital Territory – royal bluebell

- New South Wales – waratah

- Northern Territory – Sturt's desert rose

- Queensland – Cooktown orchid

- South Australia – Sturt's desert pea

- Tasmania – Tasmanian blue gum

- Victoria – common heath

- Western Australia – red and green kangaroo paw.

The most celebrated of all our native plants is, of course, our national emblem – the golden wattle – which grows naturally in parts of South Australia, Victoria, New South Wales and the Australian Capital Territory. This small tree can grow up to ten metres tall and, each spring, blooms with fluffy, yellow flower heads.

Equally evocative are the bush's omnipresent eucalypt trees. There are more than 700 species of eucalypt, or gum tree, and they can be found all over the country. Probably the most recognisable of them all is the ghost gum, which is found in central Australia and northern Australia, its startling white bark the inspiration for a thousand songs.

Another highly distinctive tree is the boab, which is found chiefly in the northwest of Western Australia. Although it grows to some 20 metres, the boab has a blobby appearance due to its thick, bottom-heavy trunk. Indeed, there's even a boab near Derby roomy enough to have been famously used as a lockup for disorderlies in the old days. The Prison Tree draws plenty of admirers each year.

You don't have to become a botanist to appreciate the natural beauty of Australia and to understand the significance of its plant life in our development as a country. From the spinifex and the saltbush to the bottlebrush and the legendary coolibah, Australian flora is a huge part of what this country is – and could play an equally huge part of what your trip becomes.

PHOTOGRAPHY

The beauty of your surroundings, and the varied and enjoyable company you'll now be keeping, could well inspire you to take your photography more seriously.

Many grey nomads seize the opportunity offered by their trip to understand truly what makes a good photograph and to capture the wildlife, lakes, rivers, mountains and memories forever. Those who go to the trouble of moving beyond automatic focus mode are sometimes able to produce some quite extraordinary shots. Indeed, the photography of some grey nomads has begun to appear in newspapers and magazines.

One of the dilemmas many older travellers face is whether to update their camera. Even though the film camera you've used for the past 20 years to record the family growing up may still be taking great pictures, this could be time to go digital. Prices keep plummeting and the money you save on developing costs will soon pay for the cost of purchase. It's truly liberating to be able to shoot endless pictures and then simply delete the ones you don't like. Now every echidna sighting, every camp, every campfire and every new companion can be safely snapped and downloaded to the laptop for posterity.

So while the rellies might not yet be champing at the bit to get an invite to your holiday photos evening, they might – just might – be starting to dread it a little less!

Selecting a digital camera

Digital cameras are available in a dizzying array of makes, models, and sizes with heaps of features, options and accessories to choose from. Before you go shopping, try to think about how much you'll use the camera, what you plan to do with the photos you take and what your budget is. Then you can find a model that suits your needs. Before you make a decision, here are a few things to consider.

- *Pixel count* – do you hope to create high-quality prints or enlargements, or perhaps submit your photos to magazines or photography contests? If so, opt for a high pixel-count camera. It'll provide you with high-resolution images and the capacity to produce high-quality photos and enlargements.

- *Batteries* – most digital cameras use AA-sized batteries but because of their many power-hungry features, such as the LCD display, the flash and the zoom, it's easy to go through batteries quickly. If possible, opt for a camera that can use rechargeable batteries and always take a couple of spares along.

- *Flash* – many digital cameras come with an automatic flash function that cannot be turned on or off. If you want control over your flash, ensure the camera you choose enables you to override the automatic settings.

- *Zoom* – the zoom function is often advertised as being 12× or more but this may not be a true reflection of the camera's zoom capability. Ensure you check with the supplier to determine whether the zoom number refers to 'digital zoom' or 'optical zoom'. Digital zoom is actually a magnification of the pixels themselves, not a magnification of the scene you want to photograph.

- *Memory card* – one of the best features of digital cameras is the capability to delete photos you don't want and to store the photos you wish to keep. Investing in a large-capacity removable memory card (at least 256mb) enables you to store more than 200 photos between downloads – a hugely attractive feature for travellers who may not always be in a position to download the contents of their card.

- *Movies* – some digital cameras have a limited moving picture function which enables you to take short movies with your camera and play them back, complete with sound, on a computer. The quality may not be as good as footage taken with a dedicated camcorder, but it certainly can capture the basic feel of a moment.

HISTORY

A journey through Australia is a journey through time. It's impossible not to be caught up in the history of this land as you sit in an outback pub and imagine the characters that have drunk there over the years, as you travel through a small town and wonder at the 19th-century architecture, as you visit the desolate cattle stations and wonder at the men and women who helped build modern Australia.

Aboriginals are believed to have lived in Australia for up to 60,000 years and their population at the time of European settlement is estimated to have been around 300,000.

Their numbers now are much reduced, thanks to European violence and European disease. As you visit Aboriginal settlements, it's difficult not to ponder history and how the arrival of the Europeans has had such an impact on this ancient culture.

Similarly, a visit to Cooktown and to Botany Bay will evoke images of the great British explorer Captain Cook and his mighty *Endeavour*. A visit to the formerly brutal, albeit beautiful, penal colony of Port Arthur in Tasmania will recall the harshness that once characterised Australia. And what of the explorers? What of sailors Bass and Flinders? What of Sturt, Eyre, Leichhardt, Burke and Wills? How can you not marvel at their bravery and fortitude as you visit some of the desolate country they travelled through, dreaming of discovering a great inland sea?

What about a visit to the old Melbourne Gaol, where the infamous bushranger Ned Kelly met his end? And what of the goldrush towns of Ballarat and Bendigo? What of all the agonies and ecstasies experienced by those who dared to look and to dream?

What of the numerous war memorials dotted across the

country and the hundreds and thousands of names of those who fell fighting in the two great wars, Vietnam and elsewhere?

What better way could there be to understand the pastoral history of inland Australia, or the desperation that drove bushrangers to crime, than getting out there and visiting these places? However many books you've read about Australia's past, history will never seem more alive than when you see where it was made.

Contact information

Local libraries and tourist information centres are good places to start researching regional history. They can point you in the right direction to find attractions, too.

Historical Society and heritage websites are also useful for history buffs as they contain details of upcoming events, exhibitions, publications and other interesting information. Check these out at:

ACT	www.canberrahistory.org.au
NSW	www.historycouncilnsw.org.au
NT	www.historicalsocietynt.org.au
QLD	www.queenslandhistory.org.au
SA	www.environment.sa.gov.au/heritage/index.html
TAS	www.thra.org.au
VIC	www.historyvictoria.org.au
WA	www.histwest.org.au

GEOLOGY AND GEOGRAPHY

There's a lot more to Australian geography than knowing the capital cities of all of the states. Many grey nomads choose to use their trip to get to grips with how this land was formed and how it has been shaped by climactic and geological changes. There is now an enormous amount of information available to make this pursuit easier and more enjoyable. National parks often have information sheets and explanatory signs. In the Flinders Ranges, for example, it's fascinating to learn about how geological upheavals formed these remarkable mountains so many million years ago, and even to wander around finding fossils of ancient water-dwelling creatures, remnants from a time when this part of inland Australia was covered by a giant sea.

From the salty expanses of South Australia's Coorong National Park and Lake Eyre, to the tropical lushness of Queensland's far north and the mighty rivers of the east, Australia is a fascinating and surprising geological and geographical treasure box just waiting to be explored.

Did you know?

- The highest temperature ever recorded in Australia was 53°C in Cloncurry, Queensland, in 1889.

- Marble Bar in Western Australia is normally known as the hottest place in the country, thanks to 160 days in a row where the mercury topped 37.5°C.

- The lowest recorded temperature was in Charlotte Pass in New South Wales in 1994, a bone-chilling –23°C.

- The average annual rainfall in Australia is 165 millimetres.

- Australia, covering more than 7.6 million square kilometres, comprises five per cent of the world's land area.

- Australia is the sixth largest country in the world, and is the only one of the top six that is completely surrounded by water.

- The coastline around mainland Australian and its islands measures a total of 59,736 kilometres. (So why does everyone have to turn up in Broome in August?)

- Uluru covers an area of 3.3 square kilometres, and 9.4 kilometres around its base. It rises 345 metres above the plains and extends several kilometres below the surface.

- Australia's highest mountain is Mount Kosciuszko, at 2228 metres. The world's highest mountain, Mount Everest (8848 metres) is almost four times as high.

- Australia is the lowest continent in the world, with an average elevation of only 330 metres.

- Australia's longest river is the Murray–Darling River, measuring an amazing 3750 kilometres.

- Wallaman Falls near Ingham in Queensland is, at 305 metres, Australia's tallest waterfall.

- Apart from Antarctica, Australia is the driest continent in the world, with about 35 per cent of the continent receiving so little rain, it's classified as desert.

- The lowest annual rainfall occurs at Lake Eyre, in South Australia, which has an annual mean precipitation of about 100 millimetres.

- The highest annual rainfall occurs at Tully, in Queensland, with annual mean precipitation of well over 4000 millimetres.

- The dog fence is more than 5000 kilometres long and was built to stop dingoes attacking livestock. It runs from Jimbour in Queensland to the Great Australian Bight in South Australia.

- Australia's largest lake is Lake Eyre in South Australia, which covers 9500 square kilometres.

- The largest land-based national park in the country is Kakadu, which takes up some 20,000 square kilometres of the Northern Territory and is home to a frightening number of the world's fiercest mosquitoes!

- The tallest trees in Australia can be found in the Styx Valley in Tasmania. The *Eucalyptus regnans*, known as the mountain ash, can reach an imposing 96 metres.

- Australia's most remote town is Birdsville, situated between two deserts in far western Queensland.

- South Australia's William Creek on the Oodnadatta Track reputedly has the lowest population of any Australian town.

PLAYING CARDS

A pack of cards offers more than the possibility of a thousand different games. On the 'big lap', a pack of cards offers the possibility of a thousand different friendships. For many grey nomads – even those who haven't played whist or rummy since they were children – cards can quickly become one of the greatest pleasures of an immensely pleasurable trip.

If it's been so long since you've played you've forgotten the rules, there are some useful books on the market, like *Hoyles Rules of Games,* that will soon get you back in the swing of things. Once you've invited one set of fellow travellers over for a game of bridge, you'll find you've started a tradition that will last for as long as you stay in that camping spot. Put simply, cards are a lot of fun.

READING

Never had the time to read *War and Peace*? That excuse is out the window now. Always promised yourself you were going to read the complete works of Shakespeare but the moment was never quite right? Well, it is now.

After years of running around after family and stressing out at work, reading for pleasure is right back on the agenda. Many people on the road choose to use their extra time to rediscover lost loves – reading being chief among them.

You'll be amazed by how many lively conversations you'll have with fellow nomads about the merits or otherwise of this or that author. An active book-swapping scene is happening in the parks, and many small towns and caravan parks will have a book-exchange program. Some local libraries allow visitors to join and borrow books, and cheap books are often on offer at op shops.

BOATING

Taking a tinny along with you can help open up a whole new world. Rivers and waterways can be explored at your leisure and your fish-in-the-freezer count should rise substantially. It's not all plain sailing, however. Lugging a tinny on a roof rack around Australia will add substantially to your already significant fuel costs.

Really, the decision about whether or not to bring a boat depends on how much you think you're going to use it and how much added pleasure you'll get out of it. To some, it would be unthinkable not to get out there chasing the big Top End fish from their boat, while others say that, although it would sometimes be nice to have one, this doesn't justify the overall hassle. If you'd just like to get out on the water occasionally, it may be equally as cheap to hire a boat now and again or to go out on a fishing charter. Who knows, you may also be able to hitch the occasional ride with other travellers. Weigh up the pros and cons carefully.

One note of caution. Water offers both pleasure and peril. You can even count crocodile attacks among the latter, as previously described in Chapter Seven. As you'll be launching in unfamiliar waters, make sure you take the time and trouble to talk to locals about currents, creatures and conditions. Make sure, also, you carry with you all of the relevant safety equipment, including an emergency communication device – better to be safe than sorry.

CYCLING

The subject of bikes has already been touched on. While not as big a commitment as carrying a boat, bikes are certainly not something you want to bring along unless you're going to get some good use out of them. Again, they do have the potential to enrich your travelling experience as you explore national park and state forest trails or perhaps cruise along the beachfront boardwalk – but only if you really ride them! Unfortunately, way too many well-intentioned grey nomads never manage to get their bikes off the bike racks. You can spot the unused, gleaming new machines on caravan-mounted bike racks in camping spots across the country. If you're keen cyclists or want to be keen cyclists, then great, take the bikes along and you'll no doubt enjoy hour upon hour of great exercise, good fun and spectacular scenery. However, if you're unsure, don't fall in love with the idea without testing out the reality. Take a few days to ride around your home before you actually pack the bikes for the trip.

Remember as well that bikes can be targets for thieves, so make sure you keep them securely locked.

JOURNAL WRITING

Keeping a journal of your travels is an absorbing hobby and an effective way to keep a record of your adventure. No matter how well you think you'll remember a particular event or a certain person, the mind does play tricks and the memories do fade. Keeping a journal is a sensible activity that will keep it all alive, so that you'll always know what you were doing on that day exactly six months or a year ago. Journals are also a useful place to record the finances of your trip.

There are no hard and fast rules for keeping a journal. Different people use them for different purposes and in different ways. Some people swear by a laptop, others write longhand. Some people set aside a certain time each day and keep up with their journal religiously, recording all of the people they meet and all of the things that happen. Others just make an entry now and again when something very special or out of the ordinary takes place.

Just remember that however much you write, you'll always wish you'd written more. Your trip won't last forever but – with the help of a journal – the pleasure you get from it will.

9

Drama-free travelling

Safety first

The sheer distance involved is only one of the factors that can turn the reality of a big trip around Australia into something very different from the way it was imagined. Occasionally, living the dream can seem like very hard work indeed. Driving long distances can be quite stressful, particularly if you're not used to towing a caravan or driving a big vehicle such as a motorhome.

There's absolutely no point driving all the way around Australia in two months just to say you've done it. Be realistic. If you've only got two months, don't spend it sitting in the car day after day, week after week. If you want to set yourself a schedule, make sure it's one that allows you time to relax.

Apart from the enjoyment factor, slowing your pace is also a major safety issue. When you're driving on narrow roads, corrugated roads, or wet roads, you must never go at a speed faster than you feel comfortable with, particularly when you're handling a large rig. It's when drivers override their own inbuilt road safety instincts that accidents happen. It's always better to make one extra unplanned overnighter than to risk life and limb.

Most grey nomads have already learned these lessons through a lifetime of driving, and older motorists are considered to be more responsible on the road, a perception borne out by accident statistics.

Age, though, does bring with it a reduction in sensory perceptions, which most definitely affects our driving abilities. Ensure you have regular eyesight check-ups to monitor and correct any deterioration in vision.

Travelling in convoy with friends or as part of a self-drive tour requires extra care. Allow plenty of space between your vehicles so that other road users can overtake you individually if they need to. Also, take special care when turning right in case someone three or four vehicles behind you is seeking to overtake exactly at that moment.

Above all, get into a defensive driver's mindset. On the busy highways surrounding our cities you'll come across anxious, impatient motorists or maybe you'll be tailgated by giant road trains on the Stuart Highway. Your priority is always the safety of yourself and other road users.

General tips for a safe trip:

- Relax.

- Be courteous to other road users.

- Don't drive too close to the vehicle in front.

- Keep your distance from vehicles being driven erratically.

- Plan as much as you can to avoid peak-hour traffic.

- Drive at a speed you're comfortable with.

- Take regular breaks.

TOWING

Just because someone's been driving for the past 30 or 40 years, it doesn't automatically mean they're going to find towing a caravan or camper trailer a 'piece of cake'.

Pulling a van is a particular skill and takes some getting used to. Practise with a few shorter trips before taking your van on the long hauls. Most importantly, as ever, don't drive too fast. Some manufacturers apply restrictions to the speed at which their caravans can be towed. If these are ignored, you may find your insurance and warranty is invalid.

Start by determining whether your rig is set up properly in the first place. Your caravan and towing vehicle should look level when viewed from the side. If the back end of your towing vehicle is sagging, you have too much weight on the towbar and both your braking and steering will be impaired. A weight distribution hitch – which is essential for the bigger vans – can make a massive difference and helps to ensure that all four wheels of your car are taking the weight.

The way you pack your van can also have an important bearing on the way in which it tows. First and foremost, don't overpack. Try to store things as low as possible, too. A lot of nomads say that having their water tanks full when travelling helps to reduce sway and makes for a smoother, less unpredictable ride. This is because the water tanks normally sit low.

Of course, this will add to your van's overall weight and your fuel costs.

Manufacturers recommend that you pack about 60 per cent of the weight in front of the van's axles and about 40 per cent to the rear. If too much weight is in the back, the coupling can lift up and cause problems.

Strong winds or even the air movement of another vehicle passing you can cause even more instability. A vehicle moving in the opposite direction can push you towards the far side of the road while, conversely, an overtaking vehicle can suck you towards the middle of the road. The only thing you can do is to stay alert, try to anticipate problems, and keep a firm grip on the steering wheel.

Towing tips

- *Weight* – ensure you tow within your specified weight limits. As mentioned in Chapter Two, your towing vehicle has a maximum towing capacity; your tow bar has a specified weight limit; and your caravan also has a maximum load limit specified by the manufacturer. Find out what your limits are and stay within them.

- *Packing the load* – pack the caravan so that the heaviest items are low and centred over the caravan's axle.

- Ensure the towing vehicle and caravan are level when hitched up and viewed from the side. Any sagging at the back or front of the van may cause sway and affect steering and braking. If you detect sagging, check tow ball height, tyre pressures on both vehicles and weight distribution. If you still have a problem, you may need specialist advice.

- When you have a caravan or trailer in tow, try to travel more slowly than you would normally. Lower speeds put less stress on you and the vehicle and also save on fuel.

- Towing a van makes acceleration and braking on your vehicle much slower. Leave at least 60 metres' stopping distance between you and the next vehicle – more in bad conditions. The faster you're going and the wetter the conditions, the more road you'll need to stop.

- Make allowances for the extra length of your rig and your reduced acceleration when entering traffic.

- Sudden movements may lead to loss of control. Brakes, accelerator and steering should all be applied gently to ensure a safe and smooth ride.

- *Reversing* – reversing is one of the most important skills you'll use on your trip, as many camping spots require precise manoeuvring. Take your time and enlist the help of your partner to guide you. Hand signals are generally easier for the driver to follow than a command shouted over the noise of an engine. Before you become a full-time grey nomad, practise reversing in a vacant car park, turning the vehicle left to point the caravan or trailer right and turning right to point left.

- *Up hills* – when approaching a hill, and provided it's safe to do so, increase the vehicle speed slightly so as to make it easier to get up the hill. Always select a lower gear if the vehicle speed drops off noticeably.

- *Down hills* – travel at a lower speed and use a low gear travelling down hills. Excessive speeds or sudden braking on a downhill stretch can result in uncontrollable caravan sway.

Never overtake a slower vehicle when going down a steep hill.

- *Overtaking* – overtake other vehicles with extreme caution. Remember that your acceleration is considerably reduced and the greater length of your rig means you must travel further before you can return to the left.

- *Corners* – remember the trailer/caravan when turning corners. The trailer will take a shorter line and you must compensate by steering the vehicle on a wider path.

- *Poor conditions* – be careful when driving in poor conditions or in high winds, as their impacts are magnified when you are towing a caravan. Swaying is more likely in high winds, particularly side winds or when you are passing approaching larger vehicles.

- *Sway* – if your caravan does sway, try to avoid applying the tow vehicle's brakes. If the van has independently controlled brakes fitted, apply them firmly, otherwise accelerate gently or continue steadily until the swaying stops.

Towing courses

There are lots of specialised towing courses available which offer practical tips, techniques and hand-on experience for anyone who wants to sharpen their towing skills. Before you book in, though, check the course contents, whether the provider has accreditation and where and how the courses are conducted.

Check the internet and your local directory to find a course near you.

Types of road

From the jam-packed four-lane-plus highways around our bustling cities to the single-lane goat tracks of the bush, you'll encounter a large variety of roads on your travels. Despite their different challenges, with a little commonsense you can negotiate all of these happily and safely.

The major highways of Australia are increasingly busy places full of in-a-hurry motorists, time-pressured truckies and chilled-out holidaymakers. Consider other road users when you're on the highway, particularly if you're travelling in a caravan convoy with other nomads or if you're travelling at peak times.

Once you get away from the major population centres, the roads will become less busy but normally much narrower. Some so-called main roads are effectively single-lane tracks that require you, or an oncoming vehicle, to pull over to avoid a collision. If the oncoming vehicle happens to be a monstrous road train zig-zagging from side to side, it's probably safest if you're the one to pull over!

None of this is a real problem as long as you're not in a hurry and you're in the right frame of mind. Not only will you be keeping yourself safe, you'll also have the pleasure of receiving a wave of acknowledgement from a happy fellow traveller. What more could you ask for?

On dirt roads, swirling dust can make visibility a real issue, so always drive with your headlights on. And always expect the unexpected. What seems like a good surface one minute can throw up a nasty pothole or a deep patch of bulldust the next.

When you drive on corrugations, you must be especially careful, particularly when towing. Although some argue that driving a little faster helps you to glide over the bumps, speed can also result in a loss of traction and a loss of control. Also, although it's tempting to veer all over an empty road to avoid the worst of the corrugations or the potholes, things can change quickly. Always keep to the left-hand side of the road.

Dirt roads are notoriously tricky to plan for. You may meet someone at a camp who travelled down a given track a few weeks ago and described it as a 'highway'. Then, when you get there, it's a bone-jarring, tooth-loosening disaster zone. It depends on when the last time the grader came through, how much traffic has been across the road, and what the weather has been like. A sprinkling of rain can turn a dirt road into an ice rink in minutes. Then, once the road dries again, it may have turned into a corrugated nightmare. At the risk of repeating ourselves, always take local advice before taking dirt tracks.

The more remote the area you're driving into, the more careful you have to be about the provisions. Ensure that you carry plenty of food and lots of drinking water.

Earlier in the book, we discussed the importance of having an emergency communication device when you travel in remote areas. Bringing along a UHF radio, an HF radio, a distress beacon or a satellite phone may save your life (see Chapter Two for more details). Spare tyres, parts and tools that you should carry are discussed later in this chapter under 'Maintenance'.

Contact information

New South Wales
Website: www.rta.nsw.gov.au/trafficreports
Tel: 13 27 01

Northern Territory
Website: www.ntlis.nt.gov.au/roadreport
Tel: 1800 246 199

Queensland
Website: www.racq.com.au/travel and follow the road conditions
report link.
Tel: 1300 130 595

South Australia
Website: www.transport.sa.gov.au and follow the quick link to
road reports and traffic restrictions.
Tel: 1300 361 033

Tasmania
Tasmanian road reports are contained on various local coun-
cil websites. The Department of Infrastructure, Energy and
Resources (DIER), provides information on road ownership.
Website: www.transport.tas.gov.au
Tel: 1300 135 513

Victoria
Website: www.vicroads.vic.gov.au and follow the link to latest
traffic and road conditions.
Tel: 13 11 70

Western Australia
Website: www.mainroads.wa.gov.au and follow the link to road
and traffic information.
Tel: 1800 013 314

4WD TRACKS

Four-wheel driving is great fun and can enrich your trip but care
must be taken. A few tips for negotiating 4WD tracks safely are:

• Always make sure you have enough food, fuel and water.

- Carry recovery gear – if you don't have a winch, at least bring a snatch strap.

- Take a well-equipped first-aid kit.

- Take spare tyres.

- On many off-road surfaces, it pays to reduce your tyre pressures to increase traction, so bring along an air compressor to pump them up again.

- Always drive with your headlights on as there is often a lot of dust about, making visibility difficult.

- If you're going to do a lot of 4WDing, spend the time and effort to research the most appropriate tyres for your needs. The more rugged tyres can provide that vital extra traction in certain situations.

- Above all else, remember that a 4WD is a vehicle just like any other. It's not invincible and can get bogged, roll, and crash.

Driving techniques

- *Creek crossings*: Always get out and check the depth of creeks and the condition of the bottom before attempting to cross. If you're in any doubt, don't go for it. Spray the electrical components with WD40. If the water's quite deep, wrap the front of the car in a tarp or similar to stop the water flowing around the back of the radiator. Low-range second gear is normally the best option. Enter slowly, keep up a constant speed and don't attempt to change gear.

- *Steep hills*: Try going up in low second. If you lose traction, stop and reverse slowly down and consider trying again. Go down in a low gear and let the engine do the work for you. Try not to brake too much and don't use the clutch.

- *Sand driving*: Lower your tyre pressures to around 16psi, depending on your load. Try to stay in the wheel ruts of previous vehicles, if possible. The secret is to keep the vehicle moving. If you lose traction, don't rev the engine as your wheels will bury. If you do get stuck, rock backwards and forwards, as this can help give you the momentum to 'escape'. You may need to dig your way out.

FATIGUE

When it comes to outback driving, or indeed any long-distance driving, the biggest killer by a long way is fatigue. Many motorists, including grey nomads, try to push on a little bit further than they know they should, in order to get that extra 100 kilometres down the road or to make that better camp. You shouldn't need a doctor to tell you that driving while tired has a serious effect on your decision-making abilities and reflexes, and is extremely dangerous. The consequences of a reduction in concentration, lessened judgement and slower reactions are potentially fatal. When you're travelling, and maybe taking long bushwalks, spending all day outside and receiving lots of sun, you probably need more sleep than you've been used to having. Most people require a good seven or eight hours of sleep a night. Make sure you get it, particularly if you're planning a big day's driving when you wake up.

Beating fatigue

- Plan your trips carefully to make sure you don't have to drive for ridiculously long periods.

- If you are able to, switch drivers regularly and give everyone a chance to enjoy the scenery from the passenger's seat.

- Try to take a break from driving at least every two hours. Get out of the car and walk around to get the blood circulating and loosen up stiff limbs.

- Keep your fluid levels up. It does help.

- Be on the lookout for fatigue danger signs. Excessive yawning, sore or drooping eyes, cramps, aches and pains, loss of concentration and generally erratic driving are all indicators of fatigue. If you experience any of these symptoms, pull off and take a break.

- For all sorts of reasons, try to avoid driving at night. You're certainly more prone to doze off or to suffer from fatigue during your normal sleeping hours.

ROAD TRAINS

Coming across a road train swaying along on a narrow outback road for the first time is an exciting experience . . . but the novelty soon wears off!

They pull as many as three-and-a-half trailers, weigh as much as 146 tonnes, can be up to 55 metres long and are a very intimidating sight indeed. Given their dimensions, it is no surprise that they are very difficult to drive and to control.

A lot of grey nomads have horror stories to tell about a near miss with a road train but, occasionally, the close thing becomes something more . . . a real-life tragedy. Even a sturdy 4WD is going to come off very much second best in a collision with a road train, so show them the respect they deserve.

The cost-effective transport provided by road trains offers an economic lifeline to many small rural communities, and has been doing so for many years. It is important to appreciate the vital role these giant vehicles have in the bush, and to understand properly what a demanding job their drivers have.

Basically, all motorists who see a road train snaking towards them on a narrow or one-lane road would be well advised to pull over and wait for it to pass. Bear in mind that these monsters, and their multitude of wheels, will kick up a cloud of dust on a dirt road that, as well as limiting your vision, could hide all manner of rocks and debris bouncing along towards you.

While it is easy to say that road trains should be more prepared to slow down, you have to remember that it can take some 15 kilometres of road for them to reach their cruising speed – it's no wonder their drivers don't like to reduce speed unless they absolutely have to.

Caravanners, in particular, have to take extra special care when thinking about overtaking trucks or other long vehicles. Not only is the acceleration considerably reduced by the weight of the van, but the extra length means a tremendous distance has to be covered before it's possible to move back into the left-hand lane.

According to the authorities in the Northern Territory, motorists need to be able to see at least one kilometre of clear road ahead in order to be able to overtake a road train safely.

Similarly, you should constantly monitor your rear-view mirror to spot a truck preparing to overtake you. The greater the difference in speed of the two vehicles and the further they are apart while passing, the safer the situation becomes. If you're towing a caravan or a camper, you should apply some power when the other vehicle starts to pass. There's less chance of sway occurring if the caravan is being pulled rather than it pushing onto the car.

If you've got a UHF radio in your vehicle, it's always worth monitoring as it can give you an idea when a truck is heading your way.

Sharing a road with trucks – advice from the Australian Road Train Association

- Keep left – give yourself and oncoming traffic a decent margin for error.

- Keep your distance – tailgating the vehicle in front reduces your chances of stopping in time and doesn't allow the driver in front to see you properly.

- Check your caravan – ensure your vehicle and van are properly prepared. Extend rear-view mirrors so you can see behind.

- Give trucks space – allow extra space at intersections for turning trucks. They can legally use both lanes when turning.

- Don't cut in – trucks need more space when stopping, so don't cut in at lights and roundabouts.

- Indicate your intentions – let other vehicles know what you're doing by always using your indicators when turning, changing lanes or overtaking.

WANDERING WILDLIFE

Because many roads are unfenced, cattle or other animals may wander into your path. Stay alert and keep your speed sensible. If you do come across a herd of cattle, move through it very slowly and the animals will spread to let you pass.

The risk of actually colliding with wildlife is highest at

dusk and dawn. Kangaroos and wallabies are perhaps the most likely animals for you to run into and they can cause a lot of damage to your vehicle and to your health. A bull bar offers a measure of protection but it's best to avoid driving at high-risk times and miss these creatures altogether. If you do drive in the dark, look out for the light reflecting off animals' eyes as this is often the first indication that they're about.

Even though hitting a kangaroo is awful, it's far from the worst thing that can happen. It's not uncommon for grey nomads to run into wild camels on outback roads and the consequences can be severe.

Remember also that other animals and birds often feed on roadkill, so be careful. The eagles on the Stuart Highway may be masters of judging the speed of oncoming traffic but even they sometimes get it wrong – and consequently make big holes in front windscreens.

ROADSIDE ASSISTANCE

Sooner or later, most grey nomads who travel long-term will journey through some pretty remote country with limited facilities and services. Breakdowns in the wilds do occur and, when they do, being armed with a good roadside assistance policy can make a big difference to your wallet and your peace of mind.

Each state and territory has a motoring organisation that offers its own array of roadside assistance policies with its own specific features and pricing structure. However, all states have reciprocal agreements with one another so if you're a member of, for example, the NRMA in New South Wales, you'll receive roadside assistance at a similar level of care from the RACV in Victoria.

In most places, the difference between the most basic cover and the most comprehensive is about $100 or less, and it's definitely worth the upgrade if you're embarking on a long journey. In most areas, the most comprehensive roadside assistance cover tends to include unlimited yearly breakdown callouts, at least 100 kilometres of free towing to authorised repairers in remote areas, accommodation for several days if you have to wait for repairs, a car rental allowance and similar cover for your van or trailer. Yearly costs for this kind of cover range from about $125 to $175.

Contact information
Australia-wide roadside assistance
24-hour emergency roadside assistance in all states and territories:
Tel: 13 11 11

NRMA (New South Wales)
Membership and customer service
Website: www.mynrma.com.au
Tel: 13 11 22

AANT (Northern Territory)
Website: www.aant.com.au
Membership enquiries: (08) 8981 3837

RACQ (Queensland)
Website: www.racq.com.au
For membership, insurance and emergencies, call 13 19 05

RAA (South Australia)
Website: www.raa.net
Membership enquiries: (08) 8202 4600

RACT (Tasmania)
Website: www.ract.com.au
Membership enquiries: 13 27 22

RACV (Victoria)
Website: www.racv.com.au
Membership enquiries: 13 72 28
RACV Total Care – Australia-wide Helpline: 1800 333 300

RAC (Western Australia)
Website: www.rac.com.au
Membership enquiries: 13 17 03

OUTBACK BREAKDOWNS

If you find yourself stranded in a remote area, don't leave the car. A vehicle is far easier for rescuers to find than a disorientated person wandering around in the bush. A car also provides shade and shelter and will probably contain sufficient supplies to see you through your ordeal.

As previously discussed, hopefully you'll have equipped yourself with some sort of emergency communication device, such as HF radio, UHF radio, satellite phone or distress beacon to contact help. If not, you'll have to try to attract the attention of passing vehicles.

In general, don't panic. Try to keep as relaxed and comfortable as possible. If it looks like you may be in for a long wait, ration your supplies of food and water.

Maintenance

CAR OR MOTORHOME

Taking off on a trip for months or years is a big step, particularly for your vehicle. It's going to be expected to perform like it's never performed before, clocking up thousands of kilometres in rough country, day after day after day. As mentioned previously, a troublesome vehicle can break the bank and destroy a trip so it's worth taking a little bit of time to keep it happy.

First, ensure your vehicle is thoroughly inspected and tuned up by a professional before you set off. It may also be worth having a wheel balance and alignment done.

Once on the road, continue to perform regular maintenance tasks and checks on your vehicle (see below for a suggested list). Catching problems early may prevent serious and expensive damage in the future.

The RACV suggests the following maintenance checks at these intervals:

Weekly

- Engine oil level

- Radiator coolant level

- Windscreen washer fluid

- Lights

Monthly

- Tyre pressure

- Automatic transmission fluid level

- Brake and clutch fluid level

- Power steering fluid level

- Brake pedal travel

- Radiator coolant level (for overflow reservoir type)

- Battery electrolyte level

- Wash the car

Six-monthly

If you don't have your car serviced by a local dealer every six months, it's advisable to change the engine oil, the air-cleaner element and the spark plugs and to check a number of other items. These are normally done automatically as part of a dealer's serviced schedule. If you're smart, you won't overlook them.

- Change engine oil

- Change the air-cleaner element

- Check spark plugs

- Check and replace fan belt/drive belts

- Check radiator and heater hoses

- Clean battery terminal and top

- Replace windscreen-wiper blade inserts

Occasionally, grey nomads who've previously been too busy with other aspects of their lives to devote much time to mechanical matters decide they want to learn how to perform a few maintenance tasks and fix a few minor problems themselves when they travel. Many local TAFEs and community education centres offer automotive maintenance and troubleshooting courses that provide participants with some basic knowledge of mechanics. Having the know-how to change the oil and oil filters, lubricate points and install replacement hoses provides a sense of empowerment, as well as the potential to save both time and money.

CARAVAN

If you're towing, don't forget to look after the van as well. A professional should service your caravan before you embark on your journey – and at regular intervals if you're on a long-term trip. The brakes, especially, should be inspected by a specialist. The following are some of the main items to check on a regular basis and then refer to a professional if required:

- Jockey wheel – ensure handle and wheel turn easily and apply lubrication if necessary.

- Wheel bearings – check there's no excessive free play in the wheels and ensure there's sufficient lubrication.

- Safety chain – check for any signs of rust on your safety chain and on all fixing points.

- Water tank and fittings – check hoses for leaks, signs of wear and for any mould growing inside. Also ensure clamps are tight and connections don't leak. Empty and flush out your water tank periodically to maintain the purity of your water supply.

- Van exterior – check regularly for cracks in the aluminium sheets or signs of corrosion in the roof. Check all joints and seals for signs of cracks, holes and water damage – once water has seeped through, things can deteriorate quickly. Also, it's worth giving the van a wash now and again to protect the paintwork.

- Windows – check glass for cracks and ensure seals are free of damage and fit properly, both inside and outside.

- Van interior – check flyscreens are intact; ensure fridge and stove remain firmly fixed, especially after rough roads; check around windows, hatch and corners for signs of water damage. If water appears to be leaking through, address the problem immediately.

- Gas cylinders – check date stamped on the cylinders to ensure they're not out of date. Keep gas bottles and couplings covered as much as possible.

- Gas connections – ensure connections are tight; test by putting a little water and washing up liquid on fittings to see if any bubbles appear.

- Gas regulators – check for signs of rust. Any problems with the regulator or any other elements of your LPG system should be addressed by a qualified person.

- Locks and hinges – ensure van door and cupboard doors are sufficiently lubricated to avoid jamming.

Note that your van manual may contain more specific advice regarding maintenance; please check it for your own manufacturer's recommendations.

Before setting off

There are a number of tasks and checks that must be done every time you set off, whether your stay has been for one night or one month. Many grey nomads find that using a departure checklist helps them to remember everything and to split the jobs with their partner more easily. Develop a routine and keep the list handy.

Departure checklist

- Ensure coupling is securely fastened.

- Check safety chains have been properly connected.

- Check trailer brake and light connections are secure and that all lights work.

- Check gas cylinders have been turned off and are secured.

- Ensure steps have been raised.

- Check TV antenna is in travel position.

- Ensure refrigerator door is closed and locked.

- Ensure cupboard doors have been closed and secured.

- Ensure electrical cords have been disconnected and stored.

- Check roll-out awning is stored away and locked in travel position.

- Remove jockey wheel and store in secure location.

- Check front and rear stabilisers are in the travel position.

- Ensure roof hatches and windows are closed.

- Ensure handbrake of trailer has been released.

- Check that brakes are working.

- Secure van door.

- Remove and store chocks.

- Ensure load is properly secured.

- Take a final walk around the van before departure to confirm nothing has been missed.

TYRES

A set of new tyres on your car, your van or your motorhome can cost you a small fortune. Nevertheless, tyres are a key element to your safety on the road. At 100km/h the average tyre turns around 50,000 times per hour, so its condition can change quickly. It's absolutely vital that you check your tyres regularly, particularly if you're getting off the bitumen.

Terrific tyre tips

- Check your tyre pressure, including the spares, at least every fortnight. Always conduct checks when the tyres are cold. Carry a reliable gauge with you and, if you're going to remote areas, an air compressor.

- Maintain the recommended pressure. Check with your owner's manual to confirm you're using the correct tyre pressure for the load you'll be carrying.

- Check the sidewalls for cuts and damage as these can cause tyres to blow out.

- After each trip, check rims for buckles, cracks or other damage.

- Check the tyre treads for uneven or excessive wear and separation. The minimum legal tread depth is 1.5mm. Uneven tyre wear may indicate a wheel alignment problem.

- Have a regular check that your wheel brace and jack are where you expect them to be and are in good order.

- Dust gets everywhere as you travel, especially when you take dirt or gravel roads. Make sure all of your valves have a dust cap and that they are kept clean and free from dirt.

- Rotate your tyres at least every six months to improve their life span.

- Try to avoid scuffing and hitting kerbs when parking your vehicle.

Spares

On long trips, especially to remote areas, it's always advisable to carry spares, as well as the tools to use and install them. Here's a list of some of the items you might need:

Spares/ Miscellaneous Accessories	Tools
Air compressor	Adjustable wrenches (large and small)
Bulbs for lights	
Fuses	Grease gun
Fan belt	Hammer
Insulating tape	Jack
Puncture repair kit	Pliers
Snatch strap	Rivet gun
Spare inner tubes	Saw
Spare tyres	Screwdrivers
Spark plugs	Set of spanners
Spray can of de-watering fluid	Shovel
Top and bottom radiator hoses and clips	Soldering iron

Tow rope	Spark plug spanner
Trouble lamp and/or torch	Wheel brace and tyre levers
Wire	

Sensible defensive driving, an understanding and awareness of other road users, and a willingness to take regular breaks can dramatically reduce the risk of being involved in a road accident. You'll be spending thousands of hours behind the wheel as you criss-cross the country and so you need to be relaxed and to be sensible. No single incident has more potential to destroy your trip than a moment of carelessness on the road. No desire to reach a certain destination by a certain time or on a certain day can possibly be worth endangering your life and the lives of others.

While breakdowns and punctures are to some extent facts of life, there are steps you can take to minimise the chances of them occurring and, if they do occur, of reducing the negative impact they have on your trip. Plan ahead, carry out regular maintenance checks and drive carefully.

10

Six of the best

Australia – with its rivers, beaches, wildlife, birdlife, mountains, history and its endless outback skies – is a nation like no other. When you add a great camping tradition, friendly people and relative safety to the cocktail of spectacular natural beauty and a wonderful climate, it is no wonder that grey nomads are heading off to 'live the dream' in unprecedented numbers.

There are, of course, as many different types of grey nomads as there are tracks and back roads to explore. No two sets of travellers are on the road for exactly the same time, in exactly the same rig or for exactly the same reason.

Similarly, there is no perfect itinerary that can be applied to every trip. It's not always best to travel from east to west or west to east; it's not always right to stay in more bush camps than caravan parks or more caravan parks than bush camps; and it's not always right or always wrong to travel with your pet. These are individual choices that you must make based on your individual circumstances. Throughout this book we have used the phrases 'must-see' and 'must-visit', but these are just phrases. There are no rules, there are no places you 'have to go' or times you have to be there. Choose an itinerary or route that best suits you and that you think will help you get the most out of your trip.

Every grey nomad and every journey is unique. Below is a brief insight into parts of six unique journeys, and into the grey nomads who undertook them. The routes have been chosen because of their iconic status, not because they are necessarily the most popular or the easiest to travel. They are just six grey nomad adventures out of the millions that have already been undertaken, and the many millions more that are yet to be enjoyed. Hopefully, yours will soon be one of them.

The Nullarbor

Crossing the Nullarbor Plain could be described as a rite of passage for grey nomads. The 1200 kilometre journey between Norseman in Western Australia and Ceduna in South Australia may seem daunting to some . . . but it is one that has to be accomplished before you can lay claim to have completed the 'big lap'.

Nullarbor means 'no tree' in Latin, and this gives a clue to what you can expect as you drive along the surprisingly good bitumen surface of the Eyre Highway. This is a vast, barren plain and – although you may see patches of low scrub and maybe some kangaroos or emus moving around – the landscape is hardly inspiring and the trip can only be described as a long, long haul.

But it is the sheer distance and the sheer emptiness that ironically give the Nullarbor its allure and almost mythical status. As with all great adventures, preparation is key. Make sure your rig is in tip-top shape, you have spare tyres and, crucially, you have plenty of water. You can forget about your mobile phone being used to summon help out there and, while you will see other vehicles, it can be a long wait for them.

Vince and Carol, both in their mid-60s, loved the adventure of crossing the Nullarbor and were fortunate that they didn't run into any problems, such as a flat tyre or a breakdown.

Vince said they weren't nervous about the trip at all, perhaps because they had done their homework and knew exactly what to expect.

'I would just advise people who are planning to cross the Nullarbor to make sure that they are aware of the distance between roadhouses so they don't run out of fuel,' Vince says. 'People should also know that there is a quarantine point and two changes of time zones . . . other than that, it is a really easy trip, it's just another road, really.'

Big trip veterans from Coffs Harbour, Vince and Carol say they just love the freedom of the grey nomad lifestyle but are quick to acknowledge that they do find it hard to be away from their five grandchildren. They also find the occasional long days of driving demanding.

The couple have so far only crossed the Nullarbor once and went from east to west, taking about three and a half days to do so.

'The countryside is much different than we expected it to be,' says Carol. 'We thought it would be completely barren, like a dust bowl, but there is vegetation along the road and the coastal scenery is fantastic.'

Of course, this is the Nullarbor's greatest secret. Too many people whiz along the highway, desperate to get to the other side, going straight past tracks of a kilometre or so that lead down to the spectacular coastline of the Great Australian Bight. Here, massive cliffs of up to 60 metres face the might of the wild southern ocean, and visitors are often lucky enough to see migrating southern right whales.

'We took lots of stops to view the Bight – we probably took every little track to the viewing area that we could,' says Carol. 'It was absolutely spectacular and, although there were no whales, the scenery was fantastic and we took lots of photos.'

For people who are keen to really understand the natural history of the coastline, it is possible to organise a visit to the Nullarbor's remote and not-easily-accessible Eyre Bird Observatory.

Vince and Carol travel in a small pop-top caravan and prefer camping in the bush to caravan parks, although sometimes they succumb to the need for a shower and a bit of luxury.

'We love the social side of travelling in a van,' says Carol. 'When you're sitting outside, people come up to you and ask where you're going and where you've been; whereas if you stay in hotels, you just close the door and never speak to anyone.'

However, the couple spent their first night on the Nullarbor camping at the Nullarbor Roadhouse, mainly because they wanted to see what it was like to stay at a roadhouse.

'The sunset was spectacular, the moon was beautiful and there were rabbits everywhere,' says Carol. 'But because roadhouses have to generate their own power, people should try to identify where the generator is so they can choose a camping spot away from it . . . although the generator powers down a bit at night, we were still aware of the noise.'

While Nullarbor roadhouses are generally more famed for their expensive fuel prices than their aesthetic appeal – some can look pretty unkempt in fact – they can be interesting places nonetheless. At the Balladonia Roadhouse, for example, there is a collection of memorabilia from Skylab on display. In July 1979, pieces of the space station landed there, putting Balladonia well and truly on the international map. From the Eucla Roadhouse, about 500 kilometres west of Ceduna, you can strike off to visit the nearby ruins of the old Telegraph Repeater and Weather Station, and from the Nullarbor Road-house you can head out to explore some of the region's caves, including the famed Koonalda Cave.

On the second night of their Nullarbor odyssey, Vince and Carol stayed at a bush camp about one kilometre off the highway.

'It was an established camp with rubbish bins around but we went further in than most people probably would, so we couldn't see or hear the road,' says Vince. 'No one else was camped nearby although we did hear a truck and a caravan pull in quite late but they left very early the next morning so we didn't even see them.'

On their last night on the Nullarbor, the couple stayed at the Fraser Range Station about 100 kilometres east of Norseman.

'We wanted to see what it would be like to stay at a station,' says Carol. 'It was very well set out with cabins and every-thing, and it looked like someone had spent a lot of time and money to make it nice . . . but it was expensive.'

And the next morning, it was all over. Vince and Carol arrived in Norseman, ending a memorable leg of an unforget-table trip around the country.

'I have to say that crossing the Nullarbor wasn't boring at all . . . I loved it,' Carol says. 'It's something we have always wanted to do although, I suppose, ultimately, the most memorable thing about the journey was the achievement of actually doing it.'

The Savannah Way

The Savannah Way stretches some 3700 kilometres from Cairns in tropical North Queensland across the Northern Territory to the grey nomad mecca of Broome in Western Australia.

It's a massive drive that takes you through spectacular national parks, sprawling outback cattle stations and historic gold mining towns. And it's a journey that will teach you much about our country's rugged geography and pioneering history.

It's an adventure that you will never forget . . . and one that you don't have to tackle in its entirety to appreciate. While some of the route is 4WD only, there are large sections that are suitable for just about any vehicle, including caravans. Many grey nomads simply travel bits and pieces of the road, some preferring to just stick to the blacktop while others are game to take on the dirt sections and some adventuresome water crossings.

Peter and Margaret, who retired in the middle of 2005 and have been travelling around Australia in their motorhome for eight months a year ever since, fall into the latter category.

'We usually travel alone, but sometimes team up with others we meet along the way for short spells or if we're venturing into extremely remote country,' says Peter. 'We bush camp wherever possible and only use conventional caravan parks as a last resort.'

The couple estimates they travel about 20,000 to 30,000 kilometres per year, mostly in more remote off-bitumen areas. After buying their OKA motorhome in 2003 as a worn-out 1994 ex-tour bus, they had the mechanicals reconstructed and then built the camper themselves, setting it up so they can be totally self-sufficient in the bush for at least four weeks. The vehicle has solar power, a shower and toilet, a 240v power inverter, and it carries up to 280 litres of water and 280 litres of diesel.

The decision to take on the Savannah Way's sometimes challenging Gulf of Carpentaria section was an easy one for this adventure-seeking couple. In early April – the very start of the season – they travelled up from Mount Isa via Lawn Hill and Kingfisher Camp to join the Savannah Way at Doomadgee. The dirt road had not been graded since the wet so they knew they were going to face some challenging conditions.

'Later in the year it would probably be generally better,' says Peter. 'But maybe more corrugated, depending on traffic.'

Peter and Margaret try to travel at times when there are not too many people about and they found the camping area at Kings Ash Bay very crowded as it is primarily a fishing camp. They left after one night and, following some stony river crossings, found complete solitude at the Calvert River campsite where they even managed to catch a couple of Sooty Grunters on lures.

However, trouble was around the corner. The down side to travelling early in the season became painfully apparent when they found muddy conditions north of Borroloola had forced official closure of the road. The barrier across the road warned them that they faced a fine if they tried to continue. Nonetheless, thanks to a little bit of satellite phone negotiation over a four-hour period, Peter and Margaret were eventually given the all-clear from the Roads Department to proceed as far as Lorella Springs station.

Once they reached the station however, it was obvious that the road conditions meant it was impossible for them to proceed – they were stuck! Happily, the couple found that if you are going to get stranded, it was not a bad place to do it.

A lot of effort is being put into setting up the station to appeal to travellers, and Peter and Margaret enjoyed spending time in the thermal pool, the waterholes and the hammocks. They stayed two weeks and were lucky enough to be able to do so free of charge in exchange for doing a variety of maintenance tasks around the place. They found themselves cleaning toilets, putting in a paved pathway, splitting rocks – and loving every moment of it. Back in the real world before retirement, Peter was a manufacturing engineer in the plastics industry and Margaret was in the childcare industry. They have since proved themselves highly adaptable and more than ready to turn their hands to anything. In the past two years, they have carried out volunteer work on cattle stations, in national parks and at the Kalumburu Mission in the Kimberley.

'So far we have not worked for wages since retirement, but expect that we might need to,' says Peter. 'We will do that rather than "constrain" our travels.'

Despite being nearly permanently on the road, Peter and Margaret have kept their house in Adelaide and return annually to spend Christmas there and to catch up with friends and family, especially their three grandchildren. On the road, the couple love to fly kites, fish, bushwalk, take photos and they have now started to write as well. It's little wonder they have fallen so deeply in love with the grey nomad lifestyle.

'There are no deadlines, no time constraints and no plans

that can't change,' Peter smiles. 'We like to grab every opportunity for a new experience or to get to know the locals.'

That was something they were certainly able to do during their prolonged stay at Loretta Springs. When the road north finally opened, the couple said their farewells at the station and travelled on to the tall sandstone columns at the Southern Lost City in Linmen National Park, and then to camp at the wonderful Butterfly Springs.

Peter and Margaret describe the Savannah Way as one highlight after another. Tiny historical townships, cattle stations, gorges, natural springs and waterholes, roadside campsites, fishing hot spots and spectacular national parks. It's all there and it's obvious that the couple will never forget their adventures on the track.

But if you ask them about their favourite places in Australia so far, they are not so sure.

'We keep going back to the Kimberley, but we also love the Pilbara and the deserts, Tasmania . . . all of it,' says Peter. 'But it's a big country, and we have lots to discover yet.' And what about the east coast? 'We avoid it,' says Peter firmly. 'There are too many "No camping" signs and too many grey nomads . . . even if we do like a lot of them!'

Great Ocean Road

The Great Ocean Road in Victoria is one of the most spectacular and famous coastal routes in the world. Little wonder then that the 300-kilometre or so drive between Torquay and Allansford near Warrnambool is one of the highlights of any grey nomad's 'big lap'.

The road itself is in fact a memorial to those Australians who died fighting in the First World War. Along its route, and in the towns it passes through, are numerous memorials to those killed in action. The Great Ocean Road snakes alongside a series of magnificent beaches, through the rainforest of Cape Otway, and then twists and turns along the entire length of the Port Campbell National Park. As it does so, it takes you past some amazing rock sculptures including the iconic 'Twelve Apostles' and 'London Bridge'.

The Twelve Apostles rock stacks were formed by the gradual erosion of softer limestone areas, creating caves in the cliffs. These caves eventually wore away through wind and wave erosion to become arches and, when they collapsed, rock islands were left detached. The cliffs rise to nearly 70 metres in some places and the highest Apostle is approximately 50 metres from base to tip.

While the length of the Great Ocean Road could easily be navigated in a day, there are numerous places to stop and camp, and to rush through this incredible part of the world would be a terrible mistake.

Helen, a 64-year-old retiree who has been travelling since the middle of 2007, was determined to enjoy all there was to enjoy along the route.

Driving a Nissan Xtrail and towing a Coromal Pioneer Compac nicknamed 'The Tortoise', Helen took the advice of some fellow travellers to drive from west to east.

'I presume this was to prevent vertigo while on the ocean side!' she says. 'I found the road easier than I expected, but was pleased that my van was only 13 feet long . . . maybe someone with a much larger van has a different story to tell.'

Helen has friends in Warrnambool and spent a week there, staying in a small central caravan park within easy walking distance of the city.

'I could have spent more time exploring this very historic

and fascinating area,' she says. 'I then travelled to Cape Otway in one day with brief stops in Peterborough and Port Campbell and much longer stops at the spectacular natural wonders along the way.'

She says all of the attractions are clearly signposted and boast good parking areas.

'No matter how many times I see these cliffs and rocks, I am always in awe,' she says. 'I had hoped to stay at Johanna but there was no one else around and the flies were really prolific so I then spent a week at Bimbi Park, surrounded by – but not in – Cape Otway National Park.'

As a woman travelling alone, Helen has some pretty clear rules about where she stays.

'I am fussy about where I camp if not in a park and, if it feels uncomfortable or there are no other campers, I will move on,' she says. 'People often suggest I have a dog for security and company but I like to stay in national parks so it is not an option.'

Helen travels with an 80W solar panel and a 150W converter so she is quite self-sufficient and able to free camp a lot. In terms of communication, she has a mobile phone, a laptop computer with a wireless modem and a UHF radio.

'I feel that as I travel on my own, commonsense and an ability to call for help if needed is wise,' she says. 'The UHF also helps in outback Queensland and elsewhere, to communicate with road trains or fellow travellers.'

Helen, who recently became a grandmother, says being a grey nomad has opened up her life to a range of experiences she would not otherwise have had.

'The freedom of time to do what one wants, to stay months in an area if it is appealing, or move on, is liberating,' she says. 'Meeting a huge range of interesting people is one of the best things about travelling as we all have the common goal of really getting to know our country.'

Helen's stay at Bimbi Park illustrates the point perfectly. While there, she says she met several couples with whom she became good friends and they helped to make her stay there an enjoyable one. So too did the koalas which were abundant in the trees around the caravans.

'It was intriguing to watch their day-to-day lifestyle up close,' Helen says. 'And the walks from the park were really enjoyable, including to the lighthouse and to the beaches, which are stunning.'

Helen also enjoyed visiting the pleasant towns of Apollo Bay, Lorne and Anglesea.

'Having been along the Great Ocean Road several times, I was feeling apprehensive when I first decided to tackle it with the van,' Helen admits. 'The only section that I didn't like was near Lorne where the rock face is on the edge of the road and it is hard to give it a wide berth.'

Of course, it is hard for anybody when things go wrong, but when you are travelling alone it is that little bit worse. Helen is philosophical though and accepts that, from time to time, little dramas will crop up.

'One time, I wrecked my clutch trying to back the van up a steep gravel road when there was no alternative after taking a wrong turn in a national park,' she recalls. 'It seemed horrendous at the time, but all ended well. I have learned if things go wrong, to stop, make a cup of tea, sit down and assess the situation before taking any action.'

Leaving the Great Ocean Road behind her, Helen knows there are still many, many wonderful places left for her to visit. She has sold or given away most of her worldly possessions and knows she has all the time in the world to explore.

'I love outback areas and red soil plains,' she says. 'And I have enjoyed the Yarra Valley in winter and spent months along the Murray, and now I am looking forward to exploring the south of Western Australia again . . . I fall in love with new places all the time.'

Helen always intended to find odd bits of work along the way but this hasn't happened as yet. Nonetheless, she is a keen quilter and hopes that once she has produced enough stock she can try selling at local markets. As well as quilting, Helen keeps busy by reading a great deal and walking every day. She also hopes to rekindle her passion for painting and to keep a visual diary of her adventures.

And when she does so, no doubt the wonders of the Great Ocean Road will feature strongly in some of her work.

'I would love to drive it again with more time to stop and spend time walking and exploring,' she says. 'I would definitely return to Cape Otway and walk the beaches and trails again.'

And her advice for those following on behind?

'Take it slowly and enjoy what the Great Ocean Road has to offer,' she says. 'Check with an information centre about all the things there are to do and don't travel too far each day.'

The Gibb River Road

The Gibb River Road is one of the most iconic tracks in Australia. Stretching for 700 kilometres or so, it connects Western Australia's remote Kimberley cattle stations to the towns of Derby and Kununurra.

Fortunately for grey nomads and other adventurers, it also offers access to some incredible scenery including Bell Gorge, Windjana Gorge and Tunnel Creek. If waterfalls and gorges are your thing, then this drive is for you.

The Gibb River Road is still basically a red earth track which is only really suitable for 4WD vehicles due to the high clearance sometimes required. Although caravans are not recommended here, you may see some travellers prepared to haul their van over the corrugations and through the dust. Some are even game to take their vans up the Kalumburu Road, on to the Mitchell Plateau and even to the Aboriginal outpost and fishing hotspot of Kalumburu itself. However, even the bravest leave the van at Prince Edward Falls camping area if they choose to take a side trip along the extremely rough 83-kilometre track that leads to the spectacular Mitchell Falls. Despite its fearsome reputation in some quarters, the Gibb River Road is not as rough as it used to be and some parts of the western section of the road are even sealed, while a few bridges and creek crossings have been reinforced with concrete.

The improvements have helped to encourage a steady stream of 4WDs and campervans along the dusty track in the season. In fact, the campgrounds fill up quickly, so you need to arrive early in the day if you want a nice spot. It's still no picnic though and the Gibb River Road is really only traversable between May and October.

If the track is an experience now, it could probably be described as a wild adventure when inveterate travellers Bridget and David took it on back in 1980. The couple from Port Pirie in South Australia have been travelling in fits and starts for most of their lives and say they have no intentions of ever stopping.

In those days, they travelled in a 1975 Nissan that would die on hill climbs due to a fuel filter blockage.

'There was no support back then so there was a real feeling of achievement when we did it,' says David. 'We had some unforgettable experiences and I still remember crossing a river and seeing a big old croc watching us at eye level, not 30 feet away!'

David and Bridget, who now travel in a Toyota HiAce long wheel base, soon to be a Mazda T4600 motorhome, admit they were fortunate to suffer no breakdowns or punctures on their trip.

'We were certainly lucky as we were the only people up there at the time,' says David. 'Looking back I would say that the whole experience exceeded our wildest dreams . . . the nights and the sounds and sights were unbelievable.'

While the sounds and sights are still unbelievable, you would certainly be very lucky now to have a Gibb River Road campsite to yourselves as David and Bridget were able to. Rural myth has it that some 350 people a night have been known to camp in places like Manning Gorge in peak season. Strange as it may seem for a road with such a wild and woolly reputation, the Gibb River Road is, to some extent, now becoming a victim if its own success. The surprisingly high volume of traffic on the road in peak periods is a testament both to the incredible beauty of the country through which it passes and the increasingly adventurous nature of grey nomads.

There is little doubt that the best time to take on the Gibb River Road in terms of climate is June or July but this can also mean clashing with school holidays and therefore running into more traffic and the flow-on problems of rougher roads and fuller camping sites.

If you travel a little earlier in the season you are likely to find the water crossings deeper, and you are also running the risk of finding some areas inaccessible. However, if you wait until later in the year, you may find the temperatures unbearably hot.

It's a dilemma, but certainly not one that should deter you from taking this trip. Some grey nomads choose to compromise. They reason that as most of the 'must-see' attractions like Bell Gorge, Tunnel Creek and Windjana Gorge are at the southern end, there is no real point in travelling the entire track. Instead, they drive along the bitumen on the Great Northern Highway, perhaps taking in the Bungle Bungles and Geikie Gorge and duck in from the southern end to get a taste of the Gibb River Road and to see the most iconic locations it offers.

Certainly, Bell Gorge is genuinely spectacular and should not be missed whether or not you are taking on the whole of the Gibb River Road. Most grey nomads camp at the Silent Grove campground which is a short drive from the gorge itself. The walk from the carpark is well worth the effort. There are no crocs here and you are free to swim in the rock pools and shower beneath the waterfalls. Yes, this is what being a grey nomad is all about!

Windjana Gorge is dark and imposing and in some ways resembles the set of a *Lord of the Rings* movie. It's famed for the sheer volume of freshwater crocodiles that can be seen sunning themselves on the banks or swimming in the water. They may not see you as 'dinner' in the same way as their saltwater cousins do, but it's still probably wise not to get too close. Tunnel Creek is not for the faint-hearted. But it's excellent fun. Take a torch and walk 750 metres through a dark cave, sometimes through waist-deep water, until it opens out again at the other end. It's eerie and interesting – as long as you don't run into some young buffoon trying to make crocodile splashing impersonations as you make your way through the gloom.

It's no wonder that David and Bridget, who both love photography and bushwalking, describe their Gibb River Road experience as 'simply unforgettable'.

And yet, incredibly, these fun-loving grandparents say they will never take the track again.

'It would only cheapen the memory of the first time,' explains David. 'I will always remember free camping all the way, alongside rivers and under amazing gum trees ... the scenery was absolutely breathtaking in parts and desperately desolate in others.'

This cheerful couple say the best thing about being grey nomads is the freedom from responsibilities and the worst, unsurprisingly, as being away from family. There is still much of this magnificent country they have yet to explore and experience ... but they're working on it!

For those following in their wheel tracks along the Gibb River Road, David has some sound advice.

'Preparation is the key, so get as much information as you can and take plenty of spares,' he says. 'And make sure you have enough time so that you don't need to rush it ... just enjoy the experience.'

The Stuart Highway

The Stuart Highway stretches for more than 3000 kilometres through the spine of Australia, from Port Augusta in the south to Darwin in the north.

The road, which has been fully sealed since the mid-1980s, is named after explorer John McDouall Stuart and largely follows his route through some magnificent yet desolate country.

It's pretty much a must-do for grey nomads and, fortunately, offers plenty of interest and excitement along the way, although the sheer distances involved should not be underestimated.

There are numerous roadhouses, caravan parks, camping spots and natural attractions to enjoy, not to mention a few interesting little towns.

Chief among these would have to be the South Australian opal mining capital of Coober Pedy. Many of the town's residents famously live underground in 'dugouts'. You can even camp underground during your stay there, although caravans have to stay on the surface.

'It was an amazing place to visit and a unique experience,' says Susan, a 61-year-old grandmother who travels with her husband Gerry in a compact motorhome. 'We met some incredible characters and it gave us a real insight into just how many genuinely different Australias there are.'

The Sydney-based couple spent a year doing their 'big lap', and are already planning another major trip.

'In many ways, that journey up the Stuart Highway was a real eye-opener for us,' says Susan. 'There was just no escaping the sheer, unrelenting vastness of the country . . . we found it fascinating.'

Like most grey nomads, Susan and Gerry took their time heading north, enjoying detours to, among other places, Uluru, Kata Tjuti, Katherine Gorge, the Macdonnell Ranges and Litchfield National Park.

'Yes, it's a long way and there's a lot of driving but you just have to be prepared for that,' says Susan. 'What I liked is that we ended up in a bit of a loose grey nomad convoy where we would meet up with the same people – almost by accident – at camp after camp.'

Susan and Gerry just pulled in at roadside stops to camp for the night on a couple of occasions and always found at least three or four other vehicles were doing the same.

'I wasn't sure how I'd feel about doing that before we set off but I have to say that I loved it,' said Susan. 'To me, it added to the sense of adventure and . . . I know there will be plenty of genuine grey nomad adventurers who'll laugh at this . . . it made me feel a bit like a pioneer!'

At popular camping areas like the famous Devils Marbles, the couple was amazed by the numbers of campers who mysteriously appeared from seemingly empty roads.

Gerry does all of the driving when the couple are on the road and he says he had to be disciplined about making himself take a break.

'Of course, it's tempting just to get as many kilometres as you can under your belt at a sitting,' he said. 'But I think that is missing out on the point to some extent. Sometimes you've got to stop just to truly experience the vastness, and the emptiness of the outback.'

While the Stuart Highway can seem quite lonely, the bitumen road surface is good and it is also wide enough for vehicles to pass each other comfortably, although it always pays to be careful when a road train is coming at you from the opposite direction. The fact that on some stretches you see relatively few vehicles, as Susan describes, adds to the sense of adventure. You'll find that most fellow travellers will give you a cheery wave as they pass.

There are roadhouses at regular intervals – normally around every 200 kilometres or so – and there are more frequent rest stops, generally just a picnic table and a rubbish bin in what can seem like the middle of nowhere.

So how did Susan and Gerry pass the long hours on the road? 'Well, we talked about the grandchildren a lot,' laughs Susan. 'And we played a game where we tried to guess how many minutes it would be until we saw the next vehicle . . . and we can't even say we did it to amuse the grandchildren!'

In between this fun and frivolity, the couple found time to relax and to enjoy some of Australia's most iconic locations, such as Uluru and Katherine Gorge. They also fell in love with the Macdonnell Ranges both to the east and west, and spent four nights at Ellery Creek Big Hole where they took numerous refreshing dips in the chilly waters.

Perhaps surprisingly, they pick out Mataranka Hot Springs – where the water is much, much warmer – as their favourite spot on the long trek north. Apart from chilling out in the famed hot pools, Susan and Gerry looked forward to the live entertainment put on at the 'resort' every evening.

'We just had the most amazing time there and met so many fantastic people to share our evenings with,' smiles Susan. 'Okay, so maybe it wasn't the purist grey nomad experience, whatever that is, and we probably spent a few more dollars than we planned to . . . but we certainly had some laughs.'

And that probably sums it up best. There is no set itinerary on a journey up or down the Stuart Highway or indeed on any grey nomad adventure. It is a trip that different people choose to enjoy in different ways. Some adventurous grey nomads like to veer off to take on parts of the Oodnadatta Track, or to go fossicking in the Harts Range, but that doesn't mean everyone has to. The most important thing is to try to decide what you want to do and where you want to go, but still try to stay flexible.

When all is said and done, when you travel the Stuart Highway, you are following in the footsteps of some incredible explorers on an epic adventure. This is an iconic journey across a continent. It's not something that should be rushed.

'I think we did feel a real sense of achievement as we saw the signposts showing the number of kilometres to Darwin drop from the thousands of kilometres into the hundreds and then into the tens,' says Susan. 'We certainly noticed it getting a lot warmer and a lot lusher as we closed in on Darwin . . . but it didn't feel like the end of a journey . . . just the start of another one.'

Cape York

Cape York is perhaps the ultimate Australian adventure destination for grey nomads – or anyone else for that matter.

The dusty, corrugated, dirt track that takes travellers north is the stuff of legend. It is not a trip to be taken lightly or to tackle without proper preparations. As well as crocs, creek crossings and camaraderie, the adventure promises sensational secluded beaches, unbelievable fishing spots and memories to last a lifetime.

Cape York is a 'big lap' experience like no other. The journey from Cairns to the tip is approximately 1000 kilometres, but the going can be slow. The vast majority of the Cape York Development Road is unsealed, although some short sections of bitumen are now being built. They can be a welcome sight after hours of bone-shuddering corrugations.

Be aware that the most dramatic creek crossings such as the infamous Gunshot are not compulsory. There are corrugated bypasses available, although most vehicles choose to travel at least some of the way on the iconic Telegraph Track.

Retired couple Trevor and Carol from Canberra were among them, but they soon found themselves horrified by the rigorous nature of the trip.

'The most memorable thing about this trip is the unbelievable corrugations, constant, with no relief for hundreds of kilometres,' says Trevor. 'It was bone breaking . . . tedious, yet I guess fun.'

He urges fellow grey nomads heading to the extreme north to carry ample supplies of food, water and fuel, and to carry basic spare parts.

'You are a long way from any road service depots but the road is relatively busy and usually someone will be able to help you with basic repairs if you have the tools and parts,' he says. 'Make sure you are physically and mentally up for the challenge, make sure your vehicle is up to the challenge; the number of roadside wrecks amazed me, just too far from civilisation to even bother recovering the wrecks.'

While purpose-built off-road campers and caravans can get all the way up to Seisia, most grey nomads – like Trevor and Carol – choose to drop their van off at a caravan park somewhere and head north with just a 4WD and a tent.

'We stayed at a few parks but usually around 3pm we found some others camped roadside and pitched the tent there,' says Trevor. 'The best thing about Cape York was probably the sheer adventure involved but I would never, ever, go back again unless we fly there or go by sea!'

In the end, the corrugations proved too much for the couple to bear and they turned southward again three-quarters of the way to the tip.

'We didn't get all the way but our trip was still relatively event free with no breakdowns or even punctures,' says Trevor. 'However, we did stop to render assistance on several occasions to others less fortunate.'

He recommends that grey nomads travel in convoy with another vehicle because, in the worst-case scenario, someone can then get help. Trevor warns there is no mobile phone coverage to speak of apart from close to 'towns' such as Weipa, Coen and Bamaga, and says hiring a distress beacon is therefore a good option to ensure you can get help, if required, fairly quickly.

Grandparents Trevor and Carol have been travelling extensively for the past decade and say Cape York hasn't been their favourite place so far.

'Actually we enjoyed our trip to the southern most point of Australia – the southeast cape in Tasmania – much more,' says Trevor. 'It has a different climate, rugged beauty, wild weather and is a damn sight easier to get to . . . and fewer people seem to want to go there!'

But still, there's something about the Cape. Retired couple Mike and Carol from Sydney, who now travel for around five months of every year, are among the many who have succumbed to its magnetism.

It was a natural fit with their on-road philosophy. 'We love the bush,' they say. 'And we love the red dust of the outback, and we love learning about our fantastic country.'

Amazingly, however, their trip to the tip a couple of years ago was their first major adventure in their then-new Bushtracker off-road caravan: a baptism of fire that they will never forget.

They travelled in a loose convoy of other off-road caravanners and, inevitably, there were a few technical problems along the way.

It started early on, when one of their friends announced over the UHF radio that the pin connecting his caravan to his car had broken and he had lost the caravan. It meant the whole group had to stay at the Kalpowar Crossing camping area for four days to wait for a spare part – a fate that wasn't actually too bad.

'Exploring the area, eating fresh barramundi caught in the river, watching the many different birds, kangaroos next to the caravans, green frogs in the bathroom, cane toads, bright stars and the space shuttle go over at night, filled in the time,' says Carol. 'And we cooked our first meal in the Dutch oven buried in the coals . . . we had lots of time to sit around the campfire and wait.'

Between them, the members of the convoy were to suffer a series of other minor problems such as punctures, suspension issues and electrical glitches, but they were all determined it wouldn't affect their enjoyment of the trip; rather, it would add to the sense of adventure. The caravan convoy even took on part of the Old Telegraph Road as they headed north.

'We were told that there was only one section that may be a little difficult so we decided to try it with the plan of turning back if it was too hard,' says Carol. 'The difficult spot was the Cockatoo Creek crossing. We looked at it, I walked the river to see the depth of the potholes and then we decided that it was safe to do. It was nerve-racking and exciting all at once. Mike drove across while I took pictures and helped direct him on the hand-held UHF.'

While the exciting creek crossings are among the most memorable moments for many Cape York travellers, there is no shortage of other highlights. Eliot Falls, Fruit Bat Falls, Captain Billy's Landing, Seisia itself, the list goes on and on. Summing up, the Cape York Peninsula offers a genuine insight into indigenous history and remote communities, as well as exposure to bona fide bush characters . . . but it's certainly not for the faint-hearted.

Index

Travel notes

Above: Eliot Falls offers a welcome respite from the dust and corrugations of a Cape York drive.

The scenery of the Flinders Ranges has inspired thousands of artists . . . and grey nomads!

Eighty Mile Beach in northern Western Australia is a top spot to catch supper.

The rugged coastline of the Kalbarri region in Western Australia.

Crossing the Pentecost River on the way along the Gibb River Road adds to the sense of adventure.

The Stockman's Hall of Fame in Longreach, Queensland, is a great place to learn about the history of the outback.

ROAD CONDITIONS PH 1300 361 033

TRAVEL ON CLOSED ROADS IS PROHIBITED
SEVERE PENALTIES APPLY

OODNADATTA TRACK

MARLA TO LAMBINA	OPEN
MARLA TO OODNADATTA	OPEN
OODNADATTA TO WILLIAM CREEK	OPEN
WILLIAM CREEK TO MARREE	OPEN
OODNADATTA TO MT DARE	OPEN
OODNADATTA TO COOBER PEDY	OPEN
PAINTED DESERT ROAD	OPEN
WILLIAM CREEK TO COOBER PEDY	OPEN
WILLIAM CREEK TO ROXBY DOWNS	OPEN

The Oodnadatta Track is one of Australia's iconic dirt roads.

Ross Robinson and Lynne De Groot

The Painted Desert is well worth a detour off the Oodnadatta Track.

Ross Robinson and Lynne De Groot

Is there really anywhere else you'd rather be?